DATE DUE

DEMCO 38-296

The Politics and Processes of Scholarship

Recent Titles in
Contributions to the Study of Education

THE POLITICS
AND PROCESSES OF
SCHOLARSHIP

Edited by
JOSEPH M. MOXLEY
and
LAGRETTA T. LENKER

Foreword by R. Eugene Rice

Contributions to the Study of Education, Number 66

GREENWOOD PRESS
Westport, Connecticut • London

Library of Congress Cataloging-in-Publication Data

The politics and processes of scholarship / edited by Joseph M. Moxley
and Lagretta T. Lenker ; foreword by R. Eugene Rice.
    p. cm.—(Contributions to the study of education, ISSN
0196–707X ; no. 66)
  Includes bibliographical references and index.
  ISBN 0–313–29572–7 (alk. paper)
    1. Learning and scholarship—Political aspects—United States.
2. Academic writing—Political aspects—United States. 3. Scholarly
publishing—Political aspects—United States. 4. College teachers—
Tenure—Political aspects—United States. 5. Performance awards—
Political aspects—United States. I. Moxley, Joseph Michael.
II. Lenker, Lagretta Tallent. III. Series : Contributions to the
study of education ; no. 66.
AZ507.P64 1995
001.2—dc20   95–16147

British Library Cataloguing in Publication Data is available.

Library of Congress Catalog Card Number: 95–16147
ISBN: 0–313–29572–7
ISSN: 0196–707X

First published in 1995

Greenwood Press, 88 Post Road West, Westport, CT 06881
An imprint of Greenwood Publishing Group, Inc.

Printed in the United States of America

The paper used in this book complies with the
Permanent Paper Standard issued by the National
Information Standards Organization (Z39.48–1984).

10 9 8 7 6 5 4 3 2 1

Contents

III. INITIATIVES FOR PROMOTING GRANT WRITING

IV. INITIATIVES FOR PROMOTING SCHOLARLY PUBLISHING

Foreword

R. Eugene Rice

The Politics and Processes of Scholarship advances in an important way the vigorous reexamination of faculty roles and rewards currently taking place in American higher education. The essays in this book move these critical deliberations to a new level of intellectual depth and raise fresh questions about the research and publication dimensions of scholarship.

During the 1980s, it became increasingly clear that the scholarly role of the professoriate had become too narrowly constricted, focusing on the publication of highly specialized articles in proliferating journals read by too few. Many faculty were publishing for the wrong reasons, that is, in order to be promoted and receive tenure in a tight labor market, rather than because they had something significant to communicate. The scholarly work of faculty had also become largely disconnected from the basic purposes of the college and university—teaching undergraduates and serving the needs of a troubled society. Legislators, regents, and the popular press turned public attention on the scholarship of faculty and began to demand changes in faculty workload, more attention to teaching, and greater relevance to society's needs. Much of the critique was ill-informed and some of it rooted in an incipient anti-intellectualism always present in the populist side of American culture, but it also highlighted a reality that was difficult to justify in an environment marked by scarce resources.

During the second half of the last decade a number of studies, including one of the academic workplace in which I was involved, called for a "broader conception of scholarship." The work of Ernest Lynton, Ann Austin, Kenneth Ruscio, Lee Shulman, Donald Schon, and others was pressing for something similar. In 1988, I was invited to The Carnegie Foundation for the Advancement of Teaching to participate in a two-year study of faculty scholarship and contribute to the Carnegie report that became Ernest Boyer's influential *Scholarship Reconsidered*.

The primary intent of *Scholarship Reconsidered* was to reframe the discussion about faculty priorities and break us out of the old teaching versus research debate. Far beyond what was expected, a serious discourse about the scholarly role of faculty and what was to be rewarded institutionally was ignited.

The Carnegie report called for an enlarged view of scholarship that goes beyond the discovery of knowledge that is new, to include the scholarships of integration, application, and teaching. Because much of the concern about the dominant view of scholarship focuses on the incongruity between what faculty are appointed to do and what they are rewarded for, much of the debate has centered on teaching as a scholarly endeavor. Because of the importance of the task and the quality of the work that has been done, the scholarly dimensions of teaching are beginning to be recognized and rewarded. The "Peer Review of Teaching" project, building on the ideas of Stanford's Lee Shulman and located at the American Association for Higher Education, is probably the best example. Sandra Elman, Donald Shon, and others have been attending to the applied work of faculty as a form of scholarship. Lynton's *Making a Case for Professional Service* provides sharpened definitions, addresses procedures for documenting applied scholarship, and gives examples of good practice, but progress is less evident.

As part of this larger reexamination of scholarship, Joe Moxley and Lagretta Lenker held a conference at the University of South Florida. Over a four-day period, faculty from the United States, Canada, the Caribbean Islands, and Africa met to discuss needed changes to the faculty reward system. The result of these discussions among faculty leaders, provosts, faculty-development specialists, editors, publishers, and development officers is this volume.

The Politics and Processes of Scholarship advances the discussion on yet another front, examining the implications of this broader view of what is honored as legitimate scholarly work and the role of publication in the academy. Obviously, research and publication will continue to have a vital place in advancing knowledge and play a key role in the evaluation of faculty work. If the effort to enlarge our view of faculty scholarship is seen as devaluing research and publication, the entire enterprise will have been seriously misinterpreted. This is not the intent. It is clear, however, that a broader view of the scholarly work of faculty will change the nature and focus of research, and, along with the technological, demographic, political, and economic pressures on higher education, will transform academic publishing. The chapters of this book give valuable insight into these changes and help us anticipate the magnitude of the transformation.

The essays in this book address the scholarship theme from a variety of innovative and challenging angles. Some, such as Ralph Norman's piece on "The Scholarly Journal and the Intellectual Sensorium," raise profound questions about the proliferation of specialized knowledge and our capacity to make public connection, to attend to the common good.

In an especially important essay, Morton Winston takes on the basic thesis of *Scholarship Reconsidered* and contends that redefining scholarship is something of a "semantic sleight of hand," and that the analysis of academic culture provided by the Carnegie report does not go deep enough. Winston argues that significant change in faculty roles and reward systems is going to have to go beyond definitional issues, and address "the power structures in the academy whose interests such reforms threaten, the disciplinary elite." Although this sounds a little like a warmed–over version of C. Wright Mills's "power elite thesis"—which can easily lead to the counsel of despair—Winston provides a careful analysis of what he calls "epistemic certification," which gives disciplinary elites formidable control over what counts as "real" scholarship, what research gets funded, and what leads to publication in the prestige journals. Winston concludes his penetrating essay by identifying leverage points that might challenge the current hierarchical structure of the academy and move higher education toward a more open and pluralistic commonwealth of knowledge.

Winston's essay, along with much of what is included in this volume, takes the faculty roles and rewards discussion beyond the conceptualization of what counts as scholarship to the department and the discipline—where faculty live and work. Winston is raising the right questions and advancing the agenda in pressing us to pick up on the more difficult challenge. This is a significant contribution.

Nothing is going to transform the world of scholarship more than the rapid rise of the networked, electronic community. I heartily recommend Section II of this book, "Scholarship in the Late Age of Print," and commend the editors for featuring it. The proliferation of electronic venues for the exchange of scholarly ideas and research is already challenging the traditional protocols of publication and review, just as electronic networking, in general, has enabled faculty to involve themselves in new kinds of scholarly communities. A new genre of scholarship is emerging that—in contrast to the kind controlled by Winston's "disciplinary elites"—promises to be not only more immediate and collaborative, but more inclusive.

Joe Moxley and Lagretta T. Lenker have given us a book that not only records the changes taking place in faculty scholarship, but advances ideas that will themselves make a difference.

REFERENCES

Boyer, Ernest. *Scholarship Reconsidered: Priorities of the Professoriate*. Princeton, N.J.: Carnegie Foundation, 1990.

Lynton, Ernest. *Making a Case for Professional Service*. Washington, D.C.: American Association for Higher Education, 1995.

Acknowledgments

For sponsoring the conference, The Politics and Processes of Scholarly Publishing, we thank the University of South Florida (USF), Division of Sponsored Research, the College of Arts and Sciences, the USF St. Petersburg campus, and the USF Division of Lifelong Learning. More specifically, we thank the special people who work for these organizations—that is, David Stamps, Rollin Richmond, Richard Taylor, Richard Streeter, Priscilla Pope, William T. Ross, and Darrell Fasching.

Without the talents and patience of Beth Dalton Williams, this book would not be possible.

Introduction

Joseph M. Moxley and Lagretta T. Lenker

Across disciplines, faculty are talking about the redefinition of scholarship. Faculty in humanities and social science departments have been particularly vocal about ways to improve both the academic reward system and the product of that system. For all around us in both our personal and professional lives, we are confronted with significant problems—the public schools' inability to teach; violent crime; the deterioration of our environment; overpopulation; racism and ethnic cleansing—that could be lessened, perhaps even solved, by the collective attention of academe. Unfortunately, however, American colleges and universities typically do not reward faculty for engaging in research or scholarship that address these kinds of problems.

Academic institutions have traditionally favored a narrow range of intellectual pursuits. Tenure and promotion committees at many universities and colleges devalue research that integrates and synthesizes theories across disciplines, trade books, textbooks, or pedagogical articles. Traditional committees and department chairs, when they assume a mentoring role, typically encourage faculty to write for specialists and to avoid writing essays or books for broad audiences. We can trace the source of this narrow conception of scholarship to approximately 1815 to 1915, when American scholars imported Germany's system of research-based graduate study and the associated ideal of "pure" research (Connors, 1991). Since the early nineteenth century, universities and colleges have encouraged faculty to ignore the problems of "society, politics, morality, and religion, even from the classroom itself, and [remove themselves] during most of their waking hours from their fellow men" (Lawrence R. Veysey, quoted in Connors, 60). Although many professional organizations, scholars, and even accrediting organizations are beginning to challenge this narrow view of scholarship, the legacy of privileging research and theory for specialists over pedagogy and other applied concerns still guides the missions of many American universities.

Rather than privileging basic research or theoretical studies, critics of higher education argue that universities should equally value applied research, community service, and teaching. R. Gene Rice, Richard Gebhardt, Robert Diamond, Ernest Boyer, Clara Lovett, and Russell Edgerton, for example, have persuasively argued that universities and colleges should reconstruct their perception of scholarship as "pure" and reconsider their perception of undergraduate teaching as atheoretical. Additional support for redefining scholarship can also be found in postmodern theories. Postmodernists have rejected the modernists' faith in objectivity and foregrounded the ideological nature of scholarship and teaching. Rather than perceiving scholarship (or teaching) as the objective illumination of *the truth*, academicians have embraced the concepts of multiple truths, of situational knowledge, of valuing the striving for truths over the expectation of uncovering a truth that transcends culture and the evolution of time and knowledge. Postmodernists have challenged grand narratives—such as Freudianism and Darwinism—because these narratives assume that human beings share universal characteristics and because these theories overlook or downplay the effects of culture, class, gender, or socioeconomic status on the development and constitution of self. As postmodern theories have transformed academic disciplines, professors have exposed the myth of disinterested science. If meaning is socially constructed by members of a discourse community, then researchers and scholars should avoid generalizing or depicting knowledge as limited to specific communities. By validating the subjective nature of interpretation, postmodern theorists have provided the theoretical ground for qualitative research methodologies and the personal essay. In short, no one form of scholarship is inherently superior; instead, all scholarship is valued by the standards of its discourse community.

While the foundations of scholarship have been battered by reformers, perhaps the greatest challenge, the challenge that truly will redefine scholarship and transform the academic reward system, lies ahead in the networked, electronic community. Thanks to the possibilities created by the Internet and multimedia-authoring software, some professors have even called for the end of scholarship as we know it. After all, the Internet permits the immediate distribution of knowledge. Via electronic conferencing programs, scholars throughout the world can engage in real-time discussions about issues of importance to them. Working collaboratively on listservs, scholars can extend the conversations in their disciplines at a pace that traditional scholarly journals cannot. If we can distribute our ideas within nanoseconds, if we can create a homepage on the World Wide Web to store our favorite essays, books, and hypermedia software, why do we need to wait months, even years, to produce books in text-bound form? Indeed, how can we *not* create a new genre of scholarship—one that is more immediate, more collaborative—than current modes of scholarship now that we can use Internet browsers to access information stored in computers throughout the world; now that we can engage in extended, text-based discussions with other colleagues at other institutions on listservs and via E-mail; and now that we can use multimedia-authoring software to develop documents that contain audio, visuals, and movies.

Reformers will certainly face obstacles to redesigning the faculty reward system so that professors are rewarded for monitoring listservs, authoring multimedia software, and organizing electronic conferences. In this late age of print, some technophobics will argue that the printed book is superior to the multimedia book. Some will argue that listservs serve neophytes who are more concerned with socializing than with debating serious intellectual questions or critiquing a canon. Ultimately, however, the new intellectual frontier creates too many possibilities for innovative faculty to ignore. If academic institutions hope to be honored and supported, if they acknowledge their responsibilities for educating students, then faculty will be encouraged to participate in computer-related research and computer-assisted instruction. Academics just cannot stick their heads in the sand on this issue—that is, if they hope to come up for air.

Along with heated discussions about ways to improve the faculty reward system, professors across disciplines have problematized their roles, questioning, for example, whether they should serve as agents of social change or as representatives of the military-industrial complex. Some faculty believe they should serve as public intellectuals. Rather than writing for a narrow group of specialists in academic journals, they hope to influence public opinion and policies by publishing trade books and articles in magazines and the op-ed pages of daily newspapers (Scott, 1994).

Clearly, current methods of defining and rewarding scholarship are not working, and the role of the professoriate will be forced to change, thanks to modern technologies and thanks to major social, economic, and environmental problems that our world population faces. Recent surveys of faculty attitudes demonstrate that faculty are discouraged from pursuing the practical implications of their scholarship, from conducting research related to their teaching, and from working collaboratively to improve their institutions, professional organizations, or communities (Boyer, 1990; Gray et al., 1994; Sykes, 1988). Present estimates of faculty productivity suggest that 10 to 15 percent of the professoriate account for the bulk of what is published (Boice and Jones, 1988; Jalongo, 1985). In turn, when the Carnegie Foundation for the Advancement of Teaching surveyed 5,000 faculty throughout the United States (1989), it discovered that few faculty had published many articles or books: 13 percent of the faculty members at four-year institutions had published no essays, 30 percent had published one to five essays, and 49 percent had written or edited no books. In turn, at two-year institutions, 52 percent had published no articles and 69 percent had written or edited no books (Boyer, 1990).

While creative endeavors cannot be reduced to quantitative unit—one major book can transform a discipline in ways a dozen minor books cannot—we clearly have some evidence that faculty could be much more productive. Those of us who provide faculty development programs understand that professors need training in writing; marketing essays, books, and grant proposals, Internet browsers, multimedia-authoring software, and electronic conferencing software. Certainly, if institutions provided more support programs for creative endeavors, faculty would be more creative and would be more likely to share their ideas in refereed journals and to work collaboratively.

To help our colleagues find their voices as scholars and teachers, we need to do more than provide useful faculty-development workshops: more professors would realize their creative potential if academic institutions rewarded faculty for conducting applied forms of scholarship or research related to teaching. Few faculty are in a position to routinely discover new knowledge, which may explain why so much scholarship is so jargon-ridden that only a few specialists can read (or care to read) it. Yet faculty can be creative in a range of ways—that is, by conducting research related to their teaching, synthesizing and integrating others' scholarship, and translating scholarship to less specialized audiences.

Also, unmistakably, public dollars that fuel major portions of academic research will go to projects perceived as having direct benefits to our society and economy. In this era of streamlining government and budgets, the academic community must demonstrate a profound value-added relationship between scholarship and quality of social life. If today's academics fail to manage this debate, surely future scholars will suffer as business and industry assume the lead in this technology and information revolution. Academic turf wars, compensation/rewards systems, and even academic freedom will become obsolete issues unless the academy firmly establishes itself as the most efficient, effective, and responsible defenders and producers of knowledge—electronic and otherwise. To make this claim, we must maintain order in our own metaphorical house. This volume, it is hoped, contributes to that elusive process.

THE POLITICS AND PROCESSES OF SCHOLARSHIP

In March of 1994, we held a conference at the University of South Florida titled The Politics and Processes of Scholarly Publishing. Over a four-day period, provosts, editors, publishers, and faculty-development specialists debated ways to define scholarship and improve the faculty reward system. Over lunches and dinners, keynote and plenary speeches, panel presentations, and open-ended discussions, we discussed many of the tough questions that contemporary faculty and university administrators are debating within the higher education community, such as

- When determining tenure, promotion, and merit pay, how much weight should universities and colleges ascribe to the scholarships of *discovery, integration, application,* and *teaching*?
- Will giving additional weight to the scholarships of *integration* and *application* inspire more faculty to conduct research and publish their results?

- What institutional and academic barriers have kept faculty-development specialists and administrators from changing the faculty reward system?
- How does one's class, race, and gender affect what gets published or funded and who gets promoted?
- How can we improve the peer-review process and the selection process for choosing editors and members of a journal's editorial board?
- How will the Internet, online databases, and electronic journals impinge on the creative endeavors of faculty, notions of intellectual property, and promotion criteria?
- What innovative faculty initiatives can colleges and universities develop to help faculty find their voices as researchers, scholars, and teachers?

Even though these conference participants represented a variety of disciplines and academic institutions from throughout United States, Canada, Jamaica, and Africa, their presentations and discussions made it clear that they shared many similar ideas about improving higher education.

Now, several years later, we present this book as a sample of our discussions, albeit a more polished sample of our ideas. In a broad sense, this book is about who we are and who we want to be. Written for faculty and faculty-development administrators, this book is about the changing, evolving responsibilities of the professoriate in a postmodern, networked world. This book analyzes ways to redefine scholarship, suggested alternatives to improve the academic reward system, explores the impact of technology on scholarship, and presents innovative faculty-development initiatives.

REFERENCES

Boice, Robert, and Ferdinand Jones. "Why Academicians Don't Write." *Journal of Higher Education* 4: 2 (Fall 1988): 4–46.

Boyer, Ernest. *Scholarship Reconsidered: Priorities of the Professoriate.* Princeton, J.J.: Carnegie Foundation for the Advancement of Teaching, 1990.

Connors, Robert. "Rhetoric in the Modern University: The Creation of an Underclass." *The Politics of Writing Instruction: Postsecondary.* Gen. ed. Charles Schuster. Portsmouth, N.H.: Boynton/Cook Publishers, 1991. 55–84.

Gray, Peter J., Robert C. Froh, and Robert M. Diamond. "Myths and Realities." *Institutional Priorities and Faculty Rewards.* Syracuse, N.Y.: Syracuse University, Center for Instructional Development, 1994.

Jalongo, Mary Renck. "Faculty Productivity in Higher Education." *Educational Forum* 49 (Winter 1985): 17–182.

Scott, Janny. "More Intellectuals Writing for Public Instead of Fellow Scholars." *New York Times* News Service, August 8, 1994.

Sykes, Charles J. *ProfScam: Professors and the Demise of Higher Education.* Washington, D.C.: Regnery Gateway, 1988.

PART I

POSTMODERN CONCEPTIONS OF SCHOLARSHIP

1

Avoiding the "Research versus Teaching" Trap: Expanding the Criteria for Evaluating Scholarship

Richard C. Gebhardt

Writing in *Change*, James S. Fairweather of the Pennsylvania State University Center for the Study of Higher Education noted that "Public concern about the rising costs of higher education has led academic leaders and their critics alike to examine how faculty spend their time and the concomitant institutional rewards for doing so. Particularly at issue is what Ernest Boyer calls the 'old teaching versus research' debate" (1990, 44).

One side of this debate grows from the widespread view that "teaching" encompasses holding classes and office hours and that scholarship and publishing undermine teaching. On this side of the debate stand politicians and the press when they criticize the university's reliance on teaching assistants, the sparsity of senior faculty in undergraduate classes, and academe's luxurious twelve-hour week. (An extreme illustration of this side of the debate is a plan put forward by a member of the Ohio Legislature to base faculty salaries on the student credit hours generated by each person.) On the other side of the debate, academics point out the obvious errors critics make when they leave preparation and evaluation time out of what it means to "teach a course"; exclude nonclassroom work on independent studies, theses, and dissertations from the definition of "teaching"; forget the role that research and scholarship play in qualifying a professor to develop and teach courses, direct student projects, and evaluate student work; and devalue the intellectual and social importance of research and scholarship done by faculty members.

I've deliberately drawn a caricature of a debate—wrong-headed public misperceptions versus high-minded academic principles. But there is much more than that to today's research versus teaching discussions—broad questions about the job description of the faculty member and the relationship of scholarship to other dimensions of the professor's life and work. As Russell Edgerton, president of the American Association for Higher Education (AAHE) has written, "It would be a mistake to assume that the reexamination of faculty priorities is powered only by pressures from *outside* the campus. Conflicts over what priorities faculty should pursue are occurring *inside* our campuses as well" (1993, 12). I'll not belabor this point, but I'd like to illustrate it with a few quotations. First, here is Ernest Boyer, in the preface of *Scholarship Reconsidered*: "Research and publication have become the primary means by which most professors achieve academic status, and yet many academics are, in fact, drawn to the profession precisely because of their love for teaching and service. Yet these professional obligations do not get the recognition they deserve" (xii).

And here is Clara Lovett, director of the AAHE Forum on Faculty Roles and Rewards: "At every type of institution, faculty express a longing for an older and spiritually richer academic culture, one that placed greater value on the education of students and on the public responsibilities of scholars" (1993, 3).

Finally, here is Russell Edgerton, generalizing from 50 campus taskforce reports on faculty rewards prepared between 1990 and 1993: "[T]he campus reports and surveys I studied reveal tensions between younger and senior faculty as well as between the interests of minority and feminist scholars and traditional notions of disciplinary rigor. Many midcareer and senior faculty clearly feel caged in by the reigning definitions of what scholarly work is valued" (1993, 12).

It is important to realize that Boyer, Lovett, and Edgerton are academic *insiders*, not outside critics of priorities and rewards that privilege research over teaching. The research versus teaching trap in my title, then, is not a simple conflict between the priorities and reward systems of academia and those of society at large—not just a matter of finding oneself criticized for being too research-oriented or insufficiently "productive" in teaching. Increasingly, of course, faculty members are experiencing such external criticism. But in addition, many faculty (as Boyer's quote implies) sense a mismatch between personal motives and professional rewards and feel "longing" (Lovett's word) for an academic climate that values education and public service; they feel (Edgerton says) "caged in by the reigning definitions of what scholarly work is valued" (12).

Any cage, of course, has several walls, and the research versus teaching trap many professors find themselves in is no exception. First, there are the external constraints—administrative efforts and initiatives by governing boards or legislatures to increase faculty teaching productivity in the face of financial and other pressures.

Second, there is the fact that research and teaching are competitors for the time and attention of professors. How could it be otherwise? When you are in class, holding conferences with students about course work, preparing classroom presentations and tests, and grading papers and tests, you are not doing research in the library or laboratory, or working at the computer on a paper, article, book, or grant.

Third, faculty members have good reason to protect time and attention for their scholarly projects, for there has been a dramatic increase in the role of research and publication in faculty evaluation. In 1969 and again in 1989, Carnegie Foundation National Surveys of Faculty asked this question: "In my department, is it difficult for a person to achieve tenure if he or she doesn't publish?" In 1969, 21 percent of all faculty surveyed strongly agreed, but in 1989 this response doubled, and 42 percent strongly agreed. In Ph.D.-granting departments, the response nearly tripled—from 27 percent in 1969 to 71 percent in 1989; it quadrupled at liberal arts colleges (from 6 percent to 24 percent); and it increased sevenfold (from 6 percent to 43 percent) at comprehensive institutions (Boyer, 12). Given such a shift in the importance of research at all sorts of institutions, it is not surprising to read what James Fairweather found by studying data from the 1988 National Survey of Postsecondary Faculty: "The more time a faculty member spends on teaching, the less she or he spends on research, and vice versa"; "the more time faculty spend on teaching, the lower the pay"; "[c]onversely, the more time spent on research and the greater the scholarly productivity, the greater the pay" (Fairweather, 1993, 46). Faced with such a situation, faculty have good reason to try to protect their "research time."

Fourth, the sort of scholarship most valued and rewarded is traditional "academic" work published in refereed journals and books of high reputation. At any rate, that's what 73 percent of faculty in Ph.D.-granting institutions reported in the 1989 Carnegie survey (Boyer, Appendix A–10). This research is, in one characterization, "work expected to make original contributions and additions to the body of knowledge" (Lacey, 1990, 92); in the well-known term from *Scholarship Reconsidered*, it is "the scholarship of discovery." And as I found in a survey of faculty and administrators in the field of composition studies (see Gebhardt, 1993, 12–13), it is evaluated against standards like these:

Object of Research: A rough hierarchy ranging from arcane and theoretical topics and issues (at the high end) to pedagogical matters (at the bottom).

Manner of Research: Another rough hierarchy in which rigorous "original" research has more value than rigorous secondary or summarizing research and work with a more personal slant usually has less value still.

Genre of Publication: Here, university press books and "major" scholarly articles are more important than books and articles for nonspecialists, and textbooks and other pedagogical materials bring up the rear.

External Validity of Publication: Refereeing and the reputation of presses and journals figure strongly here, as do citations by others and comments by external evaluators in tenure reviews.

Assistant professors looking toward tenure and associate professors interested in promotion understand—or come to understand—these criteria as they work to develop research records showing "important," "cutting-edge" work in high-quality refereed journals.

But as they try to develop these records (and this is the fifth part of the trap—the ceiling, I guess), many faculty are doing something they don't

particularly like. For traditional research and publishing—the scholarship of
discovery, if you will—does not fit particularly well the interests and priorities
of many faculty. This is a clear and very important theme in *Scholarship
Reconsidered*. Boyer states that 68 percent of faculty at all types of institutions
agreed that "we need better ways, besides publications, to evaluate the scholarly
performance of faculty" and that even those at research and doctorate-granting
institutions supported that view, by 69 percent and 77 percent, respectively (34).
Boyer also notes "a strong undercurrent of dissatisfaction" which one survey
respondent captured "when he wrote that today's dominant emphasis on
publication 'is seriously out of touch with what [the faculty] do and want to do'"
(29, 31–32). Such dissatisfaction is unavoidable for many faculty, if Paul Lacey
is right that only "the small number of faculty at research institutions" really
need to publish "work expected to make original contributions and additions to
the body of knowledge" and that most faculty members need "writing and other
professional activities" that are "appropriate to our work and our own inclinations
as teachers" (Lacey, 91–92). No wonder Lovett sensed much faculty "longing"
for a different sort of academy and Edgerton found faculty "feeling caged in by
the reigning definitions of what scholarly work is valued" (12).

So far, I've tried to present the "research versus teaching" dilemma we face
as complex and operating on four fronts: (1) inside academe, faculty evaluation
stresses research and publication and particularly privileges research of discovery
and prestige publication; (2) increasingly, various groups outside higher education
are finding the proportion of faculty time going for "research" to be problematic
and so are pressing for increased emphasis on "teaching" in workloads and
faculty rewards; (3) in turn, governing boards, administrators, and other academic
leaders are looking for ways to increase teaching "productivity"; and (4) at the
same time, many faculty are dissatisfied with the research and publishing
demands they are expected to meet.

No one, it seems, is happy with the present situation. So the time is ripe for
a simple, surefire solution. I'm afraid I don't have such a wonder to share here.
But I would like to sketch the sort of approach I think we need to take. In short,
we should expand the criteria we use to evaluate scholarship in order to meet
more fully faculty and public dissatisfaction with the present emphasis on the
object, manner, genre, and external validity of scholarship.

A first step toward this goal is to rethink those criteria—especially the *object*
and the *genre* of publication—in light of the widespread unhappiness with the
sort of research and publishing being encouraged by present standards of
evaluation. Why should it be the case, as Maryellen Weimer writes in a review
of discipline-centered journals on teaching, that "what faculty tend to say first is
that writing about pedagogy isn't regarded as legitimate scholarship" (Weimer,
1993, 44)? Why should it be, to use Paul Lacey's words, that "writing about
teaching and a number of other activities that keep teachers intellectually alive
and effective in the classroom are excluded from consideration by definition" in

tenure and promotion reviews (Lacey, 1990, 95)? There's really no reason for this to be the case. After all, many in the professoriate desire greater emphasis on teaching and chafe at the present restrictions about acceptable research. (And governing boards, politicians, and the public certainly favor more concern with teaching.) So why not take the "first step" recommended in *Scholarship Reconsidered* and have "faculty assessment take into account a broader range of writing," including textbooks and articles about teaching—writing that, "if done well, can reveal a professor's knowledge of the field, illuminate essential integrative themes, and powerfully contribute to excellence in teaching, too" (Boyer, 35)?

Once teaching, students, and the integration of research with theory so that both are more useful in teaching students are seen as appropriate *objects* of research, the range of appropriate *genres* of publication will begin to increase. Lacey's approach may seem a radical departure from traditional practice: "Materials that in a more rigid system of classification would be considered only under assessment of teaching" also reflect on scholarship by providing "evidence of the faculty member's quality of mind" (97). But as traditional a scholarly group as the Modern Language Association (MLA) has issued guidelines indicating that textbooks and faculty-development workshops are, in some specialties, fully appropriate evidence of scholarship ("Report"). The MLA's Association of Departments of English has spoken more broadly: "Publication need not be the only or even the most important measure of a faculty member's accomplishments. In evaluations of scholarship, different kinds of activities and products should be given credit" ("ADE Statement," 1993, 44).

Doubtless, it may be difficult, at the outset, for personnel committees to evaluate these "different kinds of activities and products." But it shouldn't take long to make adjustments in our ideas of "appropriate" scholarship and genres of publication—that is, if we want to.

Scholarship Reconsidered provides a useful start, with its treatment of the scholarship of integration, application, and teaching. Faculty often pursue such scholarly agendas through conventional means—journal articles, books, and convention papers. Clearly, these can be evaluated by such traditional standards as currency, significance, professional influence, and the rigor and reputation of journal, press, or conference. Even when they find expression in less traditional publications—internal study documents, for instance, or curriculum development materials—research and scholarship focused on students and teaching can be evaluated against traditional standards appropriate for the author's methodology, and they can be sent out for peer review at tenure time. Similarly, the notes, handouts, and other materials developed for a workshop can be evaluated for currency and the aptness with which theories and research are integrated and clarified for others. In addition, people who took the workshop can be asked to comment on its significance and usefulness.

Ultimately, I expect *three new* criteria will evolve for evaluating scholarship. In addition to object, manner, genre, and external validity of published scholarship, I believe that the evaluation of research and scholarship will increasingly stress the *relationship* of research and publishing to the faculty member's teaching; the mission of the institution (university, college, department); and the needs and expectations society has of higher education.

The Relationship of Research to a Scholar's Teaching

This criterion would be fairly simple to apply in merit, tenure, and promotion reviews. On the one hand, is there evidence in course syllabi, lectures, handouts, paper assignments, and the like that the faculty member's scholarship is influencing what or how she teaches? Department committees could look for such evidence in a teacher's merit or promotion file, and sample teaching materials could be sent for external review of how well they reflect current scholarly trends.[1] On the other hand, is there evidence of carryover from teaching to scholarship: reference to class situations that raised or clarified the question behind an article, use of student comments or examples, conclusions that include pedagogical implications, and the like? Chairs and personnel committees could look for such things at the same time as they are considering the substance and significance of a faculty person's scholarly record. External evaluators could be asked to do the same.

Clearly, in either internal or external reviews, a shallow, confusing monograph published by a vanity press would not provide evidence for tenure just because it bears a strong relationship to the author's teaching. But a solid, refereed article that connects to its author's teaching might, quite reasonably, be taken as stronger evidence for promotion than a solid, refereed article with no such connection. Similarly, a textbook—a genre of publication closely connected to teaching—would merit much more serious consideration in personnel reviews if it grew out of current research and theory in its field than if it were based on outmoded or discredited views of its field.

The Relationship of Research to the Institution's Mission

This criterion would figure prominently in the sort of review I have just suggested. Depending on the role that undergraduate teaching plays in an institution's mission, a department could give the relationship to teaching more or less weight, in relation to traditional tests of scholarship. This probably would mean that the "relationship to teaching" criterion would have less impact on the evaluation of scholarship at research and doctoral institutions than at two-year, liberal arts, and comprehensive institutions. But wherever teaching is part of a department's mission, this criterion could be important.

Imagine an associate professor of history who teaches graduate courses and directs dissertations on nineteenth-century America and who also regularly teaches courses taken by undergraduate majors preparing for high school teaching certification. Is it inappropriate—and irrelevant in her promotion review—for this person to do research into ways that high school textbooks oversimplify the causes and outcomes of the Civil War; to address this problem in her classes and prepare her students to work professionally with limited textbooks; and to publish a solid article on all this in the national journal *The History Teacher*? Answering only from the twin perspectives of its research and doctoral education missions, a department might answer "yes" and dismiss all this work during promotion review. But why should this be the case? Why shouldn't the department's role in undergraduate education and its mission in the training of future teachers also figure in promotion review? Both should, just as most doctoral and research departments of English and mathematics have missions in general education, basic skills education, and secondary teacher preparation that are quite relevant in merit, tenure, and promotion reviews.

The Relationship of Research to Society's Needs and Expectations

Basic skills, general education, the preparation of school teachers—these are all things society, broadly speaking, expects from higher education and for which public institutions receive financial support. There are many other such needs and expectations. Some of them are quite lofty—for instance, research to increase America's industrial productivity, solve environmental problems, improve human health, broaden literacy, and address widespread social inequities. Others are mundane but deeply felt by taxpayers, legislators, and parents of students: that undergraduates should work closely with faculty members, that teaching should be central in the job description of professors, that students should leave college with the education, values, and skills to get and succeed in a job of their choice. It's an oversimplification to say that higher education faces criticism and economic restrictions today because it has failed to meet such expectations, but this clearly is part of the reason.

"In just a few decades," to use the words of *Scholarship Reconsidered* as it traces the evolution of U.S. higher education, "priorities in American higher education were significantly realigned. The [initial] emphasis on undergraduate education" was "overshadowed by the European university tradition, with its emphasis on graduate education and research" (13). Boyer's book sounds this note of caution: "At no time in our history has the need been greater for connecting the work of the academy to the social and environmental challenges beyond the campus. And yet, the rich potential of American higher education cannot be fully realized if campus missions are too narrowly defined or if the faculty reward system is inappropriately restricted. It seems clear that while research is crucial, we need a renewed commitment to service, too" (xii). As we evaluate scholarshp, we should keep in mind this caution against overly narrow academic missions—and "inappropriately restricted" reward systems—as well as this call for greater connection of the academy to the surrounding society.

We should give due credit to solid, effective "applied" scholarship—like the hypothetical historian's efforts to make a difference in the way the schools teach history.[2] We should also take a hard look at "specialist" or "theoretical" biases in the way we think about our disciplines and evaluate research and publication in them.

Regardless of our academic disciplines, we would do well to attempt the sort of analysis Rutgers University English professor George Levine offers in an influential publication of the Modern Language Association: "[T]he two functions of English departments that institutions and the culture as a whole endorse, and pay for, are perhaps the two to which we as research faculty members are least committed. One is the teaching of writing as a basic skill that all educated people need to acquire, and the other is the teaching of literature as it is widely understood by those who don't make the study of it their profession" (1993, 44).

Analogous statements could be made about most academic fields. We should try to locate such areas of mismatch between academic rewards and public expectations. In addition, we should look for ways to reflect the needs and expectations of society in our departmental guidelines for evaluating scholarship and in departmental reviews for merit, promotion, and tenure. Even small adjustments would be a good start toward the goal Levine offers: "We must learn to build departments whose interests and objectives are less at odds with their immediate public responsibilities" (45).

Doing this, like all the innovations sketched here, seems reasonable to me, caught up as I am in the enthusiasm and idealism of writing this chapter. The key question is, "Do we *want* to?" Do we want to expand the criteria we use in evaluating scholarship? Often, I think academics say "no" to this question because we fear or resent "outsiders" criticizing what we do. But it seems clear that many college and university professors themselves yearn for broader standards of evaluation that better fit their careers as scholars. I hope that we will find ways to respond affirmatively to the many faculty members who would welcome and endorse expanded criteria for evaluating scholarship.

NOTES

1. Peer review of teaching is "the single most promising trend" Russell Edgerton found among recent campus studies of faculty reward systems (1993, 20). My approach would help further that end as well as show how course materials can be a form of the "scholarship of teaching" (see Boyer, 23–25).

2. On "the Scholarship of Application," see Boyer, 21–23.

REFERENCES

"ADE Statement of Good Practice: Teaching, Evaluation, and Scholarship." *ADE Bulletin* 105 (Fall 1993): 43–45.

Boyer, Ernest. *Scholarship Reconsidered: Priorities of the Professoriate*. Princeton, N.J.: Carnegie Foundation, 1990.

Edgerton, Russell. "The Reexamination of Faculty Priorities." *Change* (July/August 1993): 10–25.

Fairweather, James S. "The Nature of Tradeoffs." *Change* (July/August 1993): 44–47.

Gebhardt, Richard C. "Issues of Promotion and Tenure for Rhetoric and Technical Writing Faculty." Studies in Technical Communication. Denton,Tex.: CCCC Committee on Technical Communications, 1993. 9–15.

Lacey, Paul A. "Encouraging and Evaluating Scholarship for the College Teacher." *Excellent Teaching in a Changing Academy: Essays in Honor of Kenneth Eble*. Ed. Feroza Jussawalla. New Directions in Teaching and Learning, No. 44. San Francisco: Jossey-Bass, 1990. 91–100.

Levine, George. "The Real Trouble." *Profession 93*. New York: Modern Language Association, 1993. 43–45.

Lovett, Clara M. "Listening to the Faculty Grapevine." *AAHE Bulletin* 46, 3 (November 1993): 3–5.

"Report on the Commission of Writing and Literature." *Profession 88*. New York: Modern Language Association, 1988. 73–74.

Weimer, Maryellen. "The Disciplinary Journals on Pedagogy." *Change* (November/December 1993): 44–51.

2

Disciplinary Associations and the Work of Faculty

Robert M. Diamond

FACTORS INFLUENCING WHAT FACULTY DO

Disciplinary associations have historically played a major role in determining the priorities of faculty and, in those professional fields where accreditation is involved, in determining the content and scope of courses and curricula. As institutions, faced with both internal and external pressures to place greater emphasis on teaching and applied work or service, attempt to relate what faculty do more closely with their institutional mission, the role of disciplinary associations has been the center of increasing attention. To facilitate these changes and to be more sensitive to the needs of their own members, a number of associations have begun to develop and disseminate statements that describe the work of faculty in the discipline. These statements, developed with support from a national project, promise to have a direct impact on faculty work and priorities.

There are five variables that influence how faculty spend their professional time: (1) formal assignments; (2) criteria for faculty rewards; (3) priorities of the discipline; (4) personal priorities; and (5) available time and resources. Some of these are outside the faculty member's locus of control and others are external to the immediate context of the institution. These variables and their influence over faculty work change over time in response to external circumstances and fluctuate with the stages in a faculty member's career. Consequently, the focus or balance of work is dynamic rather than static. Figure 2.1 illustrates the forces that influence faculty work.

Formal Assignments

Perhaps most significant among factors that influence how faculty spend their time are formal assignments, ranging from assignments to teach specific courses, to serve on particular committees, and to advise an identified number of students. Assignments are based in part on the priorities developed at the institutional level and then passed on to the school/college and department levels. Priorities or goals of this nature might include improving the quality of undergraduate teaching, increasing the amount of external funding the unit receives, or becoming more active in community service or outreach activities.

Figure 2.1
Factors Influencing What Faculty Do

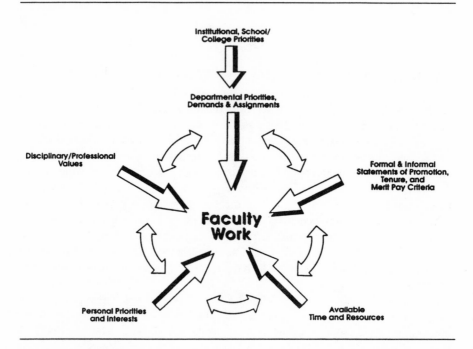

Criteria for Faculty Rewards

A second variable affecting how faculty spend their time resides in the formal or informal statements articulating the criteria that will be used for making promotion, tenure, or merit pay decisions. If, for example, grants or refereed publications are perceived as being the primary factor in determining faculty rewards, a faculty member would be ill-advised to spend his or her discretionary time on other activities that have little impact on these crucial decisions. Faculty understandably devote their time to activities that promise a payoff for them.

Priorities of the Discipline

A third variable that affects how faculty spend their time is the recognition given to particular activities by the faculty member's discipline. Disciplinary associations and professional organizations influence the standards for promotion and tenure decisions and professional mobility by establishing scholarly traditions and practices that set the standards for the academic discipline. It is an interesting and perhaps unfortunate paradox in higher education that the factors that influence how a faculty member spends his or her discretionary time can be impacted to a great degree by influences external to the institution that employs them. These external priorities may be quite different from the priorities of the institution or academic unit.

Personal Priorities

The fourth set of variables affecting faculty work are the personal priorities and interests of the faculty member. Some faculty devote a great deal of time to their teaching, to involvement in interdisciplinary projects, or to professional work in their communities. Faculty may make these choices conscious of the risk of jeopardizing pay increases, promotion, and even tenure. Some faculty are motivated by the enjoyment of teaching, the challenge of working with students, and the thrill of experimenting with new instructional approaches. It is these activities in which they have decided to invest their energies. Other faculty are motivated by the pleasure and challenge of research and discovery. When they have a choice, faculty spend their time on activities that provide them with so-called intrinsic rewards—a sense of accomplishment or satisfaction accompanying activities with particular features or characteristics. Faculty gravitate toward work that provides them with pleasure and fulfillment.

Available Time and Resources

The last of the five variables is the most pragmatic of the list—the faculty member's discretionary time. Public opinion to the contrary, most faculty are extremely hard working. Workload studies reported in November 1992 note that faculty, on average, work more than fifty hours per week.[1] Time, however, is finite. One of the greatest challenges a faculty member faces is determining how to spend the discretionary hours that are available. A faculty member's choices are impacted significantly by available resources, including laboratory equipment and supplies, clerical or graduate assistant help, space and facilities, or travel funds.

Some Observations

None of these influencing factors exists in isolation from the others. The values of the scholarly community, as articulated by the disciplinary association, can have a direct impact on the department's criteria for promotion and tenure, on the resources available for certain activities (particularly if accreditation is involved), and on the individual's personal priorities. History and acculturation are significant. Not surprisingly, faculty educated in graduate programs that are research-oriented tend to enjoy doing research. Faculty are attracted to a specific field, and they develop the skills that are necessary to be successful in that field. Problems arise when institutional priorities change and faculty are asked to spend greater proportions of their time doing work for which they received little preparation, from which they derive little enjoyment, or which is not recognized in the faculty reward system.

Another example of this interrelationship of influencing variables is in resource allocation. An institution that decides to forge a reputation as a major research center or to develop a new program in a particular discipline does so with a commitment to provide the resources necessary to accomplish this goal. The building of new facilities, the purchase of new equipment, and the hiring of key support staff all combine to make that campus attractive to the specific faculty that are necessary to develop the curriculum.

The way faculty spend their time varies or fluctuates from year to year. In some cases, the nature of the discipline determines those periods in a faculty member's career when greater emphasis is given to research and/or publication. In some fields significant scholarly activity develops over time, after the individual has had time to broaden his or her experience and to synthesize the knowledge of the field. In other areas, maximum research productivity tends to come earlier in a career when the faculty member is fresh out of graduate school and up to date in the literature of the discipline. As professional responsibilities and assignments broaden, the ability to keep up with an area of expertise becomes more challenging. It is also the case that faculty gain greater individual freedom in selecting what they do after tenure has been granted. The longer a faculty member has been in the field and at an institution, the greater freedom and choice he or she has in selecting how time will be spent.

Finally and perhaps most importantly, colleges and universities are entering a period of change that will have a direct and lasting impact on the lives of faculty—on how they work and how they are rewarded. Students, parents, and local, state, and national governments are calling for greater attention to teaching and greater involvement of faculty in community-related activities. Pressures for change are coming from the faculty as well. The majority of faculty at most institutions seriously question the perceived emphasis on research over teaching[2] and believe that many administrators give only "lip service" to the teaching mission which they personally believe is the primary role of their institution.

Many faculty in this study claim that the present reward system pays little attention to the quality of teaching, is inappropriate for many of the disciplines (the creative arts, many of the humanities, and the professions), and actually runs counter to the values that institutions say are most important. Faculty members report spending a significant amount of time on activities that (1) they do not want to engage in, and (2) they believe are inappropriate given the stated mission of their institution.

CHANGING THE SYSTEM

Recognizing that institutions will not change without the active involvement of faculty and the fact that what faculty do is determined by the faculty reward system, a number of national initiatives are underway to relate the faculty reward system more directly to the stated priorities of institutions. One of these initiatives is focusing on the disciplinary associations and the critical part they play in establishing scholarly traditions and standards of excellence for faculty work.

Describing the Work of Faculty—Statements from the Disciplines

Since disciplinary/scholarly associations play a key role in influencing the significance of particular faculty roles and their recognition in the reward system, a project was begun in 1991 at Syracuse University to work with a number of these associations in the development of statements describing the scholarly, professional, and creative work of faculty in the disciplines. Funded by the Fund for the Improvement of Postsecondary Education and the Lilly Endowment, Inc., the project was built on a number of premises: that the redefinition of scholarship will expand the range of activities that qualify as scholarly or creative faculty work and that an extension of the range of activities recognized as scholarly will change the priorities at colleges and universities, while at the same time facilitating (1) an improvement in the quality of teaching, (2) an improvement in the quality of curricula and courses, and (3) greater participation in applied work and service activities. In addition, the statements can serve as a basis for assessing the relative performance of faculty in an equitable manner.

The project assisted disciplinary associations in establishing faculty taskforces to develop and disseminate definitions of scholarly work. Included in the definition statements are lists of activities that academic departments are encouraged to consider when developing their own promotion, tenure, merit, or reward system guidelines. It was expected that individual departments would choose to value more strongly those activities that were appropriate to its specific mission, while perhaps expanding the range of activities it might value in the work of its faculty. This approach recognized the fact that different institutions and units have different strengths, resources, and priorities.

Disciplinary groups that have participated in project activities include the Association of American Geographers, the American Philosophical Association, the Conference on College Composition and Communication, the American Political Science Association, the American Chemical Society, the American Sociological Association, the National Council of Administrators of Home Economics, the American Academy of Religion, the Modern Language Association, the American Historical Association, the American Assembly of Collegiate Schools of Business, the Association for Education in Journalism and Mass Communications, the National Architecture Accrediting Board, the Geological Society of America, the Joint Policy Board for Mathematics, and the National Office for Arts Accreditation in Higher Education, which includes the fields of landscape architecture, architecture, art and design, dance, music, and theater.

The initial goal for this project was that approximately five of the scholarly associations would agree to participate. As the preceding list illustrates, the response was far more positive, ostensibly because each of the disciplinary groups identified problems for their faculty with the existing reward system. These problems are apparent when one reads the statements developed in these discipline groups:

> Geographers employed in American colleges and universities for too long have been hired to do one job and rewarded for doing another. (Recognizing Faculty Roles and Reward in Geography, Association of American Geographers, 1994)

> The debate over priorities is not discipline specific but extends across the higher education community. Nevertheless, each discipline has specific concerns and problems. For history, the privilege given to the monograph in promotion and tenure has led to the undervaluing of other activities central to the life of the discipline—writing textbooks, developing courses and curricula, documentary editing, museum exhibitions, and film projects to name but a few. (The Defining Historical Scholarship. Report of the American Historical Association. Ad Hoc Committee on Redefining Scholarly Work, 1994)

> After reflecting on its study and findings, the Committee discussed at some length a wide variety of possible recommendations. We came to the conclusion that, given the enormous diversity of institutions of higher education and departments, only one general recommendation could be made: The recognition and rewards system in mathematical sciences departments must encompass the full array of faculty activity required to fulfill departmental and institutional missions.

> We learned from our study of the rewards structure that this perhaps self-evident recommendation is being implemented in only a small number of departments, and only a somewhat larger number are even beginning to grapple with the issues it entails. There is a clear need for departments to implement the changes that are required to achieve the goal stated in the recommendation. (Recognition and

Rewards in the Mathematical Services. Report of the Joint Policy Board for Mathematics Committee on Professional Recognition and Rewards, 1994)

As these disciplinary statements were developed, the differences among the disciplines became apparent. There is no single definition of "scholarship" that will be agreed to across disciplines, and to try to establish such a definition can be counterproductive. The taskforce of the American Academy of Religion described their approach to the definition issue as follows:

> Given the unique history and place of religious studies in higher education, and the diversity of subfields, pedagogical goals and institutional linkages within the scope of the field, we are not at all sanguine that redefining the word scholarship to cover teaching or other professional activities now not normally considered as such is particularly useful or appropriate. Indeed, it could well appear disingenuous seemingly to stretch the categories like this in an attempt to gain what might otherwise be a worthy end. We would rather affirm the importance of excellence and quality in all the diverse modes of professional academic work, and redefine or open up the currently operative categories (research, teaching, service), than to create a new metacategory or taxonomy which (a) might eventually not serve its intended purpose, and (b) blur important distinctions within the types or professional work we all amend to. Our report, therefore, focuses on clarifying the scope and variety of professional academic work in religious studies with an eye especially on teaching. (Religious Studies and the Redefinition of Scholarly Work. A report of the American Academy of Religion Ad Hoc Committee, 1993)

Encouraging each discipline to describe its work in language with which it is comfortable with has ramifications for faculty serving on Promotion and Tenure Committees and the process that is used on campuses to develop faculty reward guidelines.[3]

- While some disciplines (history and sociology) were comfortable with the four categories of scholarship conceptualized by Eugene Rice and Ernest Boyer (the advance of knowledge, the integration of knowledge, the application of knowledge, and the transformation of knowledge) to describe the work of faculty, others were not (1990). The statement from the American Assembly of Collegiate School of Business used a modification of these categories; other disciplines built their statements around the traditional triad of research, teaching, and service (geography, chemistry, journalism, and religion). Still others, such as the performing and creative arts, developed a unique schema appropriate for their discipline.
- For those disciplines that have emphasized research over the last decade in order to gain "prestige," efforts to redefine and broaden the scope of faculty work represents a shift in direction that some observers view as a high–risk endeavor. A number of taskforces discussed this potential "tradeoff" before deciding to participate in the process of drafting a formal statement to expand the scope of professional/scholarly work for faculty in their discipline.

- The more comfortable a faculty member is with the present system, the greater the possibility that he or she will be resistant to change in the promotion and tenure system. It was very clear from data in the National Study that many faculty, particularly in the sciences, see their departments losing resources, and consequently power, if the present reward system is modified.

It is important to emphasize that the key decision regarding faculty rewards must be made at the departmental level where the mission of the institution, the priorities of the unit, the nature of the discipline, and the strengths of the individual intersect. The fairness of the system rests on the clarity of the guidelines that are used, the careful consideration of the individuals engaged in the process of applying them, and the quality of documentation that is required of and provided by those being reviewed. While no single factor determines how faculty will spend their professional time, having disciplinary statements available will support the development of a faculty reward system that is fair to the individual, the department, and the institution.

NOTES

1. Alcene Bycer Russel, *Faculty Workload: State and System Perspectives* (State Higher Education Executive Officers and Education Commission of the States. November 1992).

2. Peter J. Gray, Robert C. Froh, and Robert M. Diamond, *A National Study of Research Universities on the Balance Between Research and Undergraduate Teaching* (Syracuse, N.Y.: Center for Instructional Development, Syracuse University, March 1992).

3. Robert M. Diamond, *Serving on Promotion and Tenure Committees: A Faculty Guide* (Bolton, Mass.: Anker Publishing, 1994).

REFERENCE

Boyer, Ernest. *Scholarship Reconsidered: Priorities of the Professoriate*. Princeton, N.J.: Carnegie Foundation, 1990.

3

Talking about Research: Are We Playing Someone Else's Game?

Elizabeth S. Blake

INTRODUCTION

Language influences not only *what* we perceive but the *way* we perceive it, as the modern public relations "spin doctors" know well. Using imagery-filled speech is a way of making people "see" something more vividly, but it may also distort their view. Today a pervasive imagery seems to color our perception—and the public's perception—of higher education, to the detriment of the learning community and of educational values in our society. We need to be aware of the distortive imagery, the underlying values it betrays, and then consider some alternative ways of portraying what we do. The area of scholarly research and publication provides a good illustration of the problem and some examples of ways to eliminate the distortion.[1]

Taken to the point of caricature, scholarship today can become a kind of high-stakes *game* played for money, power, and prestige. One disillusioned humanist, Sande Cohen, has put it this way: "In academia, political and cultural achievement is defined as the property of prestige, what prestige owns and loans out, prestige as the final money" (1993, 27). As one listens to colleagues talking about their research in terms of the prestige, grant money, or other advantages it will bring them, it is evident that a certain imagery is predominant in their speech. Metaphors from sports and military life appear constantly. The following composite narrative is only somewhat exaggerated, concentrating images that are usually scattered over a longer statement:

The Winning Team

At our university the research group in that field is led by a *superstar* professor who has never *struck out* on a grant proposal. At national conferences she and her *team go in* with a *game plan*. In the sessions they *demolish* the *opposition* with their *rapid-fire* questioning. They *huddle* in advance of major discussions, *mapping out* their *strategy* so as to *defend* their *high ground* against potential

attacks. Sometimes one *member of the team* will *send up a trial balloon* to see
if it gets *shot down* by anyone. Her loyal *crew* find it *no sweat* to *recruit heavy
hitters* out of the best graduate schools because, naturally, everyone wants to *join
a winning team*!

Daily conversation provides other examples of the kind of metaphorical
accumulations to which I am referring:

— What's *your call* on the big NSF proposal?
— In my view, it's *dead in the water*.

— With a *scattershot* approach like that, we're sure to *flush out* some new data.
— Yeah, but it will delay us; we'll have to change the *target* date.

— Is Joe *on board* yet?
— No, he wants to *sit this one out*.

— Look, we *made our move*; the *ball's in her court* now.
— I don't think she's gonna *play*.

— To me, it's a *trap*. They want to *lure* us into *taking their bait*.
— And that will make us *sitting ducks* for the IRS, right?

— Hey, *what's the score*?
— Better *circle the wagons*. The Dean's *on the offensive* again.

The pursuit of knowledge calls for a different set of values. The mission of
colleges and universities gives priority to *learning*; it is their reason for being.
All knowledge is interconnected, and the natural description of its growth and
shaping by the human mind involves primary images of form, pattern, and light.
The passing on of knowledge from one mind to another is a collaborative act,
not a competitive one. Yet in many aspects of university life, and especially in
research, competition among scholars can put *winning* ahead of learning. By
extension, the goal of research and publication then easily becomes *success*
rather than *understanding*, triumph over others rather than cooperation with them
in a common adventure of discovery.

VALUES REFLECTED IN LANGUAGE

Competition is a widespread human activity that is especially associated with
the economic and political structure of the United States. As voters, workers,
owners, and consumers, we cooperate with each other in many group settings,
but we also *compete*. It is our typical American way of participating in what is
actually a value system that all human beings share, that is, the social-political-
economic arrangements that reflect human gregariousness, or the need for
society. For lack of a better general term, this social-political-economic value

system can be called the "Community of Power." The underlying motivation is self-preservation—the need for food, clothing, and shelter—with its built-in conflict between dependence on others and individual needs.

The simplistic chart presented in Table 3.1 sharpens the contrast in value systems to make them more explicit.[2] The first column shows the nature and some of the characteristics of the Community of Power—a value system that has justice as its ideal, or goal. The clusters of images that represent this value system in our everyday speech and writing frequently relate to sports, games, conflict, and, ultimately, war. In our social and economic "games," it is best if the opposing forces are balanced, so as to "play fair," but in the end someone wins and someone loses. Although women may point to the origin of this imagery, so pervasive today, in men's widely shared twentieth-century experiences in sports and military service, *all of us,* men and women, use such words and images more than we realize.

Table 3.1
Value System "Communities"

Characteristic	Community of Power	Community of Learning
Drive	Self-preservation	Understanding
Need	Access to resources	Order and structure
Goal	Justice	Truth
Emphasized virtues	Fairness, utility, independence	Accuracy, thoroughness, impartiality
Media of exchange	Money, goods, territory, prestige	Language, symbol systems, rhythm, design
Units	Rights, claims, contracts	Ideas, concepts, theories
Image clusters	Games and sports Military, war Conflict, struggle Competition, fair play Winning and losing Gambling, chance	Light, enlightenment Sight, picture Pattern, structure Grid, circuit, web, network Tapestry, cloth, weaving Building, joining

Images of game-playing and conflict appear in every—shall I say—*arena* of our lives. A reporter: "The city editor really *threw me a curve* with that assignment." A new employee: "For a long time, I felt as if I were *out in left field.*" An advertising expert: "The surveys show we aren't reaching people yet. Let's *bring up the heavy artillery.*" The dentist to a patient: "Today's filling may be painful. Do you want me to *knock you out* this time?" Whether we are talking about politics, or commerce, or justice, or just exchanging pleasantries, our speech is filled with indirect references to combat and competition. Is it surprising then that this imagery gets transferred into the world of scholarship? While it may not be surprising, it is dangerous. By talking about learning as if it were a series of power negotiations, we devalue our own curiosity, the natural human desire to *learn* and understand on which culture itself is built.

Learning sets up its own value system. The social-economic-political community that assures our survival is not the only values community within which we all live and function. As human beings we are also all *learners*, from the moment of birth until our death, and our thirst to know creates another powerful value system. The righthand column of Table 3.1 presents some characteristics of that second system. The Community of Learning, as opposed to the Community of Power, is based on a system of relationships of knowledge, of concepts and ideas and theories, arising from the effort to make sense of the world and think about it. The defining motivation is the desire to understand, and the goal is truth. Human symbolic systems provide not only the media of exchange, mainly language, but also music, mathematics, logic, form, color, and so on. One finds *webs* and *tapestries*, *networks* and *circuits*, the *interlocking pieces of a puzzle* gradually revealed. We speak of *shedding light* on an issue; we want to eliminate the *darkness* of ignorance. All of creation is a *seamless web*, to use Stanley Burnshaw's term (1970). Ruth Benedict's early populariza-tion of anthropology was entitled *Patterns of Culture* (1934). An astrophysicist, looking at a large quantity of computer printouts, will say, "I see an emerging *pattern* here." We ask ourselves how the courses in a new program will *fit together*, and we talk about the internal *structuring* of the theories we elaborate. And so on and on.

TWO VALUE SYSTEMS: THE COMMUNITY OF POWER AND THE COMMUNITY OF LEARNING

As the moral philosopher John Rawls puts it in the introduction to his theoretical study of the social contract, *A Theory of Justice*, "Justice is the first virtue of social institutions, as truth is of systems of thought" (1971, 3). From these two highly abstract "first virtues" come different priorities, a different perspective that colors the same events distinctively. At times we keep the two value systems I have described compartmentalized, so that issues related to our jobs, our rights, and our government are decided one way (by means of money, power, justice) while issues related to knowledge are decided in another way (by means of hypotheses, proof, facts). Yet the *same* issues can often be looked at either way, as in the case of a family inheritance, for example. One family member may be focused on who will end up as the favored heir while another is more interested in what the distribution of the inheritance reveals about the deceased. The two value systems are operative in our lives simultaneously. They should probably be more or less in balance as we go about our daily affairs.

The problem is that in recent years the values of the Community of Power—those of the marketplace and of the political arena—have become so overwhelmingly dominant in our lives that they threaten to engulf the values of the Community of Learning. Education at all levels finds itself awash in *competition*—competition for power, resources, and recognition—and drowning in the competitive imagery of the larger society. The danger is that educational values will be lost. This danger does not mean that competition has no place in shaping the institutions of higher education and their functioning as corporate entities. In his book *Higher Learning* (1986), Derek Bok makes the point well that competitive forces are a more beneficent force in the shaping of colleges and universities, as in the United States, than is the heavy hand of a national bureaucracy, as in much of the rest of the world. But he is discussing *institutions*. My concern here is for learning itself: the discovery and creation of knowledge and its transmission to others. In that quest for learning, unfortunately, we are out there playing someone else's game, so to speak, and often looking foolish to the spectators, that is, our fellow citizens.

During the 1970s and 1980s, Senator William Proxmire's monthly "Golden Fleece" awards were symbolic of the public trivializing of academic pursuits. The very first Golden Fleece award was made in 1975 to a faculty member in psychology at my own university, the University of Minnesota. (Could the fact that Senator Proxmire represented rival state Wisconsin have had anything to do with that choice?) One of the last awards, in 1988, was made jointly to the National Science Foundation and the National Institutes of Mental Health because Proxmire thought that it was a waste of government money to study sexual behavior in quail. This was notwithstanding the fact that the research being derided was expected to yield results useful to the understanding of AIDS.

The outline presented in Table 3.2 concerning two areas of the humanities, perhaps suggests why the conflict in value systems causes the public, including legislators, to trivialize scholarship and makes it difficult for scholars and ordinary citizens to communicate. The comparative illustrations are taken from history and literature.

The lefthand column lists some commonly held popular conceptions of the two fields. History consists of dates and details; literature is just old stories. Such attributes have low value in the Community of Power, making history and literature appear unimportant in the public's eyes. Generally accepted attributes of the two fields as viewed by scholars, on the other hand, give history and literature high value in the Community of Learning. Alas, the general public seldom perceives these attributes. The result is misunderstanding on both sides. More importantly, the result is a general weakening of the value system of *learning* takes place. That in turn leads scholars to try to strengthen the university's voice by casting their own statements in the imagery of the Community of Power. Some recent headlines from *The Chronicle of Higher Education* and an *AAHE Bulletin* include the following:

> *The Chronicle of Higher Education*, October 27, 1993, A8 and A31
> LINGUISTICS ON THE DEFENSIVE AT HARVARD
> HOUSE DELIVERS A FATAL BLOW TO THE SUPERCONDUCTING SUPERCOLLIDER
>
> *AAHE Bulletin*, Vol. 46, No. 4, December 1993, 12.
> BRINGING THE "TEAM APPROACH" TO GENERAL STUDIES: A WINNING STRATEGY
>
> *The Chronicle of Higher Education*, March 2, 1994, A8, A10, and A17
> SCHOLARS REFIGHT THE COLD WAR
> WHO KILLED THE SSC?
> ALL QUIET ON THE WESTERN FRONT—FOR NOW
> (about the Western Association of Colleges and Schools)

With this pervasive imagery, and the mindset it betrays, teaching and learning are devalued, while research is glorified not because of the learning involved but because of its competitive aspects. Teaching, being a less visible and competitive activity, tends to become a burden from which one aspires to be relieved. Research may not be done with dedicated, singleminded service to the pursuit of truth because research of the "right" kind brings in grant money, or patents, or royalties on publications, not to speak of recognition among one's peers. American higher education generally has acquiesced in these distortions without protest, making little effort to defend the learning values on which it is in fact founded—a curious state of affairs.

SCHOLARLY RESEARCH AND PUBLICATION WITHIN THE COMMUNITY OF LEARNING

Let us now see what happens if one looks at scholarly research and publication without distortion, as learning activities, that is, applying the values of the Community of Learning. There is no need to invoke competition to prove their worth. Research and publication by faculty are vitally important to *student learning* at both the undergraduate and graduate levels. To look at research and publication in terms of student learning is to change the priorities. This in turn leads to new insights into teaching and into the relationship of research to teaching. The three points I want to make apply most directly to undergraduate learning, since that is the area with which I am most familiar, but I think they are also pertinent to the graduate level.

Table 3.2
Valuing the Humanities

Nonintersecting Views of Two Fields		
Field	Popular View	Scholarly View
History	Chronology Names, dates, details, useless trivia A distant past	The past in context Social forces influencing the course of human events Preservation of records
Literature	Old stories Complicated rhymes Wordy documents Out-of-date information These characteristics have *low* value in the Community of Power. The perspective of the Community of Learning is absent.	Language as art Genres: prose, poetry, drama Analysis, criticism Literary history These characteristics have *high* value in the Community of Learning. The perspective of the Community of Power is recognized as inappropriate.

Thinking Aloud in the Classroom

Scholarly publishing is important, first of all, not because it brings prestige but because it disseminates ideas, revealing to one scholar how another scholar *thinks*. A university professor ought to be able to show students how he or she thinks, and the faculty most likely to do this are those who present papers and publish. Learning to think in the manner required for excellent work in physics or psychology or history is one of the most fundamental but difficult arts that an undergraduate or graduate student must master. Often there is no model to go on for undergraduates because by the time the course is taught, much of the thinking about that subject matter has already been done outside the classroom, either by the professor or by the textbook author. The students may see only the results of thinking, not the process. Faculty members need to demonstrate, repeatedly, in front of students, how scholarship in their field is conducted—that is, how their own minds work as they confront a relevant topic, question, or set of data. That means occasionally tackling new, untried problems and working them out in the classroom, even in an introductory course. Why is this not done more often? The main reason is because it is a scary business. When the professor is a publishing scholar, however, accustomed to the give and take of peer criticism, she or he may be less afraid of revealing in front of a class the hesitation, groping, and wrong turns that naturally occur.

Beginning students are made uneasy by such an apparent lack of certainty, of course, and initially may be quite critical of the faculty member. Yet "thinking out loud" in front of students is essential in demonstrating intellectual honesty and accuracy and in getting students to step "behind the scenes" of the intellectual world where they can see for themselves, early on, that currently accepted truths form a setting for people's lives which is only temporary, that the stage setting can be changed, and that they, too, can learn how the ropes are pulled.

It is not enough to teach in this way only those students who already know how the system works; there are too few such students compared with the world's need for educated people. Students who have always thought that some mysterious "they" controlled what happened in their lives need to find out where ideas come from. Then they need to try making things happen themselves in various fields of knowledge until they see that they, too, can have an impact.

Collaborative Faculty/Student Research

That leads us to a second reason why scholarly research and publication should be valued in relation to student learning. Both graduates and undergraduates need opportunities to participate in research, and faculty who are themselves active in giving papers and publishing (or creating, in the case of artists) tend to be the best at making such opportunities available. Involving students in research early on allows them to share in both the tedium and the excitement of the quest for knowledge. It tends to slow down the research, however, so that the faculty member who is oriented primarily to beating the competition to a discovery may not want to make time for undergraduates. Faculty members expect that graduate students, especially the most gifted of them, will want to follow in their footsteps, so in certain fields collaboration with them is quite common. But it is particularly those students who are *not* continuing as scholars—that is, probably the majority of undergraduate majors (at least in the traditional liberal arts fields)—who can benefit from understanding how research works because they will be better able to interpret its results sensibly later on as citizen-voters or in their work environment. Even if they do not themselves experience research directly, they benefit from hearing about it from their peers and thereby gain some sense of what professional scholarship entails.

One advantage of a small public college setting like the Morris campus of the University of Minnesota, focused on undergraduates, is that faculty make undergraduates their research partners by necessity. The undergraduates do not have to compete with graduate students who are already committed specialists in the faculty member's field. Thus, more undergraduates enjoy hands-on experience with specialized laboratory equipment or with books from the faculty member's own library, or delve into unfamiliar bibliographies and databases, or learn to work with original manuscripts and "raw" materials or natural phenomena. The students bring to their task fresh enthusiasm and a sometimes usefully naive viewpoint on the research project being carried out. The University of North Carolina at Asheville, another small public liberal arts college, is exemplary in regard to the encouragement of research and publication by undergraduates, having begun in the 1980s to emphasize undergraduate research opportunities on its own campus and become the home of the Council on Undergraduate Research and the National Conferences on Undergraduate Research. The annual National Conference now involves hundreds of students and takes place each year on a different public or private campus.[3]

The Teacher-Scholars

There is a third reason to value scholarly publishing as it relates to student learning, particularly at the undergraduate level. Since the 1950s, considerable pressure has been placed on faculty members to publish if they wish to get ahead in a university career. In other words, the forces pushing faculty into individual competition have been stronger than those of the traditional "collegium." Yet that does not mean that faculty *do* publish. In 1975 when Everett Ladd and Seymour Lipset presented the results of a 1969 Carnegie Commission survey of four-year college and university faculty members, it showed that roughly one–quarter of the faculty were publishing regularly, while the rest published rarely or not at all. Since then, the pressure to publish has increased, but it is not clear that the proportion of faculty actively publishing is higher. A more recent Carnegie survey, in 1989, showed that 97 percent of faculty value teaching and *want* to teach well. At present, the pendulum of university opinion seems to be swinging back toward concentrating more effort on teaching, nudged strongly by Ernest Boyer's Carnegie Foundation report of 1990, entitled *Scholarship Reconsidered; Priorities of the Professoriate*, and the efforts of Patricia Cross, Thomas Angelo, and others on behalf of "classroom research." Looking at faculty research from the perspective of the individual student's learning experience, one may legitimately ask: Is publishing detrimental because its competitiveness draws faculty away from the classroom? Or, on the other hand, should *all* college and university faculty members engage in publicly sharing their scholarly or artistic work because of its value in the *learning* process?

There are at least two reasons why it is important to the best possible undergraduate experience that all faculty members *do* research of some sort themselves and present that research publicly from time to time, even if they are primarily teaching undergraduates. It is not because royalties from books may augment their salaries or because publishing makes a faculty member more marketable. Faculty at the college level need to be active in some form of scholarship or creative endeavor, first of all, because they need regularly to be willing to subject their own ideas to the criticism of knowledgeable peers. Their own undergraduate students, however bright, are by definition not yet their peers in a given subject. If they were, they would not be enrolled in that course. If faculty members are going to pass judgment on student work, they must be willing to continue to be learners themselves and to have their own ideas judged by those best qualified to offer informed criticism. Without that, it is all too easy to lose one's perspective—and one's compassion and humility—after twenty or thirty years of teaching. At that point, student learning suffers.

In the second place, students need to feel that they are being guided not by people of unattainable expertise but by fellow learners who still enjoy discovery. The faculty member who publishes, and thus is part of the international "conversation" on problems in his or her field, tends to be both a model and a resource for students. The idea of the faculty member not as an authority figure but as a resource person for the individual student to consult is especially well exemplified at the public liberal arts honors college of Florida, New College of the University of South Florida. The program at New College emphasizes the tutorial mode, with the student taking charge of her or his learning, not waiting for faculty to lead the way but consulting the faculty member for guidance, information, and assistance. As a professor of biology describes it in their admissions viewbook: "Faculty serve as facilitators and mentors rather than as purveyors of information" (*The Viewbook*, 2). The more the line between faculty member and student is thus blurred, the more engaged the student is apt to become in the learning process. As many studies of college students have shown, the more actively students are involved in their own learning, the more lasting is the impact of education.[4] All three of the public liberal arts colleges mentioned so far in this essay—North Carolina-Asheville, Minnesota-Morris, and New College—stress involvement and it is a guiding principle for the recently constituted Council of Public Liberal Arts Colleges (COPLAC).[5] One of COPLAC's goals is to set institutional priorities in relation to impact on student learning.

CONCLUSION

More and more people in higher education seem worried these days about a values conflict that they sense but cannot always characterize. In the fall 1992 issue of the *NCA Quarterly*, for instance, Alexander Astin describes "two basic realities about American higher education. First is the fact that, perhaps unwittingly, we have become an active participant in the societal *competitiveness* and materialism that we see all around us. Second, and more important, is the fact that we possess a tremendous untapped potential not only for restoring a better *balance in societal values* but also for alleviating some of our most urgent societal problems" [italics added]. It's that balance in societal values that should be righted, as the academy once again centers its actions—and its words—on *learning*. As Richard Hofstadter pointed out in the early 1960s, when he published *Anti-intellectualism in American Life* (1961), this country has never been terribly hospitable to the Community of Learning in its more complex intellectual manifestations. Americans tend to prefer their Sunday afternoon football and their late-night movie violence. Still, we have managed to develop across this land a rich and diverse network of colleges and universities second to none. The challenge is to bring today's colleges and universities out of what one might call their captivity to the overly dominant values of the Community of Power and to rethink our work in terms of creating the best possible *learning* situations for our students and ourselves.

As you listen to the next research discussion on your campus, why not check the imagery the speakers use? What values seem to dominate the politics and processes of scholarly publishing for them? Perhaps you will also ask yourself, in a quiet moment, "What ideals did I go into higher education to pursue? How can I, and those I work with, be more faithful to those ideals?" We have been drawn into playing other people's games and into using the language of other people's games to describe our own. By changing our perspective and by consistently centering our work and our words on *learning*, we will strengthen the university's mission—the teaching, the research, the scholarly publishing—and we will foster the values of education more effectively in the society at large.

NOTES

1. Much of the reading and reflection leading to this essay occurred while I was on leave during the fall of 1992 as a visiting fellow at the New England Resource Center for Higher Education, College of Education, University of Massachusetts at Boston.

2. The idea of conflicting value systems functioning simultaneously in human life is adapted from central ideas in a book by Alexander Miller entitled *Faith and Learning*, originally published in 1960 by the New York Association Press. Miller's purpose was to assist church-related colleges in separating their educational and ecclesiastical missions. Miller based some of his thinking on an earlier work, *The Theological Idea of the University*, by George H. Williams (New York: Commission on Higher Education of the National Council of Churches, 1958). The two charts (Tables 3.1 and 3.2) are my own, however, as are the connections made here to speech imagery.

3. Studies have shown repeatedly that small colleges (where there is apt to be much faculty-student interaction) produce the highest percentages of Ph.D.s in proportion to the number of their graduates. A survey by Carol Fuller that appeared in 1985, *An Analysis of Leading Undergraduate Sources of Ph.D.'s, Adjusted for Institutional Size*, for example, done under the auspices of the Lilly Endowment, shows that from 1951 to 1980 the ratio of graduates of the Associated Colleges of the Midwest who received Ph.D.s was 6.9, compared with a 4.3 ratio for graduates of the "Big Ten" universities. It is reasonable to suppose that working closely with faculty members on their research when one is an undergraduate provides strong encouragement to go for a doctorate later in one's career.

4. Key references on the importance of students' involvement in their own learning are the two books by Alexander Astin which form a sequence, *Four Critical Years* (San Francisco: Jossey-Bass, 1977) and *What Matters in College?` Four Critical Years Revisited* (San Francisco: Jossey-Bass, 1992).

5. The formation of the Council of Public Liberal Arts Colleges (COPLAC) was officially announced at the Annual Meeting of the Association of American Colleges and Universities in Washington, D.C., in January 1994. Among the founding institutions were College of Charleston (S.C.), the Evergreen State College (Wash.), Keene State College (N.H.), Mary Washington College (Va.), New College of the University of South Florida, Northeast Missouri State University, Ramapo College of New Jersey, St. Mary's College of Maryland, University of Maine at Farmington, University of Minnesota, Morris, and University of North Carolina-Asheville.

REFERENCES

AAHE Bulletin 46 (1993): 12.

Astin, Alexander W. *Four Critical Years*. San Francisco: Jossey-Bass, 1977.

—. "Values, Assessment, and Academic Freedom: A Challenge to the Accrediting Process." *NCA Quarterly* 67, 2 (Fall 1992): 295–306.

—. *What Matters in College? Four Critical Years Revisited*. San Francisco: Jossey-Bass, 1992.

Benedict, Ruth. *Patterns of Culture*. Boston: Houghton Mifflin, 1934.

Bok, Derek. *Higher Learning*. Cambridge, Mass.: Harvard University Press, 1986.

Boyer, Ernest L. *Scholarship Reconsidered: Priorities of the Professoriate*. Princeton, N.J.: Carnegie Foundation for the Advancement of Teaching, 1990.

Burnshaw, Stanley. *The Seamless Web*. New York: George Braziller, 1970.

Chronicle of Higher Education. October 27, 1993: A8, A31. March 2, 1994: A8, A10, A17.

Cohen, Sande. *Academia and the Luster of Capital*. Minneapolis: Minnesota University Press, 1993.

Cross, K. Patricia, and Thomas A. Angelo. *Classroom Assessment Techniques: A Handbook for Faculty*. Ann Arbor, Mich.: National Center for Research on the Improvement of Post-secondary Teaching and Learning, University of Michigan, 1988.

Hofstadter, Richard. *Anti-intellectualism in American Life*. New York: Alfred A. Knopf, 1961.

Ladd, Everett Carll, and Seymour Martin Lipset. *Survey of the Social, Political, and Educational Perspectives of American College and University Faculty.* Final Report (based on 1969 survey). Princeton, N.J.: Carnegie Foundation for the Advancement of Teaching, 1976.

"Proxmire Says Federal Study of Quail Sexual Habits Is for Birds." *Minneapolis Star-Tribune* March 17, 1988: 3.

Rawls, John. *A Theory of Justice.* Cambridge, Mass.: Belknap Press of Harvard University Press, 1971.

The Viewbook. Sarasota: New College of the University of South Florida, n.d.

4

A Reexamination of Views of Scholarly Publishing and Our Expectations of Faculty Productivity in Light of Federal Government Support

Maggie Johnson and David Watt

> Usually it took him a fortnight to make the discovery, write the report, and have it accepted.
>
> —Sinclair Lewis, *Arrowsmith*

This description of Almus Pickerbaugh, a character in Sinclair Lewis's *Arrowsmith*, is a classic portrait of a scientist imbued with more self-promotion than talent. But if we examine the current status of scholarly publication in American universities, there is an element of truth here that we can no longer afford to ignore: it has become possible, even desirable, to realize Pickerbaugh's fictional achievements. One of us is reminded of the remarkable productivity of a particular scientist: publications bearing this person's name now exceed one thousand. A little mathematics would suggest that if this scientist were active for a thirty-year period, then a paper bearing his name appeared once every two weeks. It would be wrong, of course, to suggest that there is anything suspect about this scientist's work, but the ability to publish at this rate, an outcome that Sinclair Lewis regarded as so improbable as to define a charlatan like Pickerbaugh, is now a reality. In another regrettable case, a different scientist produced a paper on average every ten days during a two-year period, and this prolific record failed to raise any questions until a member of a departmental committee reviewing his appointment noted the duplication of data in two articles (Abelson, 1990, 216–222). Legitimate productivity at this level is, of course, still quite exceptional, but if trends in scholarly publishing continue in their current vein, it appears likely that others will match this record. According to a recent summary, the approximately 379,000 faculty ("Almanac Issue," 1993, 5) in the United States are publishing at a prodigious rate: "Each U.S. full-time college faculty member averaged two refereed journal articles and 0.6 scholarly books, chapters in edited volumes, monographs or textbooks in the previous two years according to 1988 data from the Department of Education" (Mooney, 1991, A17). But numbers are not the only issue here.[1]

The need to sustain our commitment to scholarly research and creative efforts, as Henry Rosovsky so well articulates, represents our faith in change and improvement. If the goal of our investigations is "the revision of accepted conclusions" (Rosovsky, 1980, 86), such revisions will be accepted only if they are announced and debated widely—an activity that means publication. This tradition of investigation and publication is not just a modern phenomenon. Daniel Coit Gilman, president of Johns Hopkins University in the late nineteenth century, said to faculty, "Learned publications, containing memoirs that are only meant for the scholar—positive contributions to knowledge—are the noblest fruits of academic culture" (1898, 298). The tie between research and publication, just as Gilman espoused, persists to this day. Data taken from four national surveys of the American professoriate in 1969, 1975, 1980, and 1988 suggest that an emphasis on research at all types of institutions continues to increase (DeLoughry, 1993, A14–A17). The place for research and scholarly publishing at the academic table is secure; however, our thesis in this chapter is that the need to invite other guests to this table is even more apparent now than in the past. The notion that the reward system needs revision is not new: At the time of his retirement, Gilman recognized the growing problem of fragmented research accounts (Bruce, 1987, 336). His voice has been joined by a chorus of others (Astle, 1989, 151–156) calling for change.

The professional and economic costs of sustaining this pace of scholarly publishing is high (Mooney, A17): fragmentary, disjointed, or partial research accounts that complicate the training of new scholars; marginal peer reviewing that diminishes the quality of a journal or the fairness of a proposal review; limited faculty time for other activities like student and peer contact; a proliferation of specialized journals that are infrequently cited; and perhaps most serious, a tendency to discourage long-term, high-risk research in favor of trivial, "n+1" studies whose success is assured (Hamilton, "Trivia," 1991, 63–42). The suggestion (Crawford and Stucki, 1990, 223–228; Mooney, A17) that the escalating pace of scholarly publications might also provide a temptation to publish fraudulent results is particularly troubling. The outlets for scholarly publishing have increased substantially: a study (Bieber and Blackburn, 1989) of the disciplines of biology, psychology, and English in the years 1972 to 1988 indicated that almost twice as much space was available for faculty publishing in 1988 as in 1972, while faculty numbers increased only slightly. These outlets, which possess varying standards and degrees of refereeing, provide ample opportunity for virtually any voice to be heard—perhaps at the expense of quality and thoughtful commentary. The costs that we list, however one ranks their consequences, are significant in the sense that they detract from the mission of a research university and undermine the values that we ascribe to this mission.

Universities are facing dramatic increases in the costs of maintaining publishing as an outlet for the faculty's creative activities[2] (Cummings et al., 1992; Dougherty and Dougherty, 1993, 342–346), and it is this cost factor, more than any other, that has brought the issue of scholarly publication to the fore (Noll and Steinmueller, 1992, 32–37). The situation is a complex one in which all the key players have interdependent roles and aspirations: authors who see scholarly publications as the road to advancement and professional stature; libraries that serve the faculty and define themselves in terms of the number of volumes in their collection (DeLoughry, A15–A17); companies that see the opportunity to merchandise new communication technologies; professional societies that believe their journals preserve the intellectual heritage of their disciplines; federal agencies that observe the rapidly changing nature of disciplines and the need to encourage research; and publishers who see a genuine role for their contributions as well as the growth of the "bottom line." Even the universities, although burdened with the cost of supporting, producing, cataloging, and retrieving this information, resort to publishing statistics in their internal evaluations of programs and external reports to legislatures and accrediting agencies. In fact, most universities now have "institutional research" offices charged with reducing each faculty member to so many bytes of statistical information: number of books published, number of journal articles, number of graduate students who obtain Ph.D. degrees, and the like. All of these relationships and needs serve to increase the number of scholarly publications.

Many thoughtful suggestions have been made to control the spiraling increase in traditional scholarly publishing: authors could turn to "electronic publishing" (Calabrese, 1992, 425–438; Dillon, 1991, 23–26; Metz and Gherman, 1991, 315–327; Piternick, 1989, 260–266; Stankus, 1986, 17–27); libraries could pursue "acquisition-on-demand," meaning that they would purchase individual articles rather than subscriptions (Drake, 1992, 75); libraries could form consortiums that partition holdings and share information; authors and possibly universities could assert their ownership of published information if copyright laws were changed (Eisenschitz, 1986, 263–267; Okerson, 1991, 425–438); professional societies or university presses could take charge of scholarly publishing for various disciplines; and for-profit publishers could be held accountable for price increases that outstrip inflation rates (Hafner et al., 1990, 217–223; Marks et al., 1991, 125–138; Tagler, 1989, 109–113). Publishers take exception to the last point, enumerating both the value that they add to such publications and the costs that they face (Boswood, 1986/1987, 9–17). Finally, there have been suggestions that the federal government should or will become involved in these issues (Calabrese, 199–220). Although these suggestions may have some role to play in the future of scholarly publications, they are focused primarily on the economics of the problem. None of them addresses in a substantive way the underlying problem that has driven the expansion of scholarly publications.

The source of the problem lies in the means that faculty use to evaluate one another. Publication per se is not a problem. It facilitates the discussion of new ideas and discoveries, and it is an absolute requirement for "the revision of accepted facts," Webster's definition of research (Rosovsky, 86). However, scholarly publishing has also become the *sine qua non* of assessment mechanisms in higher education and the agencies that support research in higher education. The linkage between scholarly publication and professional stature, the tie between publication and professional advancement, and the connection between scholarly publication and continued grant funding from many federal agencies are understandable, even defensible. It may well be that higher education's need for professional staff and facilities to store, manage, and retrieve this information is the primary force pushing us to reexamine scholarly publishing (Mooney A17), but it is the notion that the number of publications matters more than the content that corrupts the current system. One recent study defined research productivity as the average annual number of articles published per faculty member (Baird, 1986, 211–225).

In using publication as an assessment tool, we are often unable to make a direct, informed judgment about a scholar's publications. The specialization within scholarly disciplines complicates the evaluation process and leads to an unfortunate reliance on numerical performance measures. Any effort to evaluate the value of publications by using the citation rate is a numerical nightmare. Various disciplines use and cite literature in different ways, specialty fields and journals are not well covered in the citation databases, and the cost of doing a search to determine how many times an author has been cited can be prohibitive. A senior colleague of ours was overheard to explain how a new assistant professor might become a successful academician. Each study, this colleague expounded, should be analyzed to determine the number of minimum publishable units (MPUs) that it contained: the more MPUs, the better the study. Although it is fortunate that this cynical view[3] of the nature of discovery in an academic setting probably has little currency, the pressure to publish, and even to publish frequently, has not diminished. Academicians have come to rely on quantitative measures: publications, articles, and books; juried exhibits of creative works; performances; abstracts from conferences and meetings; numbers of graduate students and postdoctoral associates; grant and contract funds; and memberships on editorial boards, professional organizations, and national panels. The national funding agencies are not immune to this same temptation: grant renewals depend on results and particularly on published results. This litany is familiar to all faculty and every administrator, and no single stanza is more familiar to the faculty than the importance of scholarly publishing. "The reward system for scholars and scientists depends for now on traditional publication as a defining criterion for rank and status with real compensation coming not from sales but from the advancement in rank, salary, and prestige that publication makes possible" (Cummings et al., xxv).

The question is how we might escape from this numerical treadmill, given our current assessment mechanisms for faculty performance, our continuing need to evaluate one another's achievements, and our need to deal with the escalating costs. One approach that has been advanced would place limitations on the importance of numerical data and would support more qualitative measures as a means of evaluating ourselves. Scholars welcome, we are told, new efforts to emphasize quality over quantity (Mooney, A17). Stanford's president Donald Kennedy proposed a policy limiting the number of publications that candidates for tenure and promotion can submit to evaluation panels. This suggestion would presumably reduce the number of publications that a junior faculty member feels compelled to produce and would hopefully restore an emphasis on the quality of these publications. However, an examiner, who might be asked to evaluate a case for a promotion, has access to electronic databases and can, within minutes, have a complete list of the candidate's work. Whether the artifice of submitting only a few, selected papers to an evaluation panel would diminish the fragmentation of published studies, particularly in the sciences, and whether it would encourage faculty to publish complete accounts of their work is questionable. A candidate for promotion, knowing that the whole record would likely be available to a reviewer and knowing that the reviewer has likely survived to tenure at a time when quantity (and quality, of course) was an issue, would succumb to fragmentary publication. Compounding this problem, any faculty member who is persuaded that the work is a "hot" topic under investigation elsewhere will also succumb to immediate publication. Urgency, as a justification for fragmentary publication, will always be with us, particularly in today's competitive scientific environment.

Other meritorious, qualitative measures have also been considered as a remedy for the proliferation of scholarly publications. For example, the extent to which a scholar's work appears in textbooks represents an attractive means for evaluating the importance of a contribution. What greater accolade can there be than to see one's work used to train the next generation of scholars? Regrettably, however, this measure is not without its problems. Would we see increased pressures to include ever more work into textbooks? In many first- and second-year undergraduate courses, the books have already crossed the line from textbook to tome. Would such evaluation measures fit well within the six-year tenure time frame? On a practical level, in the absence of formal citations in textbooks, how would we determine who has had work included in textbooks? And how would the textbooks themselves be evaluated for quality? Still another substantive gauge for evaluating performance is a faculty member's success in training young scholars who have pursued academic careers. This measure also has some serious problems. The opportunity, much less the ability, to train students who might choose academic careers would reside largely with senior faculty undergoing promotion from associate to full professor. Such a measure would disadvantage junior faculty under consideration for promotion to associate professor. How would we weigh the relative merits of a scholar whose students chose careers at a small, liberal arts college rather than at a research-oriented university? Given these problems, turning to qualitative rather than quantitative measures seems unlikely to solve our current problems with scholarly publishing.

If we are to address in a substantive manner the problems associated with our current emphasis on scholarly publishing, we will need to alter the reward system that drives this endeavor. This particular conclusion is neither surprising nor new: Boyer's *Scholarship Reconsidered* proposes that the traditional definition of scholarship be recast as pure ("the scholarship of discovery"), interdisciplinary ("the scholarship of integration"), and applied ("the scholarship of application") (Boyer, 1990, 15–25). Although we subscribe wholeheartedly to expanding the accepted norms for scholarship, we do not advocate the categorizations suggested by Boyer. There is nothing wrong, of course, with these labels other than the obvious tendency to place a premium on one rather than another. An invitation to label is an invitation to prioritize.

Although perhaps simplistic, we advocate retaining the traditional research, teaching, and service expectations for the faculty, but we would encourage an expansion of the research endeavor to embrace nontraditional activities. Although we will describe several such nontraditional activities later in this chapter, we want to define, as well as we can, how our suggestion differs from Boyer's. The problem that we foresee with the Boyer proposal is the need to develop a new accounting system in which a faculty member would partition his efforts, on the ubiquitous distribution-of-effort form, into new categories such as the scholarship of integration and the scholarship of application. Again, we emphasize that there is nothing wrong in principle with this suggestion, but we suspect that the newly minted category, the "scholarship of discovery," will simply replace the traditional "research" category as the most prized and most valued attribute of a faculty member's record.

The success of our proposal hinges, curiously enough, on the absence of new labels and reliance on the three oft-maligned, traditional categories of teaching, research, and service. What precisely do we mean? Rosovsky (89f), in describing the factors that draw faculty to do research, points to a love of learning and professional advancement. He is careful to define academic research, with the exception of some scientists, as distinct from research for commercial or defense-related purposes. This noncommercial orientation may serve some universities well, but the commercial alternative should be given serious consideration as a form of scholarship. The distinction between academic research and commercial research insofar as the sciences are concerned is difficult. This somewhat heretical comment comes from the fact that one of us is a chemist who understands the intellectual effort that industrial and university colleagues alike have invested in the development of certain pharmaceuticals. The other is a librarian, who has had experience in both the industrial and academic situations and who believes that the research undertaken in both settings is intense and original. Would we value any less the university scientist who chose to develop a new drug over another university scientist who chose to study a problem of minimal commercial importance? The point here is that we should value both!

Faculty in the sciences and in some of the social sciences have opportunities to see their work commercialized. The federal government has initiated programs specifically for this purpose: the Small Business Initiation Research (SBIR) and the Small Business Technology Transfer Program (STTR). State governments also encourage such activity, and economic development appears among the goals in more and more university strategic plans. Only a handful of our faculty pursue these grants and have seen their ideas take shape in a new-start venture. Although encouragement at the federal, state, and, to a lesser extent, university levels exists for such activity, some faculty, even those in disciplines where this opportunity is a reality, have shunned such endeavors. The faculty rewards, in terms of recognition, advancement, and salary, for commercial activities are not accorded any particular significance. In annual evaluations, contributions along these lines would likely fall into the "service" or "other" activity; it is not something that would necessarily appear among the "research" contributions as part of an annual evaluation or distribution-of-effort. With the caveat that commercialization is not for every faculty member, we need to encourage those with the capability along these lines to look at this particular option as a "research opportunity" and encourage administrators to place such activity on the list of achievements meriting increased pay and professional benefits.

We have mentioned the federal government's role in creating SBIR and STTR programs to advance commercialization, but emphasize that these programs are very small relative to other federal investments in higher education. The host of grant and contract programs available to our faculty have had a profound influence on scholarly publishing. It would be fair to say that scientists and engineers, for whom such funding is critical, are engaged in the cyclical process of funding, discovery, publication, and continued funding. Publication remains a central activity in this process and from this vantage point must be seen as an integral part of the professional development of scientists and engineers. Any change that one makes in the ability of these scholars to share their ideas in print with others will impact this cycle. The federal government, through the review panels and study sections that award grants, has defined scholarly publications in journal format as the measure of success that will determine future funding. But the difficulty of evaluating these publications is immense. Many faculty, persuaded that "numbers count," are alarmed by a negative outcome in a grant application. "Fifty publications in four years and my grant wasn't renewed," one of our colleagues once exclaimed. Both the federal government and universities need to rethink the notion that publication is the defining act of a scholar. As part of this effort, they will need to ask if the now standard three- to five-year time frame is sufficient for activities leading to commercialization. Again, just from our particular, perhaps even peculiar, vantage point as chemists, we understand the long-term nature of studies that have led to significant new advances.

Although we have drawn our first example of a nontraditional activity from the sciences, other nontraditional activities from nonscientific areas could merit consideration in the "research" category if we could expand the narrow definition now in vogue. Many universities extol their commitment to the internationalization of the campus, and many, ours among them, maintain a number of programs to accomplish this goal. Faculty involvement varies considerably: a few may take up this activity as their principal role at the university; another larger subset participates in overseas programs; but the vast majority are connected only insofar as they have foreign students in their courses or laboratories. This activity, for those who choose to go overseas, is often seen (by those who have not participated) as something between a sabbatical and a vacation (Lively, 1994, A16). It does not have the regard, as part of the scholarly evaluation process, that we accord to other activities like publication. Yet, there are opportunities here for scholarship that we should foster. The opportunity to teach overseas, particularly in some environments, is a significant challenge that is not for the intellectually faint-of-heart: textbooks in native languages do not exist or may need revision, laboratory and clinical programs may lack up-to-date methods, and foreign agencies need advice, when requested, on investments that they might make in higher education. This activity, not unlike the commercialization activity discussed previously, often falls into a "service" category in our distribution-of-effort forms.

No single piece of technology has changed higher education more in the past two decades than the computer. The impact of computers on all aspects of university life from accounting to research has been dramatic and irreversible. And the story is not over. We have significant opportunities in the areas of distance learning, interactive video, and teaching aids across a spectrum of disciplines. We have significant opportunities for computers in preserving rare manuscripts, opening up museum collections to scholars and neophytes alike, and providing visual supplements to instructional materials. Where else but on a computer can one slow a reaction that occurs in a split second down to a time frame that can actually be seen? We have not, however, accorded these contributions anything like the status of scholarly publication. These activities, like internationalization of the campus, are often given to professional staff. Although technically competent and sincerely interested in their work, we see no reason why faculty could not be encouraged and most importantly, rewarded for these efforts.

We conclude with a final suggestion that stems from the substantial investment that the Commonwealth of Kentucky is now making in K-12 education reform. The legislature and the people of the Commonwealth expect the institutions of higher education to play a key role in this reform process. We suspect that other states have similar aspirations for their institutions. Hence, the personal interest that we have in this effort may have some generality elsewhere. If we are to expect improvements in K-12 education, in terms of technology, governance, and the quality of the educational experience, we cannot simply add this expectation to the list of obligations of the colleges of education alone. It must be a widely shared commitment. The goal of involving faculty outside of the education field has not been a complete success, however. The problem, we feel, is again the issue of the rewards that we attach to these efforts. Without suitable rewards, faculty will not participate at the level that we will need if the reform effort is to succeed.

Any single recipe to improve the problems associated with scholarly publishing is suspect. Clearly, that the assessment mechanisms we have in place at many institutions are linked to numerical data: numbers of books and refereed publications among them. The rewards and professional stature that a faculty member enjoys is driven in large measure by the publication of books and refereed articles. It is equally clear that the federal agencies that fuel much of modern scientific and engineering research are not immune to making assessments in much the same way. Both universities and the federal government have linked our assessment mechanisms and the associated rewards in such a way that the refereed, scholarly article is the *sine qua non* of academic life. The efforts of many individuals on a variety of fronts will be necessary if the technical problems, cost issues, copyright questions, and the role of publishers are to be improved. We champion an additional suggestion: broadening the restrictive definition of research to encompass activities that we could support as scholarly activity.

Although the academy accepts a variety of different activities—from textile design to entomology, from the design of theatre sets to poetry readings—as scholarly activity, publication in hard-copy format remains the defining event in a scholar's life. And it is a curious definition in a number of ways. We have situations in the engineering sciences, for example, where faculty offer such publications as key parts of their promotion dossiers, and yet other studies suggest that an enormous number of such publications are never cited in subsequent engineering publications (Hamilton, "Research," 1991, 25). It would be simplistic, of course, to suggest that low-citation indices mean the work is not read or appreciated. Nevertheless, it does raise the issue of whether publication should be accorded the primacy that it now has in the evaluation of engineering faculty. We suggest that the problem in scholarly publishing is not just the cost issue, the information retrieval issue, the role of the modern library, or the issue of who owns the copyright. The real issue is assessment and the primacy that we have accorded publication in our assessment mechanisms for the faculty. We suggest that expanding the assessment mechanisms to include commercial activities, training programs in the international arena, improvements in laboratory instructional programs, technology introduction, and contributions to the improvement of secondary school programs are worthy goals for scholars. Faculty will pursue such directions when university administrators provide the leadership necessary to raise the value of such activities and to reward those who take up the challenge.

NOTES

1. For a well-reasoned reply to concerns about the number of articles per investigator, see Eugene Garfield, "Response to the Panel on Evaluation of Scientific Information and the Impact of New Information Technology," *Journal of the American Society for Information Science* 41 (1990): 229-230.

2. Also see the Higher Education Information Resources Alliance (HEIRAlliance) Executive Strategies Report #2, "What Presidents Need to Know about the Future of University Libraries: Technology and Scholarly Communication," June 1993. For electronic text of the report, send an E-mail message to heira@cause.colorado.edu containing the following message: Get Heira.ES2.

3. In an even more cynical vein, J. Scott Armstrong has described a recipe for improving the chances of publishing scholarly research: Do not choose an interesting topic, do not challenge existing beliefs, do not obtain surprising results, do not use simple methods of analysis, do not provide full disclosure of your results, and do not write clearly. See Hamilton, "Trivia."

REFERENCES

Abelson, Phillip. "Mechanisms for Evaluating Scientific Information and the Role of Peer Review." *Journal of the American Society of Information Scientists* 41 (1990): 216–222.

"Almanac Issue." *The Chronicle of Higher Education.* August 25, 1993: 5.

Astle, Deana L. "The Scholarly Journal: Whence or Wither." *Journal of Academic Librarianship*, December 15 (1989):151–156.

Baird, Leonard. "What Characterizes a Productive Research Department?" *Research in Higher Education* 25, 3 (1986): 211–225.

Bieber, Jeffrey P., and Robert T. Blackburn. "Faculty Research Productivity 1972–1980: Development and Application of Constant Units of Measure." Paper at the Annual Meeting of the Association for the Study of Higher Education, Atlanta, Georgia, November 2–5, 1989.

Boswood, Michael. "Future of Serials, 1976–2000: A Publisher's Perspective." *Serials Librarian* 11, 3–4 (1986/1987): 9–17.

Boyer, Ernest L. *Scholarship Reconsidered: Priorities of the Professoriate.* Princeton, N.J.: Carnegie Foundation, 1990.

Bruce, Robert V. *The Launching of Modern American Science 1846–1876.* Ithaca, N.Y.: Cornell University Press, 1987.

Calabrese, Andrew. "Changing Times for Scholarly Communication: The Case of the Electronic Journal." *Technology in Society* 14 (1992): 425–438.

Crawford, Susan, and Loretta Stucki. "Peer Review and the Changing Research Record." *Journal of the American Society of Information Scientists* 41 (1990): 223–228.

Cummings, Andrew, Marcia L. Witte, William G. Bower, Laura O. Lazarus, and Richard H. Ekman. *University Libraries and Scholarly Communication: A Study Prepared for the Andrew W. Mellon Foundation.* Washington, D.C.: Association of Research Libraries, 1992.

DeLoughry, Thomas J. "Remaking Scholarly Publishing." *The Chronicle of Higher Education* December 15, 1993: A15–17.

Dillon, Andrew. "New Technology and the Reading Process." *Computers in Libraries* (June 1991): 23–26.

Dougherty, Richard M., and Ann P. Dougherty. "Academic Library: A Time of Crisis, Change, and Opportunity." *Journal of Academic Librarianship* 18 (1993): 342–346.

Drake, Miriam A. "Buying Articles in the Future." *Serials Review.* (Spring/Summer 1992): 75.

Eisenschitz, Tamara. "Intellectual Property: Regulation of Useable Information." *ASLIB Proceedings* 38, 8 (1986): 263–267.

Gilman, Daniel Coit. *University Problems in the United States.* New York: Century Co., 1898.

Hafner, Arthur W., Thomas J. Podsadecki, and William Whitely. "Journal Pricing Issues: An Economic Perspective." *Bulletin of the Medical Library Association* 78 (1990): 217–223.

Hamilton, David P. "Research Papers: Who's Uncited Now?" *Science* 251 (1991): 25.

——. "Trivia Pursuit." *Washington Monthly* (March 1991): 36–42.

Lively, Kit. "Sabbaticals under Fire." *The Chronicle of Higher Education* February 25, 1994: A16.

Marks, Kenneth E., Steven P. Nielsen, Craig H. Petersen, and Peter E. Wagner. "Longitudinal Study of Scientific Journal Prices in a Research Library." *College and Research Libraries* (March 1991): 125–138.

Metz, Paul, and Paul M. Gherman. "Serials Pricing and the Role of the Electronic Journal." *College and Research Libraries* (July 1991): 315–327.

Mooney, Carolyn J. "In 2 Years, a Million Refereed Articles, 300,000 Books, Chapters, Monographs." *The Chronicle of Higher Education* May 22, 1991: A17.

Noll, Roger, and W. Edward Steinmueller. "An Economic Analysis of Scientific Journal Prices: Preliminary Results." *Serials Review* (Spring-Summer 1992): 32–37.

Okerson, Ann. "With Feathers: Effects of Copyright and Ownership on Scholarly Publishing." *College and Research Libraries* (September 1991): 425–438.

Piternick, Anne B. "Attempts to Find Alternatives to the Scientific Journal: A Brief Review." *Journal of Academic Librarianship* 15 (1989): 260–266.

Rosovsky, Henry. *The University: An Owners Manual.* New York: W. W. Norton and Co., 1980.

Stankus, Tony. "Desktop Publishing and Camera-Ready-Copy Science Journals." *Serials Librarian* 15 (1986): 17–27.

Tagler, John. "What Are the Reasons for the Current Packaging of Journals?" *Library Acquisitions: Practice and Theory* 13 (1989): 109–113.

5

Prospects for a Revaluation of Academic Values

Morton Winston

Academe has come in for a drubbing in recent years, by voices both within and outside of the academy, who maintain that most professors are less interested in educating students than they are in writing scholarly articles and books that no one, except for a few other professors in their own narrow academic specialties, would ever want to read. Despite repeated calls for reform of higher education in this regard, relatively little has been done to alter the institutional arrangements that have created and perpetuated this situation. This is not an accident. The dominant academic ethos that values research above teaching, publication above pedagogy, and academic prestige over social relevance has been created and is perpetuated by powerful forces within the academy—mainly by "disciplinary elites" whose members wield power within the academy disproportionate to their numbers within the professoriate. Once the ways in which these elites control the processes of the academy are better understood, we will be in a better position to appreciate what will be needed in order to bring about a genuine revaluation of academic values, though we shall also understand why the chances of actually bringing about such a change are slight.

The Kuhnian idea of scientific paradigms as defining the major theoretical and methodological bases of various fields of study is familiar enough to most scholars, but less well known are the sociological correlates of this phenomenon in the culture of academia. The shift away from philosophical and theological authorities to "paradigm-based" knowledge in the late nineteenth century also led to the "fragmentation of knowledge" into many disciplinary specialties and subspecialties, each claiming a place in the curriculum, and to the valuation of discipline-based "pure research" as the *sine qua non* of academic professionalism. The discipline-based pure researchers came to be viewed as the masters of their particular disciplinary "paradigms" and thus as the source of epistemic certification. In plain English, if what makes one a "professor" is the authoritative claim to possess specialized knowledge in some particular area, and what counts as knowledge in any particular area is determined by the "paradigm" currently reigning in that domain, then only those who could claim to be masters of their disciplinary paradigms could legitimately claim to know what they profess to know. Because the intellectual capital of the academy is knowledge, and paradigms define what is known, the credible claim to mastery of paradigm-based, disciplinary knowledge is the ultimate source of authority and power within the academy.

The shift to paradigm-based epistemic authority went hand in hand with the increasing professionalization of the American academy. As Thomas Kuhn himself has noted:

> [I]t is sometimes just its reception of a paradigm that transforms a group previously interested merely in the study of nature into a profession or, at least, a discipline. In the sciences (though not in fields like medicine, technology, or law, of which the principal *raison d'etre* is an external social need), formation of specialized journals, the foundation of specialists' societies, and the claim for a special place in the curriculum have usually been associated with a group's first reception of a single paradigm. At least this was the case between the time, a century and a half ago, when the institutional pattern of scientific specialization first developed and the very recent time when the paraphernalia of specialization acquired a prestige of their own. (1970, 19.)

Demographic pressures on higher education following the Second World War, that is, the shift from elite to mass access to higher education, and more recent demands that the academy serve the interests of more culturally, racially, and ethnically diverse students, did little to change the dominance of the professionalized disciplinary elites and of the research–publishing ethos in American higher education. To quote Boyer,

> Ironically, at the very time America's higher education institutions were becoming more open and inclusive, the culture of the professoriate was becoming more hierarchical and restrictive. The emphasis on undergraduate education, which throughout the years had drawn its inspiration for the colonial college tradition, was being overshadowed by the European university tradition, with its emphasis on graduate education and research. Specifically, at many of the nation's four year institutions, the focus had moved from the student to the professoriate, from general to specialized education, and from loyalty to the campus to loyalty to the profession. (1990, 13)

This aptly describes the orientation of the groups within the academy I am calling "disciplinary elites." These elites consist mainly of senior, tenured professors holding chairs at the more prestigious research and doctoral-granting universities who, by and large, have advanced to their current position of power within the academy by successfully developing their own disciplines' dominant paradigms.[1] The way one does this, of course, is by delivering invited lectures and talks on the circuit of speakers hosted by the major research universities, by

giving lectures and symposia at major professional meetings, and, most importantly, by the writing and publishing of learned articles and scholarly books in
which authors attempt to shape the opinions of other professional practitioners
of their disciplines. The journal article is the unit of capital in the academic
marketplace; it is the record of one's "research" at the frontiers of knowledge of
one's discipline, and it is thus the basis of any credible claim one might have to
be one of the keepers and shapers of the disciplinary paradigm. However,
individuals rarely become members of their respective disciplinary elites only
through publishing in specialty journals. The single-authored scholarly book is
the real marker of academic prestige and respectability, but only, of course, if it
is published by the "right" university press, and only then if it is favorably
reviewed by acknowledged masters of the field in the leading scholarly journals
devoted to that subject. Thus, research and publication have come to be regarded
as the necessary activities of those who aspire to power within the academy, for
only through them does a professor have the chance of becoming a member of
a disciplinary elite.

The power that the disciplinary elites exercise within their academic communities depends essentially on their ability to perform the "certification function."
According to the dominant ethos, since only members of these elites can
authoritatively lay claim to being real "experts," only they possess the authority
to certify what counts as knowledge. Disciplinary elites use their control over
epistemic certification to maintain their hegemony within the academy by
deciding which practitioners will be certified as "professional experts," whose
works will be published, and, what other activities of professors will be rewarded
within academic institutions.

First, they control the graduate curriculum, and consequently they define what
it means to be a scholar in a particular field by controlling both the canons of
scholarship and admission to graduate training at the doctoral-granting
institutions. Of course, they also control who gets to hold the Ph.D. offered in
their discipline, and thus control access to the basic credential needed to enter the
academic job market. Graduate training leading to the Ph.D., the initiation ritual
in which young scholars are socialized into the values of their particular
professional subcultures, is the basic way in which disciplinary elites replicate
themselves and hold sway over the entire academy. The graduate student's senior
professors and dissertation advisor function as his or her link to the elite culture.
Favored students are invited to join the elite by being touted to other members
of the disciplinary elite at other major research universities. Others are given
their degrees along with polite letters explaining that they will probably make
good teachers at lesser institutions. Still others are encouraged to pursue other
professions. During the socialization process the greatest rewards go to those
students who most completely adopt the values and beliefs of the local
disciplinary elites—that is, those who most completely buy into the dominant
ethos. However, the candidate member of the elite must now prove him- or

herself by publishing good articles in respectable journals and writing a well-reviewed scholarly book or two. Without these necessary credentials, even the most promising of junior scholars will not succeed. Even with them, many scholars will not succeed if they fail to cultivate the right networks. Given that we have now had several generations of college teachers who have entered the academy by this route, is it any wonder that "research" and "publication" are by now widely regarded as the dominant values within the academy?

Second, the disciplinary elites also typically control access to publication for other professors by functioning as editors or editorial review board members of the major specialty journals in their fields, and by serving as consultants and editorial advisors to most major university presses. Maintaining an ethos in which publication, preferably publication in prestigious specialty journals, is taken to be the *sine qua non* of academic success thus serves the interests of the elites since it forces other professors to seek their certification. Without such certification, that is, being able to say that so-and-so has *published* articles in such-an-such important, selective, and "peer-referred" journals, practitioners of the discipline know they cannot advance in their disciplines, or, in many cases, even retain their teaching positions at their smaller, less prestigious, more teaching-oriented institutions. This arrangement serves the interests of the elites more than it does the academy or society as a whole, since, by forcing other professors to seek their certification, they both legitimize their own claims to expertise and exercise control over what ideas and opinions get a chance to shape the discipline's paradigm. Thus, thinkers whose ideas are not in keeping with those of the disciplinary elites can be effectively marginalized, the current paradigm can be protected, and the members of the current elite can maintain their authority within the academic system.

Third, the disciplinary elites exercise power within the university itself through their ability to generate both prestige and external funds through grants that they prepare for review by other members of their disciplinary elites at other universities who serve on external grant review panels. Not infrequently, the career track of a successful disciplinary specialist will lead to a chairmanship, a deanship, a provostship, or even a college or university presidency. Such positions exist at many universities mainly to protect and serve the interests of the academic departments from which their current occupants came and will soon return. These administrators can therefore be relied upon to uphold the "research ethos" within the institution. The interests of academic administrators frequently coincide with those of the disciplinary elites since the administrators need to bring in new sources of money to make their institutions prosper, and the members of the local elites help them do this by getting external grants from which the institution takes its cut. Nowadays, institutions on the make—that is, second- and third-tier doctoral-granting institutions, and not just the prestigious, well-endowed, private research universities—want to recruit "top researchers" in various disciplines because they know that through them their institutions have the best chance of winning competitive grants. These grants will bring money in to the institution, enable these researchers to carry out and publish more research, and thus bring more prestige to the institution, which in turn will help it attract more "top researchers," who will get more grants, publish more research, and so on.

Together, these three forms of epistemic certification give disciplinary elites formidable control over the academy. Most students entering the academy are unaware of these priorities within the faculties and administrations of the institutions in which they enroll. But they learn soon enough that they must either take their degrees and seek employment outside of the academy, or become graduate students and assimilate to the cultural model of the "research professor." Prospective college and university teachers quickly learn that they cannot get a Ph.D., cannot get a teaching job, get a grant, get published, tenured or promoted, unless they pay obeisance to the research ethos and to the members of their disciplines' elite. At the same time, members of these elites invite each other to deliver lectures on their campuses, organize conferences at which other members of the elites can present their work, and jockey for power and influence on journal editorial boards, grant review committees, and the boards of their professional associations. These are forms of social cooperation by which the members of disciplinary elites maintain their advantage over professors who are not members of the elite. Members of elites are able to do this, in part, because they have enacted the research-publishing model so well that they have now been rewarded with reduced (or nonexistent) teaching loads, and cadres of graduate students teach their classes and do their grading for them.[2] Given competing demands on a professor's time, it is obviously much easier to stay abreast of new developments in one's field, and thus to "publish new research," if one has these advantages than not. Thus, in the realm of intellectual capital as in the realm of real capital, the rich get richer while the poor get poorer, while the dominant ethos is passed onto a new generation of scholars who internalize these values and pass them on to their own students, if they get the chance.

The current power structure in the academy thus consists of self-perpetuating, interlocking directorates of tenured, senior professors (most of whom by the way, despite much talk of diversity, affirmative action, and multiculturalism, are still mainly white males). They exercise control over the processes by which younger people are trained in particular disciplines, the access that other scholars in their fields have to publication, and the major sources of external funding of the university.[3] These directorates form the "invisible university" in that their members tend to have greater loyalty to their extended disciplinary community than they do to their local institutional culture. Their primary academic role is to protect and advance the interests of their disciplinary paradigm rather than to educate students who are unlikely to specialize in their disciplines, contribute to the general intellectual life of their campuses, or work for the benefit of society as a whole. The hold these disciplinary elites have over American higher education accounts for why the ethos that values "published research" over "teaching" and "service" is dominant. It also explains why this situation is not going to be materially changed simply by redefining the term *scholarship*.

Some readers are no doubt thinking that I have overdrawn this picture of the modern academy, turning it into a caricature of the real thing. What is the point of demonizing those of our colleagues who really do excel in scholarship by labeling them as members of these disciplinary elites and by suggesting they are involved in some sort of conspiracy to maintain control over the academy? Isn't this really all just "sour grapes" from someone who resents not being a member of the very groups of professors he is attacking? After all, can't anyone who has enough talent, drive, and ambition become a "published scholar" and thereby enter the elite ranks of his or her discipline?

As to the first objection, while the view presented here is only a sketch, it is not one that is all that inaccurate. The academy is a hierarchical and an elitist institution, one in which success is measured not in dollars or political power, but in terms of prestige, rank, and intellectual authority. Is it any surprise, therefore, that those who possess these markers to the greatest degree are also those who are in the best position to control the distribution of these markers to others? This is one respect in which the academy differs significantly from the marketplace or the political arena. Someone with a clever and original idea for a product or a new way of marketing an existing product can make a fortune if she can attract enough buyers. Similarly, in democratic societies politicians can be elected if they attract enough votes (whether or not they have any new ideas). But success for academics comes not from the acceptance by consumers (i.e., one's students) or by selection by a broadly enfranchised electorate (i.e., other members of the faculties to which one belongs), but through a series of certifications granted by relatively small groups of specialists who decide if and when someone will be graduated, hired, published, tenured, promoted, and so forth.

Being a specialist who is in a position to exercise such judgment is itself a form of power, and given that there is no real competition that would dethrone those who achieve such positions, is it any wonder that the academy continues to operate according to this guild-like system? As I have tried to suggest, this system did not spring into being overnight but has been developing for over a century. The current members of the disciplinary elites are themselves products of a system that was already in place when they arrived in the academy as green undergraduates. As each new generation of students enters the academy, those who aspire to become professors themselves must allow themselves to be seduced by this same ethos. The professor's only responsible recourse is to pass on the publishing-research ethos to his or her graduate students, for to do otherwise is to do them a disservice and virtually guarantee their failure. That this describes the process by which most all of us came to be members of the professoriate is, I submit, not really a distortion of the truth.

I am *not* arguing that there is no value in published "research," nor that disciplinary researchers should have no place in the academy. I am arguing that this ethos should no longer dominate the academy the way it has for most of this century, and that it should give way to a more pluralistic and egalitarian academic ethos of the kind described by Boyer in which other professional activities of professors, teaching, interdisciplinary integration, and application of knowledge to real social problems would receive the recognition (and rewards) they deserve. In particular, I am offering at least a partial explanation of why the values of the academy are the way they are and why these values are so difficult to change, despite repeated calls for change and widespread support within the professoriate for such changes.

Those voices in the academy who have been calling for change are not really asking for something that is all that radical or would seem all that difficult to achieve. All they seek is the recognition that various kinds of professorial activity—teaching classes, grading papers, advising students, taking part in departmental and school governance, organizing and attending campus events, doing volunteer and community work, and so on—are valuable and ought to be regarded as such. These activities are valuable in their own right, or because they contribute to other things that are valuable, but they need not derive their value from any relation they might have to getting oneself published.

Finally, I am not attempting to demonize our colleagues who do frequently publish and who do hold positions of influence and prestige in various disciplines at the more elite universities. Nor am I suggesting that their contributions are not valuable ones. Surely research and publishing are also worthy activities for professors to pursue. But they are not the *only* worthy activities, and they should not be regarded as such. They are in fact currently overvalued relative to other kinds of professorial activity within the academy. To suggest that those, like myself, who share the view that publishing is overvalued relative to these other activities, are just indulging in sour grapes is really to misunderstand what it means to revalue values. Judged from within the value hierarchy of the dominant ethos, publishing is the single most important activity of the professor. Consequently, the judgment that publication is overvalued within the academy can only be the result of an "outer" or external judgment based on a different table of values from the one that dictates that publishing is most valuable. But, if one rejects this value hierarchy and holds instead that various other activities of professors, teaching, advising, curriculum development, faculty governance, community and volunteer service, and so forth are also, and independently valuable, (whether or not they can be aptly renamed types of "scholarship") then, the fact that someone has not published, or published that much, or published in the "right places," does not and should not matter, so long as he or she has done these other sorts of things and done them well. That is, if one holds the (really quite reasonable view) that one's *not* being a well-published, research scholar *does not entail* that one is an academic failure, there is nothing to be sour or resentful about. That some readers may have difficulty in seeing such a judgment as anything more than sour grapes bespeaks more about their own lack of insight and the depth of their own socialization into the dominant ethos than it does about any deficiency in my argument.

Having described the nature of the power structure in the academy which created and perpetuates the dominant ethos, and having clarified this view and defended it against misunderstandings and objections, I would now like to briefly suggest some ways in which the power that these elites exercise over academic life might be decreased. If the analysis presented here is remotely on target, then any chance there is of bringing about a revaluation of academic values will derive from the possibility of challenging the right of the disciplinary elites to claim exclusive control over the various certification functions of the academy. This is so because the reward structure of academic life depends essentially on certification. Thus, in order to change the reward structure within the academy to better accord with a more pluralistic and egalitarian table of values, it is necessary to deny partisans of the research-publishing ethos control over certification.

If, as I have suggested, the dominant ethos is propagated through graduate education, it would seem that a good way to break the hold of the disciplinary elites, as well as to avoid producing yet another generation of alienated young scholars, is by reforming the way in which graduate students are trained. According to the dominant academic culture, graduate training should primarily prepare students to contribute "new knowledge" to their disciplines. Consequently, graduate education must culminate in the writing of a doctoral dissertation and the awarding of a Ph.D. Given that it is highly unlikely that one could do away with the dissertation or the Ph.D. as the dominant certificate, the next best thing would be to reform the way in which the Ph.D. is construed and granted. One needs to redefine graduate education as primarily preparation for future college teachers, and not solely as preparation of future disciplinary researchers. In addition to a significant research project, for example, there could be a requirement that graduate students demonstrate that they can prepare and teach three different courses at the undergraduate level, with their performance in these preparatory courses being closely monitored by a committee of experienced professors, through the use of self-evaluation, peer evaluation, and student evaluation instruments designed for their disciplines. Graduate students could be asked to serve as members on various standing departmental and school committees. They could also be invited to participate in campus projects directed toward bringing about curricular or pedagogical reforms, or to serve as members of the committees or governing boards of professional societies. A few graduate programs I know of have been moving in this direction; several others have altered the dissertation requirement so that it consists of three journal-length papers rather than a book-length opus that is likely to go unread.

These are steps in the right direction but do not go far enough. In any case, attacking the problem at this level is not the best option. Given the current dominance of the research-publishing ethos, graduate students who are not schooled in accordance with it will be placed at a relative disadvantage in an already very competitive academic marketplace. Graduate students and new Ph.D.s are the least powerful and most vulnerable members of the professoriate, and it would be unfair to burden them with the risks and costs of bringing about the proposed reforms and changes within the academy. These risks are better borne by more senior members of the academic profession—ideally by those whose academic credentials, as judged relative to the dominant ethos, are already beyond reproach. Thus, while graduate education certainly needs to be reformed, this should not be done first, for to do so would unfairly disadvantage the least secure and most vulnerable members of the profession.

Another obvious pressure point is the academic department itself, the institutional stronghold of the disciplinary elites. In this case I recommend that we frankly acknowledge that there is, and should be, a division of labor among the members of a typical university department, and that this should reflect more than merely the division of the academic field into various subspecialties. In a typical university department, there are individuals who excel primarily at writing and publication, others who excel primarily at teaching, and yet others who excel primarily in various kinds of service, both to their institutions and to the wider communities to which they belong. Individuals of each of these kinds should be recognized as valued members of the university community, and each department, division, and campus should institute policies by which individual contributions in each of these areas can be recognized, valued, and rewarded.

Boyer suggests a number of concrete reforms, for instance, the idea of "creativity contracts" in which "faculty members define their professional goals for a three-to-five-year period, possibly shifting from one principal scholarly focus to another" (1990, 48). Under such a system, reappointment, tenure, and promotion decisions would be based on the faculty members' achievement of the goals that they had set for themselves under their personalized creativity contract. Their performance as professors would not be measured against the abstract, and generally unfulfillable, demand that professors should excel equally in research, teaching, and service (leaving it up to the individual professor to guess, given his or her particular institutional culture, what the real weights of these various activities are). Instead, they would be judged (and rewarded) according to their success in being the kind of professor they had chosen to be. Boyer's idea of creativity contracts needs to be widely institutionalized within the academy and connected to real rewards such as tenure and promotion. That is, a professor should be able to gain tenure and promotion by demonstrating exceptional classroom skills, by contributing to college governance, or by applying his or her expertise to a wider social project, and not just by garnering publications. Such a system would also benefit more senior professors who might want to make a career change in midcourse, or pursue interests and opportunities that would take them away from their word processors for a while.

This brings us, at last, to the theme of this book—the politics of scholarly publishing. Since control over access to publication is a principal lever by which the disciplinary elites maintain their hegemony within the academy, challenging these elites entails denying them this control. The way to do so is to democratize the process of selecting editors and editorial board members and advisors, and to institute a kind of affirmative action for categories of scholars who rarely receive invitations to sit on such panels. Rather than selecting editors and editorial board members by means of the self-perpetuating "old-boy networks" consisting of other "publishing scholars," that is, other members of their disciplines' elites, major journals should hold elections periodically in which candidates for editorships could be selected by members of the relevant scholarly communities. Certain slots on editorial boards should be reserved for women and people of color, while others should be set aside for faculty members who teach at two-year and four-year undergraduate institutions. Putting faculty members on editorial boards in proportion to the class of institution that has subscriptions to the journals would ensure that the most prestigious journals, being also those with the widest circulation, are also most representative. Most importantly, the class of individuals who regularly serve as editorial reviewers should be greatly enlarged. Who are the "peers" in "peer review"? Generally, these are other published scholars in the field whose work is known to the editor. But why not have manuscripts submitted for publication reviewed by the people who are their primary users, namely, the teachers of those subjects? Perhaps reviewing duties could be shared among members of those academic departments whose libraries maintain subscriptions to the journal. Similar schemes should be applied to grant review panels, as well as to the executive and program committees of the major academic professional organizations. Such changes would help broaden and democratize the process by which scholarly work is granted the *imprimatur* of publication. In this way, the exclusive control over this important form of certification is taken out of the hands of the disciplinary elites.

These suggestions will no doubt call forth howls of protest about the need to maintain "academic standards" and "qualifications" and "competence." In fact, the louder the howls of protest raised against any suggested reform, the more likely it is that we have indeed hit a pressure point. If we are really serious about changing the culture of academia, we must be prepared to take up battles of these kinds and pursue our goals in the face of determined and powerful opposition. With each of the various certifications, some people in the academy will argue forcefully for maintenance of the status quo, and this will nowhere be more true than in the arena of scholarly publication. Fortunately, there may never be a better time to join this battle than at present.

A major force accelerating the democratization and decentralization of publishing is the technological conversion presently taking place from paper-based to electronic-form publishing. Electronic publishing, distributed worldwide on the Internet, can enable more scholars to participate directly in the work of advancing knowledge than ever before. Journal articles prepared in electronic form and sent out on the Net for comment and review can potentially reach a much wider group of scholars, with quicker turnaround, than by using the older paper-based book technology that is so thoroughly under the control of the disciplinary elites. By thus expanding the invisible university electronically, its membership can also be made more inclusive and participation can become more open and democratic. Scholars with particular areas of research can participate in online interest groups, join listservs, and read and contribute to conferences, bypassing the control of the editors and the academic elites entirely. The time-honored process of memorializing thought in words on paper can give way to more interactive, multimedia "publications" in which authors and their audiences participate in the search for meaning and knowledge, and convey their results in images, software, and virtual conversations. Teachers will soon be able to assemble electronic-form texts into custom-published anthologies for use in their courses, and scholars in separate disciplines will be able to communicate and exchange ideas with each other in ways that bypass the current rigid division into departments of knowledge. Besides the academic department, the electronic frontier is the most important battleground in the struggle to reform academic values.

But given the many different ways in which disciplinary elites now function to maintain their position of hegemony within the academy, I am not hopeful that change will come about easily or quickly. I do think there are signs in the wind that changes of the kind suggested here may come to pass. Several graduate programs have initiated programs to train graduate student how to teach (Wilshire, 1990, 76). In addition, there are now specialty journals devoted to teaching issues in various disciplines as well as many new electronic journals; there are also societies, such as the Professional and Organizational Development Network (POD), which are working to change the culture of the academy to make it more hospitable to those who do not buy into the dominant ethos. If these trends and movements continue, we may yet witness another transformation of the academy away from the specialism and professionalization that has resulted in the modern mega-multiuniversity—the equivalent of an assembly line for students. Instead, the academy may come to resemble the small, customized "quality circles" in which scholars with various kinds of disciplinary expertise can quickly and easily move among various interest groups in pursuing their search for knowledge, and in which the current hierarchical structure of the academy is replaced by a more egalitarian and pluralistic commonwealth of knowledge. In order for such a transformation to occur a genuine revaluation of academic values needs to be enacted. Doing this revaluation requires an understanding of the forces that have shaped and perpetuated the dominant ethos, together with an analysis of how this ethos can be effectively challenged and undermined. Agents of progressive change need to find each other, organize, and mobilize their resources to effectively advance this program, if the dominance of the research-publishing ethos within the American academy is ever going to be effectively challenged and broken.

NOTES

This is a revised version of a presentation entitled "The Politics of Scholarly Publication: Critique and Reform," which was delivered to the Politics and Processes of Scholarly Publishing Conference held at the St. Petersburg campus of the University of South Florida on March 14, 1994. Since delivering this talk, I have benefited from discussions on these topics with Nancy Nersessian and Stephanie Gibson, and from some comments by anonymous reviewers forwarded to me by the editor. I alone, however, am responsible for the views presented here.

1. There are two important exceptions to this generalization: the highest academic honors are granted not to practitioners of what Kuhn calls "normal science," but to those exceptional individuals who are either the founders of new paradigms in new disciplines or subdisciplines, or to those rare "scientific revolutionaries" who create new paradigms that displace the existing disciplinary paradigms in already established fields of inquiry. The more common route into the academic pantheon is the former: here practitioners of a discipline can "make a name for themselves" by developing a particular line of inquiry or a particular subspecialty within the broader discipline. Sometimes this leads to the formation of a new discipline or subspecialty, which then can set up its own new society, journal, and elite, train new students in its paradigm, and attract new scholars to labor in its vineyard. Thus the tree of knowledge has grown in this century, with new elites, new journals, new professional societies, and new departments being added to the university phone book every year.

2. Bruce Wilshire cites a study from the U.S. Department of Education which revealed that in 1986 the proportion of parttime teachers and universities was 58 percent. Wilshire comments, "When teaching assistants are added, about two-thirds of the work force is either part-time or irregular, and, it is safe to say, receives less than half the total remuneration" (note 78).

3. The disciplinary elites have been slow to respond to the demands of women, blacks, and other minorities to allow them a place in the curriculum. This is so because both women's studies and black studies programs are viewed as inherently subversive in that they seek to transform the power structure within the academy. Institutions that have responded to these demands have generally done so by admitting only a few women and blacks into the ranks of elite professors, while also making it abundantly clear that the continued status and power that these individuals enjoy depend in large part on their being loyal to the disciplinary research ethos. Thus, in effect, by assimilating their leaders into the ethos of these elites, these movements have been coopted.

REFERENCES

Boyer, Ernest. *College: The Undergraduate Experience in America*. Princeton, N.J.: Carnegie Foundation for the Advancement of Teaching, 1987.

—. *Scholarship Reconsidered: Priorities of the Professoriate*. Princeton, N.J.: Carnegie Foundation for the Advancement of Teaching, 1990.

Kuhn, Thomas. *The Structure of Scientific Revolutions*. 2nd ed. enlarged. International Encyclopedia of Unified Science, Vol. 2, No. 2. Chicago: University of Chicago Press, 1970.

Wilshire, Bruce. *The Moral Collapse of the University: Professionalism, Purity, and Alienation*. Albany, N.Y.: State University Press of New York, 1990.

6

The Dialectic of Feminism and Scholarship

Patsy P. Schweickart

What about publishing and editing feminist scholarship? The short answer is that it is a booming business. One speaker at the Scholarly Publishing Conference gave the following three-point advice to new scholars: find an area, do a thorough literature search, and stick to it. He added that it would be wise to pick a "stable" field of study. This, of course, is excellent general advice. I would add that anyone in search of a good area of study should consider women's studies. Women's studies has been, and is likely to continue to be, a good, fertile, stable field. Volumes of excellent women's studies scholarship are being published every year; a lot more is being done, and a lot of exciting work is yet to be done. Searching the literature is both overwhelming and inspiring.

The long answer to the question, "What about editing and publishing feminist scholarship?" would begin with the sentence: Feminist scholarship is problematical. I don't mean the obvious—that feminist scholarship is problematical from the point of view of traditional scholarship. I mean that feminist scholarship is problematical from its own point of view.

Last year, Christina Sommers,[1] a professor of philosophy at Clark University, published several articles ridiculing feminist scholarship. The object of her ridicule is its hybridity, which was played out as a comic spectacle at the 1992 National Women's Studies Association Conference at Austin. Sommers' good faith may be suspect, but I would argue that in representing feminist scholarship as laughable, she is only exploiting a problem that is well known to feminist scholars themselves.

We see this contradiction clearly if we draw two lists of words, one associated with feminism and the other with scholarship:

Feminism	Scholarship
Political	Academic
Engaged	Detached
Interested	Disinterested
Action	Words
On the side of the oppressed and marginal	Professional
Against authority	Claims/invokes/trades in authority
Transgressive/subversive	Disciplined
Aspires to be inclusive and accessible	Discourse of an intellectual elite
Engaged in the community	Invested in the academy
Radical/committed to changing the world	Has interest in preserving its accomplishments and place in the academy, and, therefore, in preserving the academy itself

The contradiction, the double consciousness and divided allegiance, in feminist scholarship is most palpable in women's studies programs. It is often enacted (to the amusement of unfriendly observers) at the meetings of the National Women's Studies Association (NWSA). This contradiction constitutes my job as editor of *NWSA Journal*.

One way to resolve the contradiction would be to sever one pole from the other, but this would be unfortunate for both feminism and scholarship. I see that my job as editor is not to remedy the contradiction, but to orchestrate it, to let it play itself out, to give feminist scholarship the space to realize itself as the dialectic of feminism and scholarship.

Defining feminism has been a problem from the beginning in part because we try to phrase the definition as a set of statements. I would define feminism as an ensemble of contradictions. Feminists differ as to where they stand regarding any component of the ensemble, but we all feel the pressure of the contradictions in the ensemble. The contradiction in feminist scholarship described above is only one component of this ensemble. Feminists feel it, though differently, whether they are in the academy or in the "community."

In an early essay, Mikhail Bakhtin (1981) presented a wonderful formulation of the relationship of art to life: he said that the relationship is, or ought to be, characterized by answerability. I like the word "answerability" (I can't claim anything about the Russian original) because of its oddity—or, to use a Bakhtinian word, its novelty. The more normal word would be "responsibility." Bakhtin's word carries the sense of accountability—art holds life into account and vice versa; but it also recuperates the dialogic moment—the responsiveness that has been eclipsed in the normal contemporary uses of the word "responsibility" by the emphasis on its legalistic sense as synonymous with liability.

Following Bakhtin, I would define feminist scholarship as a project oriented toward producing answerability between on the one hand, scholarship and the academy, and on the other, the domain signified by the list labeled "feminism," which I would now re-code as "Life." Or, invoking another Bakhtinian formulation, feminist scholarship becomes the interanimation of feminism (or "Life") and scholarship; feminism is a novelizing force (one among others) on scholarship. Although my remarks pertain specifically to feminist scholarship, the orientation toward answerability between life and scholarship is characteristic of scholarship at its best—that the ideal of answerability informs the vocation of the scholar. Feminist scholarship is a novelizing force precisely because it accentuates the contradiction that constitutes the scholarly project. Feminists in the academy often seek relief from this predicament by coding their work as "teaching." The idea of "feminist teacher" is not as disconcerting as the idea of "feminist scholar." "Teaching" modulates the contradiction, it mitigates the discomfort of "scholarship" because it is apparent that it implies answerability. Not surprisingly, the function of teaching as a middle ground between scholarship and life, the academy and the general public, is a prominent theme in scholarly discourse.[2]

Feminist scholarship is also problematical because it is devoted to interdisciplinarity and multiculturalism. I address these two issues together because, formally, they are similar problems—stemming from the investment in diversity. Why is the commitment to diversity a problem? Let us look at the opposite value, namely, "coherence." According to the standard argument, diversity comes at the cost of coherence.

This apparently sensible argument bears reexamination in two parts—theoretical and practical. In the theoretical argument, coherence equates with consistency of logic and values. According to conventional wisdom, valid knowledge has to be coherent, which is to say, consistent. According to the story, Western civilization originated with the Greeks, survived the ordeal of the "Dark Ages," and had a Renaissance; then came the Age of Reason and the Enlightenment, which ushered in the Modern Age and the Industrial Age, and brings us today to what some call the postindustrial or postmodern world. This central narrative underwrites the coherence of traditional education. Of course, the plot twists and turns—each stage represents a conflict of forces. Temporary setbacks to progress occur. There are villains and heroes; victory is never certain, Western civilization is always precarious, always a target for barbarians, always susceptible to decadence. After all, the viability of any story depends on drama. And minor themes and subplots exist—the stories of women and "minorities"—but attention to these, though permissible and even laudable, must never undermine the coherence and centrality of the foundational narrative. Otherwise, we risk epistemological and moral relativism, and all that goes under the name of "civilization."

The appeal of this central story—its claim to validity—rests on its narrative coherence. But this coherence comes at a price. An education governed by the storyline described above produces knowledge pertaining to a narrow area at the cost of producing and reproducing vast areas of ignorance. The other argument against diversity is a practical one, having to do with product consistency. According to the argument, in the old days, we could tell what a graduate learned in college. There was agreement, *at least*, about the *basics*. College-educated people shared a commonality of knowledge and experience. Now, as a result of multiculturalism and diversity, the curriculum has become cluttered with all sorts of things, and the idea of a common educational experience and shared knowledge has become meaningless. For example, we no longer predict what an English major would learn in college. She might take courses in Native American literature, women writers, African-American writers, Asian-American writers, Chicana lesbian literature, film, popular culture, cultural studies, the discourse of the body, and so on, but she could graduate without encountering Chaucer, Milton, Wordsworth, Hawthorne, Emerson, and even, God forbid, Shakespeare. All this diversity crowds out the basics. There is no longer any consistency in the product of higher education.

This scenario is excessively alarmist. In fact, the canon is alive and well in all the academic disciplines. But suppose that the alarmists are correct—that students come out of college knowing all sorts of different things and that no area of knowledge is shared by all. Some English majors will know a lot about Milton but not about Asian-American literature; others will know a lot about Asian-American literature and hardly anything about Milton. But why is this so bad? Given that there is so much to know, why is it practical to devote the largest amount of effort in producing an educated population that shares a small area of knowledge and vast areas of ignorance? There is a lot to learn, but fortunately, there are also a lot of us. It seems more practical and efficient to distribute different areas of knowledge—and different areas of ignorance—among different people. This way we can cover for each other. There would not be consistency of knowledge, but neither would there be consistency of ignorance.

Another side to the practical argument against diversity rests on the widely held belief that shared knowledge is a prerequisite to communication. In order to communicate productively, so the argument goes, two people need to start from some area of fundamental agreement—about facts, premises, and values. If we do not agree on anything, then we cannot talk, we cannot even disagree meaningfully. Communication depends on an economy of agreement.

Perhaps this is so. But we need to ask whether this situation is necessary and desirable, or whether it stems from a cultivated disability. Difference is often the starting point of communication; shared knowledge is something produced and negotiated in the process of conversation. In this view, communication implies trading in difference, and the mark of an educated person is the capacity to communicate profitably with someone whose areas of knowledge and difference are supplemental to his own. The degeneration of the ability to communicate across differences is part of the cost of the homogeneity encoded in "coherence."

The commitment of feminist scholarship to interdisciplinarity and multiculturalism requires a revision of the idea of coherence. To the extent that it is
encoded with the values of consistency and homogeneity, coherence is not
practical at all—its costs are high and its benefits dubious. However, rather than
banishing coherence from our lexicon of intellectual values, let us revise its
meaning to indicate not the value of narrative singularity and seamlessness, but
rather the value of connectedness, in particular, of connectedness in the sense of
Bakhtin's idea of answerability, or interanimation of various discourses. In short,
our model for coherence should not be that of a story but that of a conversation,
where coherence is produced by means of mutual responsiveness.

What does this mean, specifically, in terms of my conduct of my job as editor
of *NWSAJ*? A few years ago, we asked referees, Is this manuscript interdisciplinary? "Interdisciplinary" was generally interpreted as touching at least two
disciplines. Many manuscripts were rejected because they failed the test of
interdisciplinarity. For example, sociological research using quantitative methods
was generally rejected for being too inaccessible to the general reader. At the
same time, the editorial board continually bemoaned the lack of good social
science articles in *NWSAJ*.

When I became editor, I instituted a change in the criterion of interdisciplinarity. Now, any article may be written entirely within the framework of a particular
discipline. The question is whether it will be useful to our "interdisciplinary
readership"—that is, one that is made up of scholars, each a specialist in a
particular discipline, but conversant, or able and motivated to be conversant, with
others.

NWSAJ is also committed to multiculturalism and to being responsive to the
diversity of women's perspectives and experience. We ask our referees to
comment on whether and to what extent a manuscript takes account of
differences of race, class, sexual orientation, age, and so on, and we advise our
authors to avoid taking any group of women to be representative of all. Yet, it
is not always possible to thematize race, class, and sexual orientation. Moreover,
the mechanical gestures to indicate sensitivity to these issues or ritual authorial
self-identifications as lesbian, white, middle-class, and so on, can hardly count
as satisfactory approaches to cultural diversity. The heterogeneity of the category
"women" poses a complicated theoretical and practical challenge for feminist
scholarship which is beyond the scope of this chapter. However, within the
specific domain of my work as editor of *NWSAJ*, multiculturalism may be
approached by analogy to interdisciplinarity, not whether an article incorporates
the diversity of women's perspectives, but rather, whether it addresses itself to
a multicultural readership, one constituted by people of a particular race, class,
gender, sexual orientation, age, and the like, but able to converse with representatives of different constituencies.

To a large extent, both "interdisciplinary" and "multicultural" readership are
regulatory ideals; they are indicative of what we want to develop, rather than

what we, in fact, have. I see it as an important part of the project of *NWSAJ* and of women's studies to develop a community of scholars with the ability to interact productively with people who hold very different bundles of knowledge, experiences, needs, interests, methods, and sensibilities. Concretely, I have in mind a specialist in literature who can appreciate and profit from a sociologist's expertise in statistical methods, ask pertinent questions, form reasonable judgments (however provisional) regarding the plausibility of the results presented, and figure out useful connections to her own work. Conversely, I have in mind a sociologist whose expertise is in quantitative analysis and who realizes that the work of literary critics represents an important resource for her own work, who reads works that would supply the subjective dimensions that are not amenable to quantitative analysis, and who takes pains to inform her work in order to make it answerable to the work of scholars who employ different approaches to the study of social phenomena. I also have in mind white scholars who are answerable to the work of black scholars; heterosexual scholars who are answerable to homosexuals; and conversely.

In conclusion, when I accepted the editorship of *NWSAJ*, I did so with considerable anxiety. I thought it likely to be a tedious and thankless task that would take time away from my own work. For the most part, this has been the case, but three years into the job, to my surprise, I find that I truly enjoy editing. Trying to puzzle out the nature of this peculiar pleasure, I realized that an editor is like a talk show host charged with orchestrating a conversation among a heterogeneous constituency. The pleasures of editing have to do with the pleasures in heteroglossia (to use another term from Bakhtin), in encountering, in being surrounded by voices that are not my own. I do not mean the pleasure of learning from others or even of caring for others—although editing offers these also. I mean something prior, a pleasure that I believe is at the root of sociability, namely, the pleasure in the sheer otherness of the other.

NOTES

1. "Sister Soldiers," *New Republic*, October 5, 1992, 29–33. Sommers has written a book incorporating some of the material in this article: *Who Stole Feminism? How Women Have Betrayed Women* (New York: Simon and Schuster, 1994). The book was reviewed by Nina Auerbach in *The New York Times Book Review*, June 12, 1994, p. 13. Auerbach's review begins: "On the evidence of this book, Christina Hoff Sommers is a wallflower at feminist conferences. In revenge, she attends them obsessively, writes down all the stupid things she hears and now has spewed them back." See also "A Rebel in the Sisterhood," by Barbara Carton, *The Boston Globe*, June 16, 1994, pp. 69 and 74.

2. Constructing a definition of feminism has been a longstanding problem for feminist scholars. In another essay, I construct a definition of feminism by means of a series of tropes: feminism is a text characterized by a particular thematic structure represented as an ensemble of contradictions; feminism is a writing project (not a text but an activity);

and feminism is a novel, a mode of discourse that is constituted by the interanimation of various discourses.

REFERENCES

Bakhtin, Mikhail. "Art and Answerability." *Art and Answerability*. Trans. V. Liapunov. Eds. Michael Holquist and Vadim Liapunov. Austin: University of Texas, 1990.
—. *The Dialogic Imagination*. Trans. Caryl Emerson and Michael Holquist. Ed. Michael Holquist. Austin: University of Texas Press, 1981.
Schweickart, Patrocinio. "What Are We Doing? What Do We Want? Who Are We?: Comprehending the Subject of Feminism." *Provoking Subjects*. Ed. Judith Kegan Gardiner. Champaign: University of Illinois Press, forthcoming.

PART II

SCHOLARSHIP IN THE LATE AGE OF PRINT

7

The Scholarly Journal and the Intellectual Sensorium

Ralph Norman

On a recent trip to Chicago, as my plane left Cincinnati, I settled in for a long-overdue browsing of the latest *Critical Inquiry*, which has become a preeminent journal of critical theory in the United States and other English-speaking countries. Distracted perhaps by the noise within the cabin and the shortness of the flight, my first inclination was a lazy one, to inspect the book advertisements at the back of the journal. These pages serve as a sort of diminutive catalogue of the book displays we find at Modern Language Association (MLA), American Psychology Association (APA), and American Academy of Religion (AAR) meetings. In former days, this run-through of the scholarly discussion provided a pleasant and reasonably carefree exercise of notetaking. Which titles would I go looking for at the booksellers or my university library, or perhaps order directly from the publisher? This time, amid the astonishing cornucopia of new titles, I was beset by a series of curiously discomfiting reflections.

Somebody—the universities, the foundations, the professional societies, the American taxpayer—had been generous well beyond the fondest imagining of all previous generations to the cause of theory in this country. Scholars of every persuasion, whether of the newer dispensations or the old, had quite obviously been enjoying ample time to produce whatever criticism they needed or wanted to produce. For a reader, it was the equivalent of a Saturday morning at the market in Chalons-su-Marne. There was too much of it, but it all looked inviting.

The winter 1994 issue of *Critical Inquiry* contained thirty-four full pages of advertisements for recently published books. From Carolyn J. Dean's *The Self and Its Treasures: Bataille, Lacan, and the History of the Decentered Subject*, published by Cornell University Press (1992), to Volney P. Gay's *Freud on Sublimation: Reconsiderations* (1992), there are ninety new or recent titles available to the interested scholar. These titles include *Reading Against Culture: Ideology and Narrative in the Japanese Novel* (Pollak, 1992), *Dreams of Authority: Freud and the Fictions of the Unconscious* (Thomas, 1990), *Telling the Other: The Question of Value in Modern and Postcolonial Writing* (McGee,

1992), and *Delicate Subjects: Romanticism, Gender, and the Ethics of Understanding* (Ellison, 1990) (all from Cornell University Press).

Then, from Duke University Press have come *Text: The Genealogy of an Antidisciplinary Object* (Mowitt, 1992), *Transgressions of Reading: Narrative Engagement as Exile and Return* (Newman, 1993), *Mutual Misunderstanding: Skepticism and the Theorizing of Language and Interpretation* (Taylor, 1992), *Narrative Innovation and Incoherence: Ideology in Defoe, Goldsmith, Austen, Eliot, and Hemingway* (Boardman, 1992); *Apology to Apostrophe: Autobiography and the Rhetoric of Self-Representation in Spain* (Fernandez, 1992), and *Commentary and Ideology: Dante in the Renaissance* (Parker, 1993). And from Stanford: *The Politics of Truth from Marx to Foucault* (Barrett, 1991), *The Dark Side of Reason: Fictionality and Power* (Lima, 1992), *Institutionalizing English Literature: The Culture and Politics of Literary Study 1750–1899* (Court, 1992), *The Transformation of Intimacy: Sexuality, Love and Criticism in Modern Societies* (Giddens, 1992), *Sodometries: Renaissance Texts and Modern Sexualities* (Goldberg, 1992).

Imagine, on the conservative side, that for each of these titles several dozen more journal articles and essays addressed to the same or equivalent topics must have been published at about the same time.

I have not subjected the reader to this list as part of a technique of what some of our colleagues call "quote and gloat." Nor am I deriding any of these titles as unnecessary, effete, obscure, or in any other way a symptom of the excesses of humane scholarship in American research universities. On the contrary, part of what is going on here reflects the work of the first heady decade or two after a new set of terms and methods has taken hold, where scholars can go back over the entire canon of texts, and a great many that were never in the canon, and get fresh mileage out of looking at old favorites in the new vernacular. It is not unlike what went on in biblical criticism for a quarter of a century after the discovery of the Dead Sea Scrolls. Suddenly, in light of a new set of documents, everything was up for grabs and reinterpretation. The difference here is that the texts are old and familiar, but the scholarly arsenal itself has been remodeled and refurbished.

You are no doubt thinking that any rhetorical effect I may have been looking to achieve with my lazy-man's list has long since been ruined by the kind of numbers we ingest daily as to the extent of the information revolution. We get the news, for instance, that at any single moment between 10 and 20 billion "information packets" are surging through the electronic networks. Everyone knows about the present glut of learning and about its electronic solution. We are told, for instance, that 5,000 journals are now being produced in the field of history alone. Who's afraid of an array of titles in literary theory when the cyberprophets have been beguiling us with talk about the limitlessness of Internet journalism? If you had ever been even close to the Frankfurt Book Fair, you would know how extensive a business book publishing is. You would understand, in short, how flimsy is the tiny digest you offer up out of your casual tourist-class reading.

But that rebuke is off to the side of what concerns us just now. The kind of scholarship represented in the books on my list is not additive and cumulative. Its producers do not see themselves as marching, even asymptotically, toward far-off closure. A good portion of the work on this list is aimed at what you might call the Public Square of cultural attention. There is a genuine sense in which almost every one of these titles makes its bid for discussion and public space. All the talk here is of "discourse" and "contest" and "inscription." It makes sense to have published these books if and only if there is some reasonable expectation of their being awarded space and attention.

Let's rephrase that. A radical dissonance exists between the implicit ambitions of these works and any conceivable conditions under which these books, as any sort of collectivity, are likely to be distributed and consumed. There is indeed something askew about any sentence that includes both the term *critical discourse* or *public discussion* and the words *distribution* and *consumption*.

Let's put the matter yet another way: sooner or later, the politics and processes of scholarly publishing will run up against the notion of *economy*. Much notice, of course, is given to one kind of economy, that of book costs, publishing and distribution, and it is within this economy that the prospect of electronic publishing may be imagined to provide a certain measure of relief. But there is another kind of economy, and it is far less amenable to the same fix or manipulation. This is the *economy of attention*.

There are important reasons for believing that attention—personal attention, public attention—is not unlimited. It is a renewable resource to be sure but not an infinitely renewable resource. No society can attend to everything at once, much less value everything at once. At any moment in the life of a people, its *cultural budget* is always in place and in effect. The cultural budget is its disposition of a scarce resource, namely, its attention, its habit of attending to a certain group of ideas, arguments, images, and other contents rather than to others. There will be such a budget whether or not anybody knows it or senses it or admits it.

We can multiply indefinitely the number of electronic transmissions we get into motion. We can store a huge number of journal or other articles, and we can multiply the number and size of such journals. But we cannot increase the number of hours in the day, nor can we do much to change the physical limitations of the body. If this is true of one body, it is also true of the collection of bodies that constitutes a commonwealth.

Schoolchildren, for example, have only so many hours within the curriculum of so many years in which they can be taught some body of literature, some extent of geography, and so on. This, of course, is what we mean by the pedagogical, not to say human and logical, problem of the *canon of texts*.

It is true even of the most assiduous scholars that they can only read so much text. We have studies that show that scholars do not actually read very much text, or at least that they read only a very small portion of the text that is available to them.[1] *For a wide and complicated series of reasons, we are producing a much greater volume of text than anybody is reading or able to read.* To use a term to which Walter Ong some years ago gave currency in describing what was happening to embodied sensibility in the twentieth century, the *intellectual sensorium* is clogged, glutted, surfeited, full, overstuffed, bloated, teeming, overabundant, overflowing.

Should this situation be a worry to us, and, if so, what kind of worry? It is a very large worry for the kind of scholarship I have cited, and precisely because it is a worry there, it is worrisome for anyone who cares about the health of our public life. Clearly, the problem preceded the advent of the computer and of electronic technology. Electronic technology has in fact come into existence in part to help solve this problem. May we expect it to do so?

To see more precisely where the problem may lie, let us back up to look at the favored metaphor of the day. It is so universally favored that, as often happens, its very function as a metaphor grows ever less visible. Then we will examine a couple of other metaphors against which the first should be played out and tested within the present sensorium.

The computers of the advanced nations of the world are said to be part of a vast and intricate connection that is being heralded as the "information superhighway." What we most require from a revolution in the shape and scope of our information is a way of putting that information into the service of the common good, of having it contribute to a broadly public and political deliberation about the ends of the society. The connection that most urgently needs building is the *public* connection, the fabric from which the ancient republicans took their name: the *res publica*. But there is probably nothing more injurious to that fabric than the superhighway.

The superhighway as all of us are coming to know it—Westerners, Easterners, Eurocentrists, Asiatics, denizens of the Third or Fourth World, whether we are drivers and passengers on the Pacific or the Atlantic Rim, or caught up in the traffic of a megalopolis somewhere else—is jammed with conveyances of every description, and in each of these, to be sure, behind the wheel or windshield, there rides a mother's son or daughter. But a great crowd of people does not in itself create a public place. The people within these conveyances are unable to regard each other or to be regarded, to address or be addressed, that is because they do not and cannot appear. They are unavailable to each other for any public purpose beyond the grim ceremony of transit itself. They have no way of enjoying that amplitude of conversation and regard that we have long supposed necessary for membership in the life of the city.

Nor are other essentially public virtues like generosity and compassion much more in evidence or demand on the superhighway, those dispositions that a reasonably enlightened citizenry might be expected to show toward strangers or toward the weaker brethren.

It may be objected that these are wildly misplaced expectations, that they represent a confusion of means and ends, that highways and computers are mere conveyances. Who ever supposed that bare technology would furnish or reflect the deepest, widest ambitions of a society? As for supercomputers and super-highways, what they convey is a partial aggregate of the privacy that is available within a community, its sum of private messages, goods, and enjoyments. These together, and these alone, will constitute the common good, if there is to be any such thing.

This is a brave response, and a predictable one, but it won't wash, at least not in the present instance. In these hard-driving technological times, the distinction between means and ends has fallen on dusty days. Nowhere has the distinction been more contaminated than in the encroachment of the superhighway on the landscapes and cityscapes of the late twentieth century. To ponder that encroachment is to be reminded that for some time we have had trouble figuring out where cities leave off and not-city (formerly the "countryside") begins. It is to be reminded of cities bereft both of centers and boundaries, and of great concrete connectors stretching from unplace to noplace and back again without benefit or hint of that elusive civility students of community call the space of appearance. In this picture, means and ends have been reversed or ground into a more or less indistinguishable mix where nothing can be made out except the means. No, it is unlikely that the public part of an age of information (if the coming age is going to acknowledge a public part) will lie in its likeness to the open road of interstates and autobahns.

Still, it would be foolhardy not to grant that there is something compelling about the metaphor. Information networks and superhighways are the servants of speed and immediacy, the shortest distance between two points, the race against time and limitation and scarcity. These are the familiar imperatives of the industrial age, recast as primary demands of the age of information. The master imperative that moves both ages is probably the drive and promise of *total connection*, the prospect of a rational and fully administered society. This is the imperative identified in differing ways by twentieth-century critics of totalization such as Theodor Adorno and Walter Benjamin.

Within managed capitalist and postcapitalist societies, according to these critics, a curious thing occurs. The public sphere of appearance is replaced by what looks like its opposite, that is, by the sphere of the private. The notion of a commonwealth of ends as Immanuel Kant used that idea collapses into a series of sites and opportunities for individual gratification. As compensation for the loss of the space of appearance, the administered society allows its private individuals a range of fugitive pleasures and distractions. In our time, there are few more telling experiences of this privileged isolation than that of driving your closed sedan down the freeway, taking care to mind the traffic fore and aft, all the while luxuriating in the choicest sounds of your desiring.

We now learn that these private moments can be expanded into opportunities for buying and selling stock, shopping, checking the weather forecast, approving invoices, balancing checkbooks, briefing the boss, debriefing subordinates, registering for classes, consulting library catalogues, reading seminar papers, playing chess, learning Japanese, or researching scholarly interests. We learn that all of this will be literally as well as metaphorically possible while riding the freeway.

The grim ceremony of transit is to be transformed into the performance of a free and conscientious, if not altogether joyous, technical repertoire. The loathsome repetitions of commuting are to be translated into the profitable rituals of total-quality time management, and the society that has gone out with Proust in search of lost time will have found a way to retrieve it, although not exactly in the manner he prescribed.

To turn to the language of ceremony and repertoire is to be reminded that any society worth our desiring must keep the ritual energies of its people engaged. That is because ritual has enormous, but by no means always controllable, power to organize and most often to expand the available information. The excitement many of our most imaginative and productive scholars report on their adventures in electronic connections is based, it seems to me, in part on their delight in finding that the very apparatus they might long have associated with Big Brother, Big Business, Big Military, the corporate establishment, has become a source of at least semisubversive liberation. They seem able to recover for scholarship some of its performative and ritual possibility. By performative and ritual possibility I mean precisely the sense, which is absolutely central to ritual performance, that *somebody is watching and responding, that the work of inquiry has some prospect of being a social and possibly public act.* Or more prosaically, they have the sense that as scholars they are making a world happen. The work of scholarship, some say, is rightly in verbs and actions; the nouns, products, pronouns will follow. But it is also apparent that the speed with which all things electronic can be made to happen, and the intolerance for leisure, the impatience with indolence or reverie which it seems to engender, threaten to circumscribe the range of performance and rob the solitary ritual of its breathing room. The wholly managed society reneges on its permissions; negotiations between the reality principle and the pleasure principle sooner or later break down, and management's arbitration fails. Mademoiselle's petite bloomery turns into the little shop of horrors. The ultimate virus hits the electronic system, and all the pretty horses of the attendant scholarly community are done in. With these dire possibilities at the back of the mind, the claim one wants to make for the public sphere, that it alone can accommodate the full breadth and implication of ritual performance, might need to be reasserted in some new form.

During the fateful years between 1924 and 1940, Walter Benjamin labored on a series of reflections about the shopping arcades of the nineteenth century and about what these and other urban *Passagen* revealed as to the human and material circumstance of modern European capitalism. He had not completed these pieces, which came to be known as the *Passagen Werk*, when he died, apparently by his own hand, in late September of 1940, after having failed to get across the border out of France into Spain. Relatively few people yet knew his work.[2]

Benjamin had produced astonishingly fresh studies of Baudelaire and Goethe, of Brecht and Kraus and the German *Trauerspiel*, and essays about politics and art and storytelling. He had been close not only to Brecht and to Adorno and Max Horkheimer of the Frankfurt School, but also to his fellow Jew, Gershom Scholem, who urged him as early as the late 1920s to come and live in Palestine. But Benjamin had declined. He wanted to be a European, in the oldest and best sense of that term. He was, he told friends, "the last European." He would remain in Europe, the spiritual homeland, with the aim, as he said, of becoming the best literary critic in Germany. He never believed that these aspirations were incompatible.

Benjamin's claim that Paris was "the Capital of the XIXth Century" was not based on the part the streets of that great city played in civil unrest and revolution. He was interested rather in the way Parisians of the time were beginning to take their leisure, not so much along the boulevards but along the new indoor-outdoor labyrinth of shops, stalls, and store windows, where grand public spectacle yielded to what he called the phantasmagoria of private consumption, and where the grand avenues of the grenadiers were giving way to streets governed by a desire for a different kind of information. It is to the arcades of Paris, not to its barricades, that we must look for the most telling material clues to the spiritual condition of the Europe that was coming.

Benjamin juggled a number of different hypotheses about these clues. Ever the scrupulous, skeptical, self-critical European, he did not hesitate to offer the first and harshest refutations of the work himself. For a while he tried a version of Marxist logic on his materials, but they resisted. The emergence of the arcades was a playing out of the Enlightenment; the high claims of Citizen Reason were to be translated into the consumer demands of the bourgeoisie; the heady comprehensiveness of the Encyclopedia would trickle out into the Panoptikon, the Stereoptikon, the Diorama, and the Panorama, and photography would have to be invented; the library and the museum would enter upon their ever-quickening pace of indefinite expansion; the transported booty first of Napoleon's empire and then of his imitators would be displayed to Everyman in classrooms and lecture halls and world congresses. Soon the sheer disconnectedness of these materials from their original *Sitz im Leben* and from each other would generate within private consciousness itself the necessary and revolutionary questions that must be put to a society of consumers. The *Passagen Werk* was supposed to be a moment in this awakening to consciousness. There would be much loose energy in the play of these materials. Would it be enough to shake the foundations?

Michael Sexson, in an article reminiscent of Benjamin's work ("Miranda's Attendants: Memory, Medievalism, Cyberspace, and the Soul," *Soundings*, Spring/Summer 1994), has recently argued that the new electronic technology, which might have seemed the good fortune, if not the invention of Big Brother, offers its own special promise for shaking the foundations. He thinks that there is a notable correlation between the fabulous places described in the inward mnemonic journeys of medieval and Renaissance explorers and the cavernous inner recesses where contemporary players of electronic games go searching for demons and dragons. Sexson recalls the immense imaginative freedom exploited by Augustine in his meditations on time and memory, and then turns to Dante for a second compelling example.

Dante's interviews in hell with the great sinners of the Western world are like Benjamin's interrogations of the arcades of Paris. Indeed, Sexson refers to these moving episodes out of the "Inferno" as if they were moments in a passage through stalls and displays of the mind. Sexson is thinking of the video arcades in today's shopping malls, but his concern is to show that what these inward journeys may make possible is a subversion of the massive technological apparatus of the information age. Official corporate ideology may, despite itself, be put into the service of personal freedom. The charming and yet pitiful story of Paolo and Francesca provides the evidence.

This is not a story that Dante invented; these memorable lovers show up in Boccaccio and many other places. Dante borrows them, but he doesn't buy or own them, any more than Shakespeare bought Caesar or Wagner purchased exclusive rights to Tristan. Sexson thinks that in the *Divina Commedia* the tale gets away from Dante and takes off with moral and spiritual energy of its own. The continuing power of the story of Paolo and Francesca shows that we have whole worlds within us, to invent, rehearse, and perform even as we are engaged by the texts of the past. That possibility, and that alone, will tell whether cybernetics is cause for hope or for despair.

In Dante's version of the story, Paolo and Francesca discover they are in love while under the influence of the media then available—namely, while reading to each other the story of Lancelot and Guinevere, a story everybody else is also reading at the time. Dante says that they straightaway lay down the book and commenced the doing of what the book says young people do—not, as Lerner and Lowe have it, the way the simple folk do, but the way knights and ladies do, and more specifically the way Lancelot and Guinevere do. It is *mimesis* at first sight.[3]

Obviously, the play of energies among the arcades is not simply a retreat or an escape from the environing social circumstance and system, but a complicated echo and replication of forces within that system. Do Paolo and Francesca subvert the system, or does the system have its way with them? We begin to see why Benjamin had second and third thoughts about his project. The private and the public spheres are not sealed off against each other, nor are they mirror images either.

It is apparently as much of a mistake to think of the public sphere always as something like a forum, a debate, or a deliberation as to think of it as a superhighway. Maybe the public connection at its richest is rather the play of energies, focused now here in the arts and now there in the sciences, now here in the tone poem and now there in the painting, and only once in a while straightened and tidied up into the form of civil and deliberative convocation. If so, these energies must be kept open and in touch with one another; otherwise a single force or interest will take control of the whole. That is the danger constantly rehearsed in the science fictions that feature cyberspace and virtual reality as contested territory to be won or lost, and always against interlopers and pretenders, the embezzlers of the common good. It is, many believe, the single greatest danger in the advent of electronic scholarship and the electronic journal. When Big Brother comes around at the border checking passports and official papers for whatever form of correctness, or simply when the power has failed, we want to be able to hide the precious information under the jacket, or to read it in whispers to the beloved, or to bury it for a while in the vegetable garden. Part of what free people mean by the freedom of appearance is having the power to turn away betimes from where all the others are.

Edward Said, in his Wellek lectures at the University of California-Davis, stated that our society has tended to make every performance an "extreme occasion"—that is, a moment that distances the performer from the audience.[4] (Here he is thinking of musical performance, but I will bet he wants the notion generalized.) If Paris is the capital of the nineteenth century, it is not New York or even Hollywood that outbids all others to be the capital of the twentieth century, but Los Angeles, the invisible city Italo Calvino described as Penthesilea, a nonplace constituted totally by outskirts, a place where nobody appears.[5]

Now let us imagine that knowledge is a form of action and that performance is the highest form of action, because it is not for the sake of anything else. In a desirable society, the private and the public rituals must both enhance and restrain each other. Performance helps create the world where it will be noticed, and that is why in a desirable society no performance need ever be an extreme occasion. In its own modest way we might hope that the work of scholarship would aid and abet the creation of a such a world.

NOTES

1. See, for instance, the work of Josie Marie Griffiths in *Scientific and Technical Communication in the U.S.* (Metuchen, N.J.: Scarecrow Press, 1994).

2. Benjamin, Walter. *Gesammelte Schriften* (Frankfurt am Main: Suhrkamp, 1972), 1 Aufl.

3. Alighieri, Dante. *Divina Commedia*, translated by John Ciardi (New York: Norton, 1977).

4. Said, Edward W. *Musical Elaborations* (New York: Columbia University Press, 1991).

5. Calvino, Italo. *Musical Elaborations*, translated by William Weaver (New York: Harcourt Brace Jovanovich, 1974).

REFERENCES

Barrett, Michele. *The Politics of Truth from Marx to Foucault.* Stanford, Calif.: Stanford University Press, 1991.

Boardman, Michael M. *Narrative Innovation and Incoherence: Ideology in Defoe, Goldsmith, Austen, Eliot, and Hemingway.* Durham, N.C.: Duke University Press, 1992.

Court, Franklin E. *Institutionalizing English Literature: The Culture and Politics of Literary Study.* Stanford, Calif.: Stanford University Press, 1992.

Critical Inquiry XX, 1 (Winter 1994).

Dean, Carolyn J. *The Self and Its Treasures: Bataille, Lacan, and the History of the Decentered Subject.* Ithaca, N.Y.: Cornell University Press, 1992.

Ellison, Julie K. *Delicate Subjects: Romanticism, Gender, and the Ethics of Understanding.* Ithaca, N.Y.: Cornell University Press, 1990.

Fernandez, James D. *Apology to Apostrophe: Autobiography and the Rhetoric of Self-Representation in Spain.* Durham, N.C.: Duke University Press, 1992.

Gay, Volney P. *Freud on Sublimation: Reconsiderations.* Ithaca, N.Y.: Cornell University Press, 1992.

Giddens, Anthony. *The Transformation of Intimacy: Sexuality, Love and Criticism in Modern Societies.* Stanford, Calif.: Stanford University Press, 1992.

Goldberg, Jonathan. *Sodometries: Renaissance Texts and Modern Sexualities.* Stanford, Calif.: Stanford University Press, 1992.

Lima, Luis Costa. *The Dark Side of Reason: Fictionality and Power.* Stanford, Calif.: Stanford University Press, 1992.

McGee, Patrick. *Telling the Other: The Question of Value in Modern and Postcolonial Writing.* Ithaca, N.Y.: Cornell University Press, 1992.

Mowitt, John. *Text: The Genealogy of an Antidisciplinary Object.* Durham, N.C.: Duke University Press, 1992.

Newman, Robert D. *Transgressions of Reading: Narrative Engagement as Exile and Return.* Durham, N.C.: Duke University Press, 1993.

Parker, Deborah. *Commentary and Ideology: Dante in the Renaissance.* Durham, N.C.: Duke University Press, 1993.

Pollak, David. *Reading Against Culture: Ideology and Narrative in the Japanese Novel.* Ithaca, N.Y.: Cornell University Press, 1992.

Sexson, Michael. "Miranda's Attendants: Memory, Medievalism, Cyberspace, and the Soul." *Soundings* LXXVII, 2 (Spring/Summer 1994): 13–40.

Taylor, Talbot J. *Mutual Misunderstanding: Skepticism and the Theorizing of Language and Interpretation*. Durham, N.C.: Duke University Press, 1992.

Thomas, Ronald R. *Dreams of Authority: Freud and the Fictions of the Unconscious*. Ithaca, N.Y.: Cornell University Press, 1990.

8

Academic Publishing and New Technologies: Protecting Intellectual Property Is the Key

James Lichtenberg

The proposition that technology is about to transform higher education is not a new one. In the 1950s, television was put forward as a likely candidate—a promise that may only now bear fruit with interactive teleconferencing as part of the phenomenon of "distance learning." Needless to say, the rise of computing, especially with the advent of the personal computer, reopened these discussions fifteen years ago. Unlike the 1980s, however, when much of the discussion about transformation was merely theoretical, today it is the stuff of daily life on a growing number of campuses. According to a survey done in early 1994 by a college textbook publisher, there were already thirty 100 percent computerized colleges in seventeen states representing the full range of institutions from ivy league to urban to technical to community colleges. With each passing month, more institutions are wiring their campuses and are even beginning to digitize their libraries. In fact, an annual survey in this regard might be revealing and useful for both academics and publishers. Certainly, 1993 is the year in which the Internet went mainstream. The year 1994–1995 appears to be the year for significant attention to CD-ROM on campus—-although the long-term future of CD-ROM is still much debated.

The possibilities for scholarship, communication, advertising, commerce, and even "electronic publishing" that appear to be offered by use of the Internet are very intriguing, but they are also a little overwhelming. As Dr. Arno Penzias (one of the Bell Lab scientists who recognized that what sounded like static was, in reality, the echo of the "Big Bang") observed at a meeting in Washington: "When someone asks you for a drink, you don't give them a fire hose" (1994). Internet surfers notwithstanding, information overload is a major vulnerability in a society that creates over one trillion pages of just text a year, not to mention millions of frames of film, notes of music, folios of graphics, and so on. The steady stream of reports of disenchantment with the high volume/low quality of the "electronic dialogue" has caused some users to return to lower technology like faxes and letters.

Nonetheless, it is clear that the world is irrevocably changing. To overstate the matter slightly, we are approaching an apocalyptical moment, and the four horsepersons of the apocalypse are technology, demographics, politics, and economics. Along with the academy generally, they will transform the nature of academic publishing. Yet, if that's the bad news, the good news is that academic publishing will become even more rich, satisfying, and valuable than before.

Academic publishing represents a robust and intriguing variety that includes not only journals, monographs, and scholarly books of varying degrees of complexity (on a stunning array of subjects), but also textbooks. The key to this last kind of publishing is not only the specific pedagogical component, but also the fact that students are its primary audience. However, as new technology begins to broaden its impact in the world of academic publishing, scholars, students, and the general public may all want, and be served by, the very same product: technology will allow "access" to students and scholars across a wide range of sophistication and interest on the same platform. This projection is based on observations of some of the early example text materials in CD-ROM format which can be used at several different levels of knowledge and ability.

Although the technology of CD-ROM is projected to grow significantly in the future, it is already startling. An article in *The New York Times Book Review* by Bernard Sharratt, chairman of the Department of Communications at the University of Kent, described a CD-ROM that contains the entire National Gallery of London, all 2,000 paintings in glorious color, at the touch of a button. And this is only the top layer of this amazing disk. "Sitting in my study I have no time restrictions. I can explore the full ramifications of this extraordinary labyrinth of vivid color images, soberly authoritative biographies, history, commentary and glossary. I can browse through a million words, construct a continuous slide show of every painting, gaze for however long at my favorites, I am in danger of never reemerging" (1984, 3, 11). This disc appears to enjoy a good user interface that matches the needs and interests of the individual user. Ultimately, sources of information must be manageable and filtered, not fire hoses of data, and here is where the value that both academic and commercial publishers add will make a crucial difference. The ability to select, certify, sort, and structure is just one of the very real contributions which "publishers" will bring to content in both electronic and ink-on-paper formats. Enchantment with the potential of electronic delivery of information is not to say that the virtual will, or should, replace the real. A CD-ROM is not a substitute for the National Gallery. Nothing could ever replace the experience of meeting a late Van Gogh cornfield face to face. However, the new technologies will offer extraordinary opportunities for learning and enjoying.

Along with this intellectual excitement, there is a serious concern that all documents can be widely and instantaneously shared over networks. In other words, once it's digital, it's got legs, so how can we protect copyright? This is not an easy question to answer. In some circles, copyright is considered the problem. There is still a renegade spirit left over from the 1960s that intones: "Information must be free." Yet, how would a professor feel if the information in question was a book that she or he had spent three hard years developing and 3 million of his or her closest friends galloped away with it on the Internet? Already, there are reports of early Internet participants removing their contributions from freely accessible servers in order to "publish" them in a more traditional, and thus remunerative, fashion. In addition, professors who use the Internet for communicating with, and sending manuscripts to, their publishers, are finding systems to "encrypt" their material in order to prevent "piracy." As increasing amounts of information are sent over networks, methods will be devised to assure integrity. Otherwise, the much-vaunted information superhighway, whether national or global, would become something of a ghost road.

Rather than being the problem, copyright is actually the solution. Respect for copyright offers the framework through which the digital future of information exchange can come into being. Granted, all of us must find ways to keep information accessible. Most likely, fair return in exchange for access is the best route to take. That is the way it happens today, and we must not fall victim to the illusion that libraries offer information for "free." While students and scholars may not pay at the time of the actual "transaction" whether through gifts or grants, tuition or taxes, the payment is made for information both to the owners and those who work to deliver it. Academic librarians even talk quietly about systems to "cover their costs" and "create a surplus." In the business world, these very same activities have slightly different names—that is, revenue and profit. Intellectual property has increasing value as we move into the information age. But we will not get there smoothly if we shortchange either those who create or those who deliver it.

Taking this approach, we can seek the means to resolve our problems. Technology taketh away, but it also giveth. It creates problems, but it can also solve them. As an Charles Clark, general counsel to the International Publishers Copyright Counsel puts it: "The answer to the machine is in the machine" (1994, 35). Systems based on new technologies are being developed to make digital exchange and commerce possible. If it is possible to track exchange payment for the huge volume of telephone calls, why not intellectual property over a network? However, a new look at ethical behavior is also required. The same person who thoughtlessly "steals" a book by photocopying its contents, or sending copies along the network, would never actually do so by walking out of a bookstore with it.

Essentially, the system that protects intellectual property is the branch on which publishers and academics are both sitting. If we allow this limb to be sawed off, we will all need to find a new means of livelihood. In the spirit of Franklin Delano Roosevelt's famous exhortation, "The only thing we have to fear is fear itself," the "problem" is the mistake of considering that copyright is the problem.

In addition to being the law, copyright provides the structure that both stimulates and rewards creativity. It provides the means for compensating all concerned.

In terms of day-to-day academic life, the needs of our new era became clear following the federal court decision against Kinko's Graphic, Inc. In March 1991, Kinko's was assessed $1.9 million in damages and attorney's fees and agreed not to create coursepacks in the future without first getting permission for the use of any and all copyrighted materials (Watkins, 1991, A1, A19). Like most "revolutionary" moments, however, the situation had been building for some time, perhaps over a decade in this case, and especially during the past five years. Growing out of library reserve room materials, photocopied course anthologies were being created with little respect for copyrighted materials.

In her decision, as reported by the *Chronicle of Higher Education*, Judge Constance Motley of the U.S. District Court reaffirmed the basic purposes of copyright protection, noting, in addition, that "the company officials' insistence that theirs are educational concerns and not profit-making ones boggles the mind" (Watkins, A19). Immediately, higher education was beset by a cacophony of competing opinions from professors, administrators, copying facilities, libraries, university presses, and publishers. Yet while the need to observe copyright law may feel intrusive, the essence of it is very straightforward. Nevertheless, it is inevitable during a fundamental change in the order of things that, for the next few years, we will all be living through a period of transition.

We need to remind ourselves that the protection of intellectual property and the procedures for respecting copyright are venerable and mainstream components of Anglo-American culture. Despite legal complexities, they have never involved much rocket science or its preindustrial equivalent. The Statute of Anne of 1710 was the first copyright law in England created for "the Encouragement of Learning (and of) Learned Men to write useful Books," the goal being not only to protect authors from exploitation and poverty, but also to encourage socially useful creativity. During the centuries after Gutenberg when copying was costly, tedious, and slow, copyright issues were rarely on the front burner of the academic agenda except in the subset of issues involving plagiarism. Because of late twentieth-century technology, that courtly age is now clearly behind us.

One might suppose that respect for ownership of intellectual property, copyright, and the like, is ingrained in the very ethos of higher education. However, a funny thing happens on the way to the quadrangle. Like a stick passing from air into water, what seemed a straight line appears not to be so at all. The "bend" in the stick is, of course, the concept of "fair use," an uneasy compromise reached ostensibly to facilitate learning, but increasingly misused as technology (most recently photocopiers that turn pages automatically) provides ever easier and faster ways to duplicate and transmit. As long as the "leakage" was small, publishers looked the other way. Some faculty became accustomed to taking what they wanted and now are using the fig leaf of fair use to try and cover what is in some cases simply naked theft.

Through copyright, desire for personal gain is a legitimate and powerful motivating force in the creation of knowledge and art. I am well aware that, as part of its aristocratic heritage, the academy is diffident, or has been, about things like this kind of return on investment. In fact, part of the reason for the long-term success of higher education in America is the protection of new ideas and discoveries afforded by the Constitution through providing protection of authors and incentives for invention whether intellectual or physical. As a further consequence of this protection, the United States is a vast exporter of intellectual property earning hundreds of millions of dollars in positive balance of trade each year. In all likelihood, this creative prowess will only increase as we enter the digital era.

Thus, renaissance in the creative partnership between publishers and academics may also be at hand owing to the new kinds of academic publishing which digital technology makes possible. Such an idea may seem strange. Many faculty might ask: "What partnership?"

The creation of teaching materials is an interesting, if less salient, aspect of higher education. The collaborative partnership between professors and publishers that resulted in the post-World War II textbook has now reached a watershed. While lecture notes, classroom exercises, and the like have always been the relatively exclusive province of the individual professor, the past decade has seen a dramatic increase in publishers' contributions to faculty *teaching* materials. This has come about through the creation of supplemental or "ancillary" materials. In some cases, the ancillary package created for a textbook in some cases comprises over 100 items. It may include not only an instructor's edition, overheads, slides, test banks, and the like, but also new technologies such as computer disks, videodiscs, and other multimedia elements. The fact that such materials have generally been provided free of charge to professors, once they have adopted the textbook, has tended to mask the market significance of their innovative character and technological sophistication. While ancillaries add a significant burden to cost of creating, and thus the price, of the textbook, students are only the indirect beneficiaries of them. Professors have grown used to these ancillary materials to assist them in their courses, and occasionally the adoption of a textbook has been determined by the extent of the ancillaries rather than the quality of the text itself. The transformation of teaching materials that we are about to witness, however, is focused on multimedia and new technology elements for students, not just professors. This is the key difference. The digitized transformation of learning will change what *students* use in their dorm rooms and libraries. Already, for example, students can sit with their laptop computers under a tree in the quad reading the complete works of Jane Austen available on a computer disk. (A recent study of students in eleven introductory courses revealed that fewer than 15 percent of the respondents would choose to use their laptops outside.)

Are we facing the likelihood that teaching materials will be completely transformed? Probably not. Rather, the traditional text will be accompanied by a rich array of new materials whether supplementary text, graphics, video, photographs, or audio, taken from the realms of pure data, movies, television, art, music, historical documents and the like. Here we move toward a richness that pushes these materials far beyond their original purpose. Based on the early examples of CD-ROM textbooks, it is as if, along with the text, the professors and student have a virtual *library* of primary and secondary sources in all media through which the student can browse for hours according to interest or the professor's assignment. While this may sound futuristic, in fact, textbook publishers and editors, not "techies," are now driving the creation of new media teaching and learning materials. Even technology companies recognize that true knowledge of the subject and pedagogical insight, not random technological bells and whistles, are what is required for effective teaching materials. From the college publisher's perspective, this development breaks the mold of traditional publishing and requires a new approach to the use of intellectual property.

Two key issues remain to be resolved, which form the basis for the renaissance of collaboration between faculty and publishers. They are: (1) which of the several possible new media formats will professors and students want to buy and use, and (2) when will the market be sufficiently mature to be commercially viable? According to research by the James Irvine Foundation Center for Scholarly Technology, there is strong demand for instructional technology. There is little growth, however, in instructional development on campus. Thus, generally speaking, academia is *not* going to create these new technological materials. Instead, faculty are looking for instructional technology from other sources. Here is a point of convergence for faculty and publishers: working together can answer these questions, through continuous involvement with each other over time. We have a common goal—to harness the new media and new technology in a way that best serves the needs of scholarship and learning. Granted, this is unfamiliar territory for both parties, especially as we have grown a little out of touch, if not distrustful. Yet, just as the collaboration between publishers and professors created the teaching materials in the boom years following the Second World War, so too, this renewed collaboration should drive the development of teaching materials in new media in the new century—which may also be a new boom period. Faculty would do well to consider this opportunity and begin to engage in dialogue with publishers who will be willing to listen to their needs and concerns. Ultimately, the task is the same: to extend the frontiers of knowledge and to educate students in a profound and useful way. The classic paradigm of student and teacher on a log still holds even if the log is becoming electronic—whether a computer, a network, a distance-learning hookup, or a CD-ROM. Through these means, the professor will guide the student as well as directly instruct about the subject. As always, the institutions, professors and publishers who will be most effective in the future are the ones who are most interested in understanding these changes in the present.

NOTE

This chapter is based on an address delivered at the University of South Florida, which itself drew substantially on an article which the author originally published in the *Department Chair* journal—"Intellectual Property and the New Technologies." *Department Chair* (Winter 1994): 10–13.

REFERENCES

"The Answer to the Machine Is in the Machine." *The Publisher in the Electronic World* (1994): 35.

Penzias, Arno. Keynote Address. Annual Meeting, Professional and Scholarly Publishing Division, Association of American Publishers. Washington, D.C., Feb. 9–11, 1994.

Sharatt, Bernard. "Please Touch the Paintings." *The New York Times Book Review* March 6, 1984.

Watkins, Beverly T. "Photocopying Chain Found to Violate Copyright Law." *The Chronicle of Higher Education* (April 1991): A1, A19.

9

All Information Is Already *in* Formation: The Internet and the Future of Learned Journals

R. A. Shoaf

> keep the spice flowing
> —Frank Herbert, *Dune*

> the irritant around which a theory might grow
> —William Gibson, "Hinterlands"

We are at a crossroads, and like all crossroads, this one is dangerous; so we must be careful. Also, like all crossroads, this one may mark the spot of another human leap forward; so, we must not be too careful.[1]

The next century promises to be a radically different era in academic publishing generally and in journal publishing in particular. That difference will be owing in the main to the computer and to what we should probably begin calling "computeracy" (as we call the culture of books "literacy"). If we consider the rather remarkable fact that the era of the PC, the personal computer, is barely fifteen years old today and look, in that light, at the revolution it has effected, then I think it is easy for us to predict that within the first few decades of the twenty-first century, even more revolutionary changes will occur at every level of the academic profession.

In 1993, as vice president of the Council of Editors of Learned Journals (CELJ), I began to establish an electronic bulletin board or "listserv" for the membership of CELJ (EDITOR-L). This "listserv" was up and running by the autumn of 1993, and as of this writing about 20 percent of the membership have logged on. My goal in my tenure as president of CELJ (1994–1996) is to bring at least 50 percent of the membership online in EDITOR-L.

A few words about the Council will be appropriate at this point since they will provide the larger context of my remarks in this chapter.[2] In 1980, the Conference of Editors of Learned Journals, an MLA allied organization, was revived under the leadership of Ralph Cohen, editor of *New Literary History,* and Arthur Kinney, editor of *English Literary Renaissance.* In 1989, the organization changed its name to the Council of Editors of Learned Journals, which more accurately reflects the association of member editors. In 1991 CELJ achieved not-for-profit status.

Since 1980 CELJ has flourished. The succession of presidents from that time to the present illustrates, among other things, the wide range of literary disciplines that CELJ has been able to draw from during these years: Ralph Cohen, editor of *New Literary History* (1980–1982); Arthur Kinney, editor of *English Literary Renaissance* (1982–1984); George Simson, editor of *Biography: An Interdisciplinary Quarterly* (1984–1986); John Stasny, editor of *Victorian Poetry* (1986-1988); Evelyn Hinz, editor of *Mosaic* (1988–1990); Michael Marcuse, editor of *Literary Research* (1990–1992); John Coldewey, editor of *Modern Language Quarterly: A Journal of Literary History* (19921994); and me, editor of *Exemplaria: A Journal of Theory in Medieval and Renaissance Studies*.

Every year CELJ sponsors sessions at the annual MLA convention. One of the sessions is devoted to ordinary business. The second part of the business meeting is more exciting, however, for it is devoted to awards presentations for our very popular and highly contested annual competitions. Winners receive award certificates in five categories: Best New Journal, Best Journal Design, Best Special Issue, Best Retiring Editor, and the Phoenix Award for Journal Revitalization. Usually, around a hundred journals and editors enter into the competition, which is judged by experts from both inside and outside the academic world. Ordinarily, CELJ also sponsors one special session, devoted to a topic of interest to member editors and to publishing scholars and critics alike.

The benefits of EDITOR-L to the membership of CELJ are obvious: rapid and extensive communication about editorial problems and issues is easy and convenient through the Internet; the exchange of technical information and the negotiation of professional issues among interested parties in academic publishing are immensely facilitated by the speed and the reach of Internet.

At the same time, the Internet is still somewhat mysterious, if not, in fact, forbidding to most academics, especially academics who edit journals; the desire for more knowledge is keen, though also, in many cases, ambivalent. There are fears both vague and, in some cases, precise that the Internet will prove the undoing and elimination of many journals. It is my opinion, privately as well as in my official capacity as president of CELJ, that most of these fears are unfounded; they are misdirected energy. Indeed, many journals may modify their formats, and some journals may even abandon the paper format. Abandoning this format, however, is not the same thing as disappearing from the scene. To the contrary, in many cases, it may mean precisely the survival and indeed the rejuvenation of a particular journal. However, before any of that may come to pass, more education is needed. Only more education can begin to allay the anxieties and fears that the Internet still inspires in many.[3]

Here I cannot discuss all the issues that will need to figure in the curriculum of that education. But I do want to single out two of them for their irritancy. They are the issues of ownership, connected to but not the same thing as the legal concept of copyright, and of virtuality, what Richard Lanham refers to as "desubstantiation" (1993, 11, 18) and what I will call the New Platonism.

As Lanham also observes in his important book, the very nature of *copia* has changed: "The electronic word embodies a denial of nature: *copia* can be kept and yet given away. Electronic information seems to resist ownership" (18, 19, and see 274–276 especially).

The implications of these assertions are formidable, and I would like to elaborate on one subset of them. All information is already in formation: if information has been retrieved, then that which retrieved it has formed it, whether it is a mind or a computer or a photocell or an amoeba, and so on. It follows that the forming agent has some claim to what it has formed. But this inference is problematic. At one extreme is, say, the scholarly monograph, product of years of labor and intense dedication, every word crafted, stamped with the author's style. Surely, we would say, these words and their author should enjoy copyright. Similarly, the journal that presents a major statement of a new theory or a new approach should enjoy copyright jointly with the author. This only seems to be common sense.

And yet, seen from the other extreme, this common sense is murky at best. As cognitivism is teaching us with increasing amounts of evidence, the mind does not retrieve "raw" information: we perceive, we process, information that the brain has already formed—all our information is already in formation by virtue of having passed through a brain.[4] From this perspective, I "own" even the "tree" I "see" outside my window this morning. Just so, from this perspective, I must resign my "ownership" to the community—publish it, that is—in order to enter into any communication. Otherwise, solipsism is the result.

Somewhere between these two extremes, legal ownership, copyright, supposedly falls. But that is not precisely the issue I wish to pursue or am even competent to pursue.[5] Rather, I want to concentrate on the form in information. The computer, especially the Internet puts minds forming information in connection with each other at a speed and a magnitude hitherto inconceivable (see Lanham 19–20 for bracing comment). Communication is now virtually instantaneous and is increasing at an exponential rate: in January 1992 (one month), 9 billion packets of data were transferred over the National Science Foundation backbone in the United States, in January 1993, 27 billion were transferred, and in January 1994, 54 billion (Raish, 1994, "Introduction"). We can be confident that such doubling, in the billions, trillions, and so on, will continue in the ether for the indefinite future. If we want to communicate with each other as scholars, clearly we need (and increasingly many of us have) modems, dedicated telephone lines, and fast microprocessors.[6]

Suddenly, how much form I contribute to the information I process becomes a different matter. I may share information about *Troilus and Criseyde* with my colleagues on ChaucerNet one afternoon, and that night three, seven, or fifteen of them may embellish, redirect, and correct that information, with, moreover, the additional possible result that all of us will suddenly see a passage in the poem as none of us ever saw it before. And who owns this new word?[7] Surely, it is *ours*. Now that's an irritant, isn't it? But this irritant has actually been around a very long time. In fact, all this is a very familiar situation when we stop to think about it. Scholarship has always involved a community (if honored more in the breach) and hence communication, with its implication of corrigibility; corrigibility always has problematized ownership. I own my mistakes (as the phrase has it); the rest is the benevolence of my colleagues (we say). That remainder now confronts us as it never has before. On the Bryn Mawr Reviews Network, for example, I read a review of a book posted four weeks (not four years) after the book's official publication date—and that night I read a colleague's correction of information or claims in the review. Maybe we own nothing but our mistakes?

Because of its speed and magnitude, the Internet confronts us with one of our ideals, which we used to keep safely tucked away in the material necessities of print: rapid, corrigible communication of constantly changing information, changing because it is never singular but always plural. (That's the trick about information: it doesn't work in the singular.) Academic journals cannot much longer afford to ignore the implications of finding this ideal before us (see Lanham, 21–22). We can actually talk to each other now, in "real time" even, about what we do, and so we had best begin thinking anew about the implications of the "public-ness," the "publication," of what we do. Ours is a plural enterprise even if, with the left and the right, we repudiate pluralism.

And here is why, I think, we need to return to the metaphor of credit rather than ownership in our profession.[8] If I spend five years transcribing, glossing, annotating, and correcting Thynne's 1532 edition of Thomas Usk's *Testament of Love*, as well as W. W. Skeat's 1907 edition in tandem with Thynne's, then I receive, rightly, credit for my contribution.[9] But I do not own the *Testament of Love*. At this point, of course, copyright law can intervene with a different time scale and understanding of time. But again, I am not really addressing copyright here—I am talking about communication within the academic community.[10] In that community, credit is of overwhelming importance: just ask any dean and her T&P Committee how much they rely on the credit I as a journal editor generate for their candidates when I review, or secure an outside review, for their candidates' work. As a profession generally, academics must acknowledge that there is an irresolvable element of the free (if not also of free play) in our work. And we now have, if we will but seize the forelock, an opportunity to theorize that element anew.[11] I would hope that I and my fellow editors of academic journals would be among the first to go for it. After all, if we don't act soon, AT&T, Sony, and Microsoft et al. will do it for us.[12]

My own effort would begin with a meditation on what I think of as the New Platonism brought into being by computeracy. Lanham rightly reminds us on a regular basis that the electronic word "desubstantiates" cultural products. Hence we encounter the difficulty with the application of current copyright laws: Where's the "*substantial* similarity" (see 275–276)? But I want to continue pressing my notion that information is always already in formation to suggest that the idea Plato had of the Form is now a "virtual reality."

The Form is virtually real now, there in the ether, in the form of in*FORM*ation. And the New Guardians (I play freely with Platonism now) can materialize (if that's the word) the form anywhere they choose in as many instances—in as many *copies*—as they choose simply by pushing a button (if the satellites are working). Do we seriously suppose the New Guardians aren't at their monitors at this moment? (I play freely with the threat of fascism that I am hardly the first to have perceived as potential in Platonism.) Do we seriously suppose that the power to virtualize (the word "virtual" derives from the Latin word for "man," in respect of his "manliness" or *power*) will not be exercised? If this or that multinational company can virtualize 10 million instances of its "product" around the globe "at once," do we seriously suppose that it won't strive to virtualize 10^x billion? Consider William Gibson's vision of this (not very distant) future:

> Bobby was a cowboy, and ice was the nature of his game, *ice* from ICE, Intrusion Countermeasures Electronics. The matrix is an abstract representation of the relationships between data systems. Legitimate programmers jack into their employers' sector of the matrix and find themselves surrounded by bright geometries representing the corporate data.
>
> Towers and fields of it ranged in the colorless non-space of the simulation matrix, the electronic consensus-hallucination that facilitates the handling and exchange of massive quantities of data. Legitimate programmers never see the walls of ice they work behind, the walls of shadow that screen their operations from others, from industrial-espionage artists and hustlers like Bobby Quine.
>
> Bobby was a cowboy. Bobby was a cracksman, a burglar, casing mankind's extended electronic nervous system, rustling data and credit in the crowded matrix, monochrome nonspace where the only stars are dense concentrations of information, and high above it all burn corporate galaxies and the cold spiral arms of military systems. (1986, 169-170)

Gibson's vision is a nightmare, perhaps.[13] I'm not sure. Certainly, cyberpunk is a vision of a different space as well as a different time—a space where and a time when the boundaries between human and machine have been radically transformed (Hayles, 1990, 276-277). As Mark Rose observes, copyright

> does more than govern the passage of commodified exchanges across the boundary between the private sphere and the public; it actually constitutes the boundary on which it stands. Change the rules of copyright and the demarcation between private and public changes. "Private" and "public" are radically unstable concepts, and yet we can no more do without them than we can do without such dialectical concepts as "inside" and "outside" or "self" and "other." (1993, 141)

It is this boundary that academic editors need to begin thinking about anew because the Internet, with its millions upon millions of infonauts, will change—is already changing—not just where the boundary is drawn, but what the "boundary" is. That "boundary" will come to resemble less a property marker than the fractal-like edge between sleep and waking, where our communal dream (if we change our minds before they are changed for us) may someday differently prosper.

NOTES

1. I like to make my point about computer technology and the future (which is now) in the following way. I quote from "Voice Recognition: Coming in Loud and Clear," by Alfred Poor (*Computer Shopper* 14, 11 [November 1994, 176]): "today's hardware and software make it easier than ever to interact with a PC using voice as an alternative to keyboard or mouse input. As far as turning the tables of speech, your PC can already do a fairly good job of talking back to you" (314).

"Star Trek: The Next Generation" may have gone off the air, but then in some respects it may already have been approaching obsolescence. Asking the computer where our (Mr.) data is will soon be a commonplace in households all over the land.

2. This and the following paragraphs are taken from "The Council of Editors of Learned Journals, a Brief History," prepared for the MLA Review Committee by past president John C. Coldewey, formerly editor of *Modern Language Quarterly*.

3. This and my opening paragraphs are reprinted with permission from my Introduction to "Gonzo Scholarship: Policing Electronic Publications," the published version of the MLA panel of the same title sponsored by the Council of Editors of Learned Journals (CELJ) in Toronto, Ontario (December 1993).

4. See the helpful overview by Patricia Churchland—which is, I should say, only one of many accessible studies in this exciting field.

5. See now, in addition to Lanham, the fine study by Rose, especially his comments on the historical process by which "the 'work' as an immaterial commodity" came to be subject to copyright (131ff).

6. Jones cites an ACLS survey whose results are clearly telling in this context (note that it is not the currency of the survey but the magnitude of the results that interests us here): "The survey also documented the pronounced growth in scholarly use of computers" over a five-year period. Where 2 percent of all respondents owned or had access to a computer in 1980, by 1985 that number had increased to 45 percent. By 1985, 98 percent of respondents in research universities had access to computers, while 57 percent used computers routinely" (162).

7. See Lanham, 20–21, where he hypothesizes a similar case, of a "hypertext edition." It is probably prudent, as it is certainly ironically humorous, that I point out here that I arrived at my own positions before reading Lanham's book. In fact, for over a year now, I have been speaking and publishing on these matters in my capacity as an officer of CELJ. I take this opportunity to thank Bill Readings, editor of *Surfaces*; professors Lagretta Lenker and Joseph Moxley, organizers of the conference of which this volume is the proceedings; and John van Hook and William Baker, officers of the English and

American literature section of the American Library Association, who invited me to address their session at the Annual Convention of the ALA in Miami June 26, 1994.

8. See Lanham's mention (240) of Panurge's celebration of debt in Rabelais' Gargantua and Pantagruel, book 3. See also my *Dante, Chaucer, and the Currency of the Word: Money, Images, and Reference in Late Medieval Poetry* (Norman, Okla.: Pilgrim Books, 1983) for an extended study of the metaphor of credit in late medieval culture.

9. This is one of my current projects. METS is an initiative of TEAMS, the Consortium for the Teaching of the Middle Ages, and is under the general editorship of Russell A. Peck of the University of Rochester.

10. We should not forget what Jean-Claude Guedon observes, that it is easy to confuse diffusion with communication. They are not the same thing. Clearly, journals and monographs do communicate, but in recent decades their more obvious function has been diffusion: when journal articles take three to five years to appear (and book reviews also), we can hardly pretend that communication is a high priority. Diffusion and archiving are clearly the higher priorities. And we have lived with those priorities (if grudgingly) because they were a necessary limitation of print, its linearity and concomitant disposal of time as rigorously sequential. No more. The computer has changed all that. The virtual word disposes of time and space differently. That is why we must begin rethinking communication within our profession.

11. Lanham's project, for example, can be seen as an attempt to theorize this play element from within his career-long concern with rhetoric and the opposition between philosophy and rhetoric—see, especially, 68-72. His advocacy of the "bi-stable illusion" is an intriguing response to the theoretical problem: for a response, in turn, to it, see the illuminating and trenchant review of Lanham's book on the BMR network by O'Donnell.

12. Cf. the lengthy story on "Bulding the Data Highway" in *Byte* by Andy Reinhardt.

13. See the commentary on Gibson in Hayles, 1990: 275–278, in the context of discussing postmodernism and the understanding of metanarratives.

REFERENCES

Churchland, Patricia Smith. *Neurophilosophy: Toward a Unified Science of the Mind-Brain*. Cambridge, Mass.: MIT Press, 1986.

Coldewey, John C. "The Council of Editors of Learned Journals, A Brief History." Typescript, 1993.

Forman, Janis. "Literacy, Collaboration, and Technology: New Connections and Challenges." *Literacy and Computers. The Complications of Teaching and Learning with Technology*. Eds. Cynthia L. Selfe and Susan Hilligoss. New York: Modern Language Association of America, 1994. 130–143.

Gibson, William. "Burning Chrome." *Burning Chrome*. New York: Ace Books, 1986. 168–191.

Ginzburg, Jane C. "Copyright Without Walls?: Speculations on Literary Property in the Library of the Future." *Future Libraries*. Eds. R. Howard Bloch and Carla Hesse. A special issue of *Representations* 42 (1993): 53–73.

Guedon, Jean-Claude. "Why Are Electronic Publications Difficult to Classify?: The Orthogonality of Print and Digital Media." Copyright © guedon@ere.umontreal.ca. Web document gopher://arl/cni/org:70/00/scomm/edir/ejcg.

Hayles, N. Katherine. *Chaos Bound: Orderly Disorder in Contemporary Literature and Science*. Ithaca, N.Y.: Cornell University Press, 1990.

Herbert, Frank. *Dune*. New York: Ace Books, 1990.

Jones, William Goodrich. "Humanist Scholars' Use of Computers in Libraries and Writing." *Literacy and Computers. The Complications of Teaching and Learning with Technology*. Eds. Cynthia L. Selfe and Susan Hilligoss. New York: Modern Language Association of America, 1994. 157–170.

Lanham, Richard. *The Electronic Word*. Chicago: University of Chicago Press, 1993.

O'Donnell, James J. Review of *The Electronic Word*. Bryn Mawr Reviews <bmr@c-cat.sas.upenn.edu. BMR 94.6.16.

Raish, Martin. "Network Knowledge for the Neophyte." Version 4.0, February 24, 1994.

Reinhardt, Andy. "Building the Data Highway." *Byte* (March 1994): 46–74.

Rose, Mark. *Authors and Owners: The Invention of Copyright*. Cambridge, Mass.: Harvard University Press, 1993.

Shoaf R. A. Introduction. *Surfaces* IV, 101 (1994). Internet Access via anonymous ftp at harfang@.cc.umontreal.ca.

—. *The Testament of Love*. Kalamazoo, Mich.: Medieval Institute Publications. Forthcoming.

10

Prototypes: New Forums for Scholarship in "The Late Age of Print"

Todd Taylor and David Erben

Theorists, politicians, and futurists have offered a great deal of conjecture recently about how the so-called information or computer age will reconfigure our nations and our communities. The community of scholars is as interested as any other in what these new realms might look like. However, we no longer need to speculate so much because prototypes have already begun to emerge. While R. A. Shoaf looks at electronic journals and Richard Smyth discusses hypertext, we feel that the truly prototypic media are those that are not so much merely electronic versions of traditional print formats, but are forums that have no definitive companion in the world of print scholarship. What we identify as genuinely revolutionary in scholarship today are those forums that encourage the movement of scholarship from "the late age of print" into a new arena that can be characterized by a radical decline in hierarchical divisions within the academy as well as an abandonment of Western notions of intellectual property as we currently conceive of it. We disagree with James Lichtenberg when he writes in Chapter 8: "Respect for copyright offers the framework through which the digital future of information exchange can come into being" (91). Yet our disagreement is founded upon a fairly subtle but nonetheless crucial point. There will no doubt be an expansion, if not an eventual explosion of scholarly publication available online. But most of the publishers of these texts will do everything they can to maintain old notions of intellectual property. This means that for all the hyperbolic discussions about the information age, truly prototypic and revolution-ary forums must be defined in terms of the ways they challenge old systems. If we are to realize Morton Winston's "Prospects for a Revaluation of Academic Values," then we must begin to look at prototypic academic publishing as something other than the production of cultural artifacts in the forms of the journal article and the monograph—as something other than "vessels" of "currency" as Paul LeBlanc called them in a plenary address at a recent conference ("Writing").

The heart of this chapter is a study of one such prototypic forum in the humanities—that being the area most intensely vested in print culture. This study examines in particular an event that occurred in December of 1994 known as the Seulemonde MUD. This was a live, multilayered conversation that took place simultaneously among scholars in the humanities who ranged in status from eminent international scholar to first-year graduate student. But the December event is part of something much larger than a one-time virtual conference; Seulemonde is a polymorphous collection of a number of conversations and texts that continue to construct itself as a rambling electronic think-tank. By looking at the case of the Seulemonde Project, it is our hope that this chapter will provide not so much a vision of what things might look like in the future, but what they already look like now at the beginning of the electronic age of scholarship.

DEFINITIONS, METAPHORS, AND "THE LATE AGE OF PRINT"

Before we present this case study, we must address problems with vocabulary that we face whenever prototypes emerge on any scene. The tendency has always been to use metaphors based on old ways of operating in order to describe a new technology, and the Seulemonde Project is no exception to this phenomenon. Locomotives were first called "iron horses," and personal computers were first "microcomputers." These metaphors are all we have to work with at the beginning, but eventually, something happens: eventually, the words "locomotive" or "personal computer" develop distinct connotations and become associated with images independent from the older technologies to which they were originally compared. The same problem with vocabulary and metaphors is at hand with the prototype in our case study. We have named the Seulemonde MUD a "conversation," "conference," and "think-tank." Later, you will also see "roundtable," "panelists," "gallery," and "halls." And so, at the present, these metaphors are apt, yet we know that eventually a new vocabulary will replace the old. Eventually, the words "MUD" and "cyberspace" may be the terms we use to represent these sites for scholarship. The attention we are drawing to vocabulary is necessary because, as we present our case study, it would be very easy for the reader to be misled by the old metaphors. Even though some participants in Seulemonde appear to occupy hierarchical positions, such hierarchies are, in fact, only superficial—graduate students conversed on equal ground with scholars, senior faculty with junior, Internet experts with neophytes. The maintenance of such divisions becomes more difficult, if not impossible, as the Seulemonde conversation continues to develop even as you read this article. We need to be open-minded when dealing with vocabulary in a new medium because inconsistent metaphors and a constant "lack" while wrestling with new vocabulary are unfortunate but necessary obstacles.

But the primary argument we're trying to present in this chapter is that we believe there is a demarcation between mere electronic versions of print-based scholarship and prototypes of new species of scholarship altogether. Of course, this demarcation is going to be difficult to locate in a definitive way; nonetheless, that's the project of this chapter. We see this line as explicable if we consider ourselves to be currently operating in what Jay Bolter has labeled "the late age of print":

> Today we are living in the late age of print. And as we look up from our computer keyboard to the books on our shelves, we must ask ourselves whether "this will destroy that." Computer technology is beginning to displace the printed book. Until recently it was possible to believe that the computer could coexist with the printed book. (1990, 2)

We are not so much concerned here with whether or not Bolter's revolutionary vision will prove to be accurate in our lifetime. Rather, we would like to focus on what his passage articulates so loudly: that electronic publication and print publication are deeply antithetical and antagonist in many ways. Dating back to the scribes of the Middle Ages, moving toward the operators of the first printing presses, and continuing in the present with the authors and booksellers who comprise the publishing industry, the medium of the printed word on page maintains and supports a particular system of values. Preeminent among this system are the romanticization of individual expression in the form of the monograph; the institutionalization of intellectual capital in the form of the copyright; and the modernist obsession with unity, symmetry, order, and closure. For the most part, online versions of print journals struggle to retain these values, and hypertextual versions of most scholarly documents maintain a print-based conception of publishing as they tend to be marketed like copyrighted monographs. We should classify such work, even though available electronically, as throwbacks to the age of print. However, prototypes are already available that indicate something different—prototypes that define "the late age of print."

THE SEULEMONDE PROJECT: A DEMOCRATIC, POLYMORPHOUS CONVERSATION

On Saturday, December 3, 1994, a group of former and current University of South Florida faculty and graduate students hosted a virtual roundtable discussion or "conversation." While all of the South Florida participants were physically located in the same multimedia studio, each in front of a computer terminal connected to the Internet, other participants "arrived" for the conversation, using their computers and modems, from physical locations all over the United States. The conversation is part of a project called *Seulemonde*. Members of the Seulemonde Collective are attempting to interrogate the effects of emerging computer technology and, in particular, the Internet. In addition to virtual roundtables, the project features listserv discussion groups, publishes an electronic journal (*Seulemonde: Hyper/Text(Cyber)/Image*), and conducts interviews with interested scholars.

And so, Seulemonde is many things and many voices at once. It is so polymorphous and organic that traditional conceptions of scholarly publishing no longer apply. The electronic journal on the World Wide Web is a hypertextual collection of images, transcripts of roundtables and interviews, traditionally formatted scholarly articles, and even poetry. But Seulemonde is also a dynamic; it is conversations on listservs and MUDs. Therefore, Seulemonde is not so much a "vessel" of intellectual capital as it is a "generator," "catalyst," or "dynamo" of scholarly thought and activity.

The conference facility in which the conversation of December 3 took place is an electronic space known as a MUD, an acronym for Multi-User "Dungeon" or "Dimension." The Conference Facility MUD program is run on a computer, a Unix machine that contains a port enabling users to connect to it with their computers and modems (as long as they have access to the Internet). After users connect to the MUD, they are asked to provide a name and a password. Then they type commands, text, and actions with their keyboards, which, in turn, appear in the MUD. When you enter the textual space of the Seulemonde MUD, you literally confront yourself: you have a race, gender, and even a short physical description (anywhere from "human" to "stocky, six feet tall"). This representation of yourself is a "character" or "persona" in the role-playing sense and may move from room to room within the virtual space of the MUD, "speak" to other characters, shake hands, wave, shout, cry. Space in the conference facility is more or less an arbitrary construct: the network of spaces that constitutes the center was arranged according to three-dimensional space—north, south, east, west, up, down—but could have just as easily been arranged according to any other scheme. Spaces or "rooms" can be locked or open; they can be public or private. A room can contain one person or one hundred; spaces can act on the people within them, arbitrarily or according to a user's possessions or actions or words. In a sense, the space occupied by the conference facility is a space in memory, since the program loads and runs in random access memory. The space of the conference facility, then, is a chip—the microscopic passageways etched into a fingernail-sized chunk of silicon. In a larger sense, however, the space of the conference facility is the chip plus the telephone lines that make up the network, since the MUD is mapped on top of the Internet. And its space includes the pathways by which users connect to it, extending even so far as to the screen on which the text generated by the facility appears to individual users. These screens may be anywhere in the world, as long as the user has access to the Internet.

In practice, the space of the facility is metaphorical and symbolic: as such, it reflects the richness or the poverty of its creators' imaginations. The shape the conference facility took on December 3 echoed disciplinary structures and practices, although this did not have to be so. Builders of this MUD chose to mimic traditional structures and practices so as to acclimate new users to a forum in which they initially experience cognitive vertigo without some touchstones from familiar places.

Seven panelists, members of the Seulemonde Collective, and approximately twenty invited guests entered Seulemonde MUD using their computers and modems. The theme of the event was identified as "The Cultural Effects of the Computer Revolution," or "A Conversation about Late Twentieth-Century Technologies of Representation." The panelists, who provided the "Center" for the conversation, came from a variety of professional backgrounds and interests, including philosophy, literature, and science. Thus, the event was interdisciplinary. The panelists' experience with the Internet and computer technology also varied greatly. All were familiar with E-mail, but only two were familiar with MUDs. Most identified themselves as "neophytes" in terms of the Internet. E-mail correspondence was established before the event, and participants were forwarded MUD names, passwords, and written instructions on how to connect to the MUD.

The textual space in which the central conversation occurred mirrored a conventional conference room surrounded by private observation galleries. The entire conference facility consisted of a series of nine rooms (these rooms exist within the computer program running the MUD), eight of which were connected to each other. The room with the panelists was not accessible from the other eight rooms. Each room consisted of a short, paragraph-length description that included directions for exiting the room. Three of the rooms—the log-in room, the bar, and one of the hallways—also contained bulletin boards where the organizers posted information for the participants. Users in these eight rooms could move in and out of them freely by issuing the proper exit or entrance command ("north," "south," "enter," etc.). The eight connected rooms consisted of a log-in room (where guests initially "arrived"), four gallery rooms for the guests (each with a moderator), a bar (where you could order a drink and chat), and two hallways. The seven panelists and three moderators from the Seulemonde Collective were situated in a room that was constructed so as to broadcast to all participants the words "spoken" by the panelists. Initially, guests in the gallery rooms could "overhear" what was going on in the main room, but they could not communicate directly with any of the panelists. Questions, therefore, from the guests had to be forwarded to the panelists by moderators situated in each of the four gallery rooms. However, the panelists and guests eventually reconvened in the hallways and bar to conduct additional discussions.

The conversation actually began the week prior to the Saturday meeting in the MUD. Panelists and guests were asked, via E-mail, to provide a short description of their experience with and interest in computer technology and the Internet. Then on Thursday, eleven questions were forwarded to the participants as a way of suggesting possible topics for discussion. The panelists responded to some of these questions in the MUD, but once the conversation started, they initiated and pursued topics at their own discretion. This prompted one participant to remark at one point: "I like the idea that we are all talking at once and then responding to different comments asynchronically." In addition to frequent meta comments about the conversations that were taking place and the space in which their conversations were occurring, the panelists discussed the effect of computer technology on classrooms, flaming, falling in love in cyberspace, the university, journals, the "body," harassment in MUDs, and the effect of computer technology on the written word. Another commented that the MUD "seems to make everyone feel like they're writing marginalia, not only spatially but temporally that to participate here is to become like a Talmudic scribe whose best effort becomes commentary on commentary that is quickly receding." Thus, the effect of technology on authorship and ownership was an important issue. Who *owns* the text produced in the MUD? A critical question was posited: "What happens when it becomes impossible to 'claim authorship' when I say 'impossible to claim authorship' I mean the hypertextual nature of this origin really makes 'authorship' outmoded, no?"

The democratic nature of the conference became apparent almost immediately. As soon as the conversation began, one panelist initiated a critique of the themes established by the moderators in the pre-conference E-mail questions: "I was struck by the questions posed before we began today. What was most surprising to me was the extent to which the framework for the questions was deconstruction. I am not at all sure this is the most helpful context for considering the distinctive features of the electrosphere." The panelists frequently "spoke" at the same time, responding not only to multiple topics but also to multiple topics generated by the same user. One observed: "It is possible to have more than one conversation with the same person at the same time, multiplied by however many persons there are."

Guests in the gallery rooms were also carrying on their own discourse, some in reaction to what was being said in the panelists' room, and sometimes not. Behavior in one of the gallery rooms became, in fact, quite playful: a food fight broke out. Here's a segment of dialogue that took place simultaneously in the main room and in one of the four galleries. Three participants could not hear what three others were saying in the gallery, but the gallery could hear the others.

Hayles [main room]: I understand lots of people say the Internet is disembodied—but in another sense it isn't at all. What difference does it make, for example, that one types the keys and sees the responses flicker on the screen? I think one of the areas of investigation it proposes is the relation of embodied practices of reading and writing—the kinesthetic, tactile, visual—and how these affect the messages and experience of the medium.

Hirsh [gallery]: Does anybody in the gallery have anything to say?

Taylor [main]: I think the issue of embodiment/disembodiment is much more complex than is usually recognized. Part of what is at stake in a variety of fields is a growing recognition of the complexity of embodiment. More precisely, physical and biological organisms and processes are beginning to appear to be information processes—thus complicating the body.

Surfus [gallery]: Well, from my experiences, I'd say that "disembodied" is generous. Like Todd says, certain institutional protocols also apply in cyberspace. I got into a discussion once with Fred Kemp before I knew he owned the list [on which we were talking]. I was reprimanded often and also right away. Maybe I'm talking more about anonymity? Still, there are those hierarchies within cyberspace that call for some amount of decorum.

Sanchez [gallery]: Embodied, disembodied—I'm not sure what, if any, useful difference can be made between the two.

Culler [main]: Cyberspace is going to have different effects, but I'm not sure it makes you feel any less of a self—the fact that you can stop looking at what others are saying at any point and type your own thoughts and then send them into space creates a little cocoon which you then release into the room—and then look up to see what has happened while you were communing with your keyboard. Of course, for good typists who never look at the keyboard, things may be different.

Sanchez [gallery]: Well, I don't know about the Internet reflecting real life. Maybe we are recreating this thing we call "real life" on the 'net, yes?

Surfus [gallery]: What's the difference?

Hirsh [gallery]: Are you talking about the difference between real life and virtual reality?

Sanchez [gallery]: The difference might be, maybe, that there exists an opportunity here to do more than reflect this already "created" phenomenon called "real life." That is, perhaps different things can be made.

As the conversations in all of the rooms wrote themselves, they were also generating a hypertext document to be published in *Seulemonde: Hyper/Text(Cyber)/Image*—a document that has links to the E-mail exchanges that occurred prior to and after the December 3 event, links to interviews with the panelists and other scholars, and links to additional Seulemonde MUD conversations that continue to take place.

Of course, this prototypic virtual space isn't exactly a land of milk and honey. The event was disrupted by technical problems as well as the chaos of operating in a new medium. And it wasn't as if the content of the dialogue set the world on its ear. But the fact that such a diverse group of scholars gathered on a Saturday morning while in the comfort of their own homes and offices and generated a two-hour conversation that has already led to additional MUDs is quite significant. No one is sure what to make of the December event or the latticework into which it continues to be woven. But those involved with the event report one certainty: it was unlike anything in which they had participated before. It is/was (even tense becomes a problem in this new vocabulary) a prototype that is defined by its lack of closure and by the way it disrupts geographical, hierarchical, disciplinary, and even temporal boundaries. Above all, it makes little sense to think of Seulemonde as a *container* for intellectual property. It is more an *un*container—an eruption of the boundaries of intellectual property. In fact, the term *Seulemonde* itself—a neologism that merges the French *seule* (self) with *monde* (world)—reflects the rather complicated blurring of the individual and the communal which characterizes this prototypic forum.

CONCLUSION: OUR RESPONSIBILITY AS SCHOLARS

This chapter argues through the example of the Seulemonde project that "the late age of print" will be characterized by an increased democratization of the enterprise of scholarship, by a decreased reliance on the system of scholarly capital organized around notions of copyright and intellectual property, and by a disruption of modernist notions of unity and closure. This means that we face some turbulent times because the relatively stable political forces that have defined scholarship are being contested. As both LeBlanc and Lichtenberg have suggested, tenure and promotion committees are going to be increasingly asking questions such as: "What do we make of scholarship in electronic forms? And how can we compare what scholars are doing electronically with what they did formerly in the stable days of print?"

The "disruption" that we confront in "the late age of print" means that we, as scholars, face an increased responsibility to make exceptionally thoughtful decisions and to assert our views instead of letting others determine our profession for us. While this may currently be the case, we can imagine a time in the not-too-distant future when policies will emerge in regard to prototypic forums for scholarship. As we see it, to suggest that we should go back to old ways and old value systems, to reassert the status of the copyrighted text as Lichtenberg argues we should, does not amount to "asserting our views." It amounts rather to hiding one's head in the sand. In other words, we currently operate in an era of turbulence, meaning that power structures within the academy are being realigned by electronic scholarship. The precedents established during this era are likely to have far-reaching repercussions toward defining who we are and what we do as scholars. And if we plan to rely on old systems, then we neglect our responsibilities.

As this volume has shown, the politics and processes of scholarly publishing are directly linked with definitions of the enterprise of scholarship. In closing, we have a definition that we would like to promote: scholarship is defined by taking calculated risks and exploring prototypic situations and ideas—and such explorations are our *responsibility* as scholars. If the academy is unable to overcome its deep-seated ties to the system of values associated print, if it is unable to see past monographs and journal articles as defining the nature of research, particularly in the humanities, then scholars will unfortunately be increasingly constructed as workers who manufacture cultural artifacts known as texts instead of being defined as we should: as generators of thought and innovation.

REFERENCES

Bolter, Jay. *Writing Space: The Computer, Hypertext, and the History of Writing.* Hillsdale, N.J.: Erlbaum, 1990.
LeBlanc, Paul. "Writing Teachers, Writing Software." Paper read at the Politics and Processes of Scholarly Publishing Conference, St. Petersburg, Fla. March 1994.

11

Pulling Out the Rug: Technology, Scholarship, and the Humanities

Paul LeBlanc

Scholarship is the "coin of the realm" for academia, the currency that is exchanged for teaching positions, departmental resources, and institutional status. One problem with this model is that the system is a closed one, like some Cold War era Eastern Bloc economy, in which the currency is artificially supported or propped up in a way that contradicts the "real" value of that currency outside the system. This is particularly true for scholars working in the humanities. For a number of reasons that are too many and too complex to enumerate here, our society increasingly questions the value of what academia delivers. With regard to scholarship, there is increasing pressure to justify the value of that work—work most often supported through tax dollars or high tuition payments. State legislatures, businesspeople, parents of students, and the general public have come to question the value of the articles, chapters, and books that are so greatly prized within the academic system. How often has the title of a new article or book become the butt of some comedian's joke or outraged legislator's harangue? Forced to justify their scholarship, faculty in the sciences or engineering can often point to tangible results that extend beyond the boundaries of academia: a medical improvement or even breakthrough, new manufacturing processes, or better systems, for example. Faculty in law, business, and allied health can do the same, showing a connection between their scholarship and better services and processes that can be subsequently delivered to clients, customers, and patients. What do humanities scholars have to show for their work? The question forces us to confront what it is that we are about.

These questions are not new, but they are now posed with particular energy and sometimes hostility, and humanities scholars have not been effective in their response. Perhaps, more dangerously, the humanities are merely dismissed or ignored when resources or support are being allocated. Certainly, any examination of where public monies are assigned would make painstakingly clear how little valued humanities scholarship is. For example, only 2 percent of humanities research support comes from federal sources (Arms, 1993, 20). The humanities were scarcely mentioned in the original National Information Infrastructure proposal. Ironically, humanities scholars have been loath to embrace their most concrete product, good teaching, as Richard Gebhardt points out elsewhere in this collection. Or, when faculty do embrace teaching, the nature of the institutional reward structure fails to support that activity, or worse, effectively punishes it. As Ernest Boyer writes, "Research and publication have become the primary means by which most professors achieve academic status, and yet many academics are, in fact, drawn to the profession precisely because of their love for teaching and service. Yet these professional obligations do not get the recognition they deserve" (1990, xii). Certainly, young scholars who attend to their teaching at the cost of their scholarship pursue a perilous course at many institutions.

It might be argued that in many institutions teaching is prized and supported in the reward and recognition structure and scholarly activity is secondary—in the two-year schools, for example. However, these are the same schools that have heavier teaching loads, higher student-to-teacher ratios, fewer resources, more difficult to educate students, and fewer opportunities to teach upper level courses. In short, because they produce little or no scholarship, they fall at the bottom of the economic model and enjoy the least amount of reward as institutions and faculties. Graduate students rarely see appointment at one of these schools as desirable, because so little of their own educational experience reflects the value of teaching. In truth, many of the faculty at our two-year schools are overworked and underpaid.

TECHNOLOGY AND THE SCHOLARLY ARTIFACT

The economic model of academic scholarship described above is based on print technologies that have become second nature to educational culture over the last 400 years. However, technology is taking hold in academia and is effecting unprecedented change. Campuses across the country are using network and telecommunications technology to connect themselves internally, linking offices and classrooms and dorm rooms and libraries, and externally, most often connecting to each other through the Internet. The creation of these electronic or "virtual" spaces opens up new opportunities for interaction between all members of the academic community. Students can interact with each other over networks, as faculty can with their peers on campus and on other campuses, and there is considerable experimentation with using electronic space as a setting for instruction. Degree programs are now being offered online, distance learning programs are being expanded, and access to powerful databases and collections of digitized information is now readily available from campuses and from homes. Charles Moran has persuasively argued that the classroom can be increasingly understood as an electronic space defined by who is signed on electronically and not by the physical constraints of the classroom walls or the campus boundaries (1992, 7–23).

Certainly, the digitizing of information has already had significant impact on publishing, libraries, and concepts of intellectual property. The changes in these areas have dramatic implications for academic scholarship, especially for scholars in the humanities. Digitized information, whether it be the electronic version of books or journals or reference works or whatever, has self-evident appeal. Digital information is almost ephemeral; it can reside in tiny spaces (on the hard drive of a file server, on credit card size PCMCIA cards, or compact discs, for example); it can be distributed from one spot to millions of users in a brief period of time; it can be linked to other information (through hypertext links and, on the Internet, through Web servers); it can be acted upon in powerful ways (using full-text search tools and other database technologies); and end-users can reshape it in powerful ways.

When the creators and distributors of information can dispense with the physical artifacts of their trade, they see both opportunity and risk. Publishers see digitized information as a way of more efficiently delivering their published materials, offering customized materials, exploring online access to their properties, and providing a direct connection to local printing operations using technologies like Xerox's Docutext system, thus eliminating warehousing, delivery, and perhaps even bookstore distribution channels. On the other hand, they worry about protecting their properties, pricing and distribution, their core competencies in packaging information for the new environments, and a new set of competitors. Libraries see powerful ways of expanding access to information, the ability to share resources, and new, more powerful ways to conduct research. This presents a very different role for the campus library. When information has physical heft and weight, as it does in a book or journal, the library becomes a repository and offers to faculty and students *proximity* to that information. Thus, libraries compete to have the largest collection (the *Chronicle of Higher Education* publishes an annual list of library collections by size), acting as a vault, if you will, for the collected value of the scholarship the library contains. Journals, magazines, newspapers, a multitude of collections in every media, and more are now being offered in wholly digitized form either on the Internet, through commercial online services like America OnLine or Prodigy, or on CDs. Libraries, rather than acting as repositories of information in physical form, are increasingly becoming access points for information that resides on the Net, as travelers of virtual spaces like to call the aggregate collection of interconnected networks of all forms. There is serious and ongoing debate, as well as research, on the idea of a "national electronic library" to which all citizens would have access, an idea originally forecasted by David Bolter in *Writing Space: The Computer, Hypertext, and the History of Writing* (1991).

The digital or virtual era into which we are entering raises serious questions for academic scholarship. In our text-based culture, having one's work contained in physical form gave that work value, as earlier argued, and it meant that work would take some time to reach its audience (several months for many journals and longer for books). Thus, conferences became important for early dissemination of research. In print culture, annual conferences offered early access to new research, journals offered the earliest access to fully developed and reviewed research, and books sought to solidify and even institutionalize that research after it was fully matured. Having physical access to these eventually published works was important to scholars. Indeed, the greatest value accrued to those who maintained the largest collection of these artifacts. In a virtual culture, proximity is replaced by access and speed, terms that describe process and not product. The difference is critical, for scholarship in the virtual age becomes a more dynamic activity. Just as publishers and librarians and many others grapple with the opportunities and the risks of conducting their business in this new environment, so, too, should the academy reexamine scholarship in its most fundamental dimensions.

EMERGING TRENDS

Higher education will have to understand and factor a number of existing and emerging trends into its rethinking of the nature and role of scholarly activity. It is, of course, risky to build scenarios based on technological trends. (Remember Beta versus VHS or, more recently, the much heralded HDTV?) Yet much of the technology assumed in the following discussion is in place now, and there exists for each of the trends well-established practice and precedent. The major trends I predict over the next ten years are these:

The Breakdown of the Old Print-based Economy of Academic Scholarship

In many fields, print journals are already being displaced by electronic dissemination of new research, with that dissemination taking many forms. Online discussion groups, listservs (asynchronous group discussion via E-mail), usenet groups, and other Internet-based forums for professional dialogue, debate, and collaboration are increasingly the sites of the newest and most vigorously discussed research and thinking in the sciences. Virtual conferences—that have panels, registration, and question and answer periods, like any other conference—are beginning to take place in electronic spaces. Because they are not constrained by the physical limits of a conference hotel or the logistical limits of people's budgets, time, and geography, they can go on longer, include more speakers, be conducted at minimal cost, reach more people in the field, and produce instantaneous electronic or print transcripts of the whole experience. In virtual environments, scholarly activity may be a more explicitly collaborative and communicative act that is ongoing, dynamic, and that does not necessarily have its greatest value in an eventual print form (for which there is little demand in its physical state anyway). This notion suggests that libraries will become less important than information infrastructures on and between campuses. More importantly, if the value of scholarship shifts from the print *product* to the electronic-based *process*, what happens to the economic model of academic scholarship posited in the first section of this chapter?

The Growing Complexity and Challenge of Gatekeeping

In print culture, the gatekeeping process of the editorial process ensures quality and validates the efforts of the academic scholar. Gatekeeping in virtual environments is difficult in a number of ways. First, the predominant ethic of the Internet actively works against gatekeeping of all sorts. The freewheeling and strongly democratic idealism of the Net is based in part on the ability of everyone to be a publisher. That is, because there are largely no costs of production and dissemination in electronic environments, anyone can choose to "publish" his or her work for public consumption. There can be no middleperson like a publisher, library, or bookstore between the creator of information and its consumers.

Second, if scholarship becomes more of an ongoing process without the focal point of a print product (which is replaced by continuing scholarly exchange and public collaboration), gatekeeping comes to mean the control of a process and not a product. This becomes an inherently more difficult task if the process is the give and take of multiple parties. That said, moderated online discussions are becoming increasingly valued and sought after by Net users for the improved signal to noise they offer. Electronic journals are emerging, but it remains unclear whether they represent a mere short-lived analog from print culture.

The Redefinition of Intellectual Property

Intellectual property rights are being hotly debated as content creators and publishers struggle to understand how they can protect and sell their properties in virtual environments. The ephemeral nature of electronic property seems to undercut many people's concrete sense of intellectual property, although there is little rational ground for that fact. Consider, however, that many people who would not think of stealing a book routinely accept or make available copies of software for which the recipient has paid no money. How many readers of this text own a computer on which there resides software for which they did not pay? A great deal of energy and effort is being invested in systems for protecting electronic information and for collecting payment. (The former remains difficult, while the phone company has long worked out the general structures for the latter.) Fair-use policies, which are generally enforceable and limited in their impact on publishers' revenues, do not make sense in electronic environments in which a library could buy a single copy of a property and effectively make it available to every person on campus.

The Democratization of Information and Scholarly Activity

Where a faculty member works will have much less to do with the quality and kind of scholarly activity and interchange available to that faculty member. The research questions and problems that could only be addressed by those lucky enough to be at the right institutions or elite institutions will be open to any interested researchers with access to the Net. Once connected, they will be able to easily participate in the discussions of similarly interested peers, share data, attend electronic conferences, have access to others' expertise, and more. With more people working on research questions, more information should be produced and made available in a more timely fashion than is now the case. Interestingly, academic scholars may be easily joined in their dialogue by interested peers from other disciplines and by nonacademics who have an interest in the topic. It should certainly be easier to give students access to the scholarly process as conducted by professionals and to find ways to bring that process into the classroom (however that space is defined). With more parties involved in more dynamic collaboration, the scholarly process may be enlivened, becoming more spontaneous, more rhetorical, and more serendipitous.

If the above trends play themselves out as present conditions suggest, many of the goals for scholarly activity articulated elsewhere in this volume should be more easily achieved. For example, in Chapter 7 Ralph Norman describes the need to nurture young scholars and to develop in the work of many scholars a better sense of reader. In an electronic environment where scholarly dialogue is democratized, young scholars will have ample opportunity to interact with well-established scholars in their field, becoming less isolated and observing models for scholarly work and interchange. Because the interaction online is almost wholly text-based, and will remain so for quite some time, participants in electronic forums are creating "texts" with a very immediate sense of reader, and unlike most print texts, their work usually gets a response. Indeed, in Chapter 1 Richard Gebhardt calls for a speedier response to scholarly work submitted to journals. As described above, the response time to work posted in electronic environments is often immediate, and many journals have successfully compressed the editorial process by implementing electronic systems for handling manuscripts and facilitating communication between writers, editors, and reviewers. In Chapter 3, Elizabeth Blake suggests that scholars engage students in their research, an activity that is much more easily accomplished in virtual spaces. Linda McAlister wants journals to become risk takers, a quality that more easily exists in the dynamic give and take of electronic interaction (group discussion, the Politics and Processes of Scholarly Publishing conference, March 1994). In all the above cases, these thoughtful authors are struggling with the limitations of making scholarly work available in print texts, limitations that are either absent or more easily overcome in virtual spaces.

The trends described above are offered in most general terms and will eventually manifest themselves in a range of ways and to varying degrees over time. Certainly, the egalitarian, democratizing impulses underlying these trends will stand in conflict with the trends toward commercialization, regulation, and control that *always* attend the advent oi new technology. The implementation of new cardinal technologies is never black and white. That said, much of our rethinking and debate about scholarship and publication in the next century is informed by the dynamics just described.

THE PLACE OF THE HUMANITIES SCHOLAR
IN THE VIRTUAL AGE

Technology stands to redefine the scholarly publishing paradigm, complicating or even making irrelevant some of our basic assumptions about scholarship and opening up new economies of production and entirely new opportunities for scholarly activity. As these changes occur, the "economic" system of scholarly publishing within higher education will become increasingly unable to cope. Within its value system, it will have to accommodate new forms of scholarly activity that in many cases will have more practical or "real-world" value than the primary print forms of the past. If a young scholar invests herself in setting up a World Wide Web home page for rhetorical studies, for example, and maintains that page, perhaps moderating a usenet discussion, what value will that have in her promotion or tenure hearings? The activity may be as complex and valuable to her field as beginning and editing a high quality journal. Some departments are already trying to formulate policy for evaluating faculty-developed software or multimedia materials.

The questions suggested in the transformation of scholarly activity may prove particularly difficult for the humanities. First, technology is expensive, and competition for resources is often fierce on our increasingly underfunded campuses. Faculty in the sciences, medicine, business, and engineering, for example, can make a ready case for their acquisition of technology. In contrast, faculty in English, history, languages, and philosophy have not widely adopted technology (word processing aside) and are more likely to get underpowered institutional hand-me-downs or lower end machines. Moreover, the former group of faculty engage in scholarship that ostensibly has concrete application in the "real world" outside the academy. Second, if static print products give way to dynamic digital products or processes, the latter seeming less valuable because they take so long and are not at the forefront of the scholarly debate within a field, the one palpable product of humanities research is taken from the field. That possibility, combined with a growing demand for accountability, will make it increasingly hard for humanities scholars to evaluate each other's work and the value of their collective work to the culture, the latter being something at which they are already quite poor.

This situation will force the humanities to grapple with a number of important questions. In some cases, these are questions that have been long debated (such as the research versus teaching issue), and others are emerging with the development and implementation of new technology.

What Do We Produce?

Humanities scholars have long managed to fend off this question, often dismissing it as the wrong question, borrowed as it seems from business, or too crass to answer. The result has been a steady loss of students and of institutional support. Reconciling scholarship and teaching and rewarding that reconciliation may be one of the most effective ways to make concrete the contribution of humanities scholars to the creation of an enlightened citizenry. Yet that calls for a fundamental restructuring of the academic "economy" described at the start of this discussion. As Gebhardt (1994) has suggested, the relationship of a person's research to his or her teaching, the mission of the institution, and the needs of the society need to be added to the criteria that are applied to scholarly activity. Answering this question may also force us to admit that when we teach, we are about values—an admission that is a mixed blessing. On one hand, there is a pervasive desire in this culture to counter a growing sense of ennui, as suggested in our popular media and as is deeply felt by many. Positioning ourselves as addressing that need assigns great value to our work. On the other hand, the classroom is already the site of considerable intellectual bloodletting over culture wars. Putting our cards on the table, if you will, leaves faculty open to criticism and means putting down the mantle (and illusion, as feminist and African-American critics have shown us) of objective analysis with which we protected ourselves from attack.

What Passes for Scholarship?

Technology is already making available new tools and new sites for scholarly activity. These opportunities will have to be understood and factored into our academic economy. When an archeologist uses a Computer-Aided Design program to reconstruct a site, or a rhetorician moderates a four-month discussion online, or an historian collaborates with 120 colleagues to produce a polylog, departments and tenure/promotion committees will need to know how to evaluate those efforts. As Carnegie Mellon's William Arms asserts, "They (tenure committees) need to rethink the current criteria based on books, monographs, and articles and redefine scholarship to include new forms of research and instruction" (19). The same knowledge will be necessary in making hiring decisions and in training young scholars. Indeed, an attendant question may be, "What new scholarly methodologies do we need to develop?" For example, graduate research in the humanities is often a solitary endeavor, yet the scholarship on the Net may be deeply collaborative.

What Tools Do Humanities Scholars Need?

If humanities scholars are to adopt new technologies in their research activities (and convincing them to do so remains a formidable obstacle), they will need access to these often expensive technologies. Scanners, high-bandwidth Internet connections, multimedia computers, and more will be some of the tools that twenty–first century scholars bring to their work. Department chairs, as advocates for their faculties and managers of budgets, will need to be well informed and well able to articulate the needs of their faculty in this area. For the humanities in general, there is a danger that the equity gap that already exists between our richest and poorest institutions will widen further, undercutting the democratizing potential of new technology. As Stanford's Carolyn Lougee says, "Differential access to computer hardware, software, and services could also exacerbate inequalities among students, institutions, and disciplines" (1993, 16). The scholar, once largely independent, will increasingly depend on the institution for updated tools, levels of access, support, and training.

CONCLUSION

The humanities' struggle to justify themselves is not new, and the increase in pre-professional education, professional schools, and new professional certification programs has steadily increased the pressure to develop an effective response to the marginalizing of study in disciplines like literature, history, and philosophy. The integration of new technologies, however, is exacerbating the situation. As Lougee points out, "Although the humanities were at risk even before electronic information resources began their transformation of the university, the information age could put universities under increasing pressure to turn out scientists and engineers, relegating the humanities to the status of frill" (16). Moreover, technology will increasingly shift the value of scholarship from the print product to the process of making meaning, yet it will tie that process to tangible production. As print becomes secondary to digital information and interaction, it will become more difficult for humanities scholars to demonstrate their contributions in the way they have thus far, through the accumulated print artifacts they produce.

It is not irrational for humanities scholars to resist technology; there are many reasons to accept technological innovation slowly. Wanting concrete evidence of an innovation's efficacy before adopting that innovation seems reasonable enough. There are myriad examples of ineffectual uses of technology. In addition, there are boundless opportunities for poorly implementing and even misusing technology in education; of these, we should be wary. More unsettling is the idea that when technology is introduced into a workplace, workers are displaced; there are few, if any, exceptions to this dynamic. The ability to offer instruction to multiple sites from one site almost certainly means a reduction in faculty, although few technology leaders would openly admit to that almost universally accepted proposition. How to keep teachers at the heart of teaching in an increasingly technology-based delivery system will be a central challenge to the profession.

The danger to the humanities is in stubbornly clinging to print culture, which is not the same as holding on to the importance of texts. We are a technology-based culture and economy, and any meaningful productivity, even in the relatively sheltered environment of the academic institution, increasingly relies on technology. If the profession accepts this premise, then it can begin to answer the many questions outlined earlier in this discussion. More importantly, it can assert for itself a key role in the transformation of the society. Humanities scholars, more than engineers and computer scientists and businesspeople, are the best equipped citizens we have for helping to shape our information age culture in humane and healthy ways. We are, as a society, still early enough in the mass adoption of digital technology to have a healthy anxiety about it. Public policy is still being debated and formulated. The technology gap between our haves and have-nots is not yet insurmountable, although it grows steadily. As Joe Moxley and Lagretta Lenker argue in the Introduction, humanities scholars must become "public intellectuals." The societal changes brought about by technology demand their attention and energy, as do many of the other issues facing the citizenry. Humanities faculty can play an important role in addressing the serious questions before us. It is not a role they elected to play in the mass adoption of a technology like television, most often preferring to dismiss it and then to retreat to the more intellectual territory of the study or library. The culture has paid a heavy price for that abnegation. Should humanities scholars make the mistake again, the culture is in danger of becoming technologically determined and the humanities may go the way of classics departments, quaint and largely irrelevant to the culture at large.

REFERENCES

Arms, William. *The Institutional Implications of Electronic Information*. Proceedings of a Summary Conference on Technology, Scholarship, and the Humanities: The Implications of Electronic Information. American Council of Learned Societies and the J. Paul Getty Trust, 1993.

Bolter, David J. *Writing Space: The Computer, Hypertext, and the History of Writing*. Hillsdale, N.J.: Lawrence Erlbaum Associates, 1991.

Boyer, Ernest. "Preface." *Scholarship Reconsidered: Priorities of the Professoriate*. Princeton, N.J.: Carnegie Foundation, 1990.

Gebhardt, Richard. "Avoiding the 'Research versus Teaching' Trap: Expanding the Criteria for Evaluating Scholarship." Paper presented at the Politics and Processes of Scholarly Publishing Conference. March 12–14, 1994. Tampa, Fla.

Lougee, Carolyn. "The Professional Implications of Electronic Information." Paper presented at the Conference on Technology, Scholarship, and the Humanities: The Implications of Electronic Information. Summary of Conference Proceedings. American Council of Learned Societies and the J. Paul Getty Trust, 1993.

Moran, Charles. "Computers and the Writing Classroom: A Look to the Future." *Reimagining Computers and Composition: Teaching and Research in the Virtual Age*. Eds. Gail Hawisher and Paul LeBlanc. Portsmouth, N.H.: Boynton–Cook, 1992.

12

The Physicality of Research: Typesetting, Printing, Binding, Fulfillment, Storage, and Academic Snobbery

George Simson

A blue-collar perspective on the politics of scholarly publication is not only useful but also necessary. By "blue collar" I mean physicality. "Physicality" in publishing means, first, multicopy printed artifacts; second, the machines and material to make them; third, the eyes to see them and the hands to turn their pages; and, fourth, their physical storage for future use. The multicopy printed artifact is the main medium of the culture of protest and dissent because its life after production and distribution is not necessarily controlled by the original producers and controllers. Protest and dissent are the glory of Western civilization and are now becoming central to Asian civilization, as witness the brave efforts of Sulak Sivaraksa in Thailand and Baw Aung in Burma. The culture of protest is the main defense we have against caesaropapism, political totalitarianism, cultural authoritarianism, social control, aesthetic conformism, personal enslavement, and other mind-forged manacles. The European events of 1989 and the *samizdati* that preceded them are the most recent global examples of why we need real physicality. By this I do not mean the abstracted and desiccated "materiality" of the remnants of Marxism who never stubbed a toe in the search for "materiality."

We have another strong reason to think in terms of physicality and its contribution to defending against the culture of conformity. We should remember at this juncture that if we go back to Bacon and Locke, one of the patterns in the thinking of the new empiricism was between the particular, the physical, and, after some inferences further on, freedom of the individual mind. The new highway to conformity is the enormously growing industry of electronic communication; the ordinary scholar physically connects with it only by putting her or his fingers to a keyboard.

What we do not know about the electronic superhighway is the relation between the megacontrollers who will own and run the megasystem and the individual intellects fueled by dissent and steered by conscience. Scholarly journals, which collectively, though not necessarily individually, welcome the dissenting intellect, are now a series of mom and pop stores that will soon have to compete with communication K Marts and Wal Marts. Virginia Woolf could buy a pencil at a Wal Mart, but she would have a hard time placing a Hogarth Press first edition of *Prufrock* on its newsrack. The sleek academic politicians and their innumerable minions who run the university systems of such places as Texas and California, and their Ruritanian imitators in such places as Hawaii, will no doubt find it easy to side with the communication K Marts, not the communication mom and pop stores. The abstract credits of high finance and the light particles charging off satellites at 186,000 miles per second are not the sort of physicality available to the individual dissenting intellect. Conformity versus dissent is the large cultural issue surrounding the proposal I make later in this chapter for joining the football players in physicality for the purpose of expropriating some of their power.

The development of desktop typesetting in the past ten years has created a revolution by telescoping scholarly creation and typesetting. The PC with its floppy disk has liberated researchers from much of the tedium of typing multiple drafts and some of the cost of making camera-ready copy, although the capital investment still runs pretty high for a young researcher in the low-paid humanities.

There is no commensurate development of efficiency or cost reduction in printing multiple copies, binding them, or getting them to readers (called fulfillment in the trade). "Desktop publishing" as the phrase is used now is really a misnomer. What we call "desktop publishing" should be called "desktop typesetting" of a single or limited number of copies. A single issue of an ordinary scholarly journal needs between 500 and 1,000 inexpensively produced copies of about 100 pages, far too many physical artifacts for the slow and relatively delicate desktop reproducer. Typesetting is only the beginning of publishing. Four other expensive physical steps remain: rapidly and accurately printing many copies; binding them into an attractive shape of conventional size with an aesthetically pleasing cover made of fairly heavy stock; sending them to subscribers, usually research libraries and practicing scholars in the field; and storing them for a long time on shelves of research libraries whose protections from temperature, flora, and small fauna vary.

Printing a scholarly journal usually means making multiple copies on archive-quality (acid-free) paper usually by photo-offset. Although there was a time before the advent of high-end photocopy machines when companies such as Addressograph-Multilith (A-M in the trade) made relatively low-cost offset printing presses, they were lightly constructed and could not reliably handle the 100,000 (1,000 copies of 100 pages) page impressions needed for the average issue of a scholarly journal or the 2 million impressions needed over five years.

Binding a scholarly journal is essentially an appeal to the snobbery of university bureaucrats and personnel committees that invariably judge a book by its cover. That snobbery rubs off on contributors and editors who want their work recognized for its association with the appearance of good repute. The best looking journals are perfect bound, that is, bound with a square edge created by very accurately clamping fascicles of paper together with massive clamps in a large and expensive machine; gluing with a high-quality, sometimes hot, glue; and trimming precisely, most often to an impeccable 6 x 9 inches, sometimes with designs or print bleeding over the edge.

Fulfilling a subscription or other order is, unlike much of the rest of the physical publishing process, labor intensive. It is usually a minimum-wage job for short-run wrapping and stamping. Cost-benefit factors change with the number of physical copies. In the Ann Arbor area, where many journals are manufactured, mailing companies handle scores of journals for several specialized printers.

Finally, the storage of hard copies of journals has been part of the major dilemma facing the glory of American scholarship, the research library. The ongoing claims oscillating between competition and cooperation between journals and librarians have been the major physical and political issues for over a decade.

My point in presenting a tradesman's perspective (inherent in all scholarly journals) on publishing scholarly journals is that the snobberies of high-class production are a motive for high costs, which the misnomer "desktop publishing" misleads us into overlooking. Nice looking work costs a lot more. Or, let me translate that into a more elegant and soothing idiom: aesthetically pleasing appearance is the outward and tangible manifestation of an inward state of peer-reviewed grace. In publishing a scholarly journal, typesetting was traditionally about half the cost, while the printing, binding, and fulfilling comprised the other half. In the past fifteen years that ratio has been changed considerably: copy contained on a floppy disk has turned the ratio from 1:1 (typesetting in relation to the other three steps) to perhaps 1:3 or 1:4. Printing costs have gone up with the increased price of fuel, which is a major determinant of paper cost. But the exquisite academic snobbery that demands the very best binding, design, and paper keeps the cost of scholarly publication high because very few journals can afford the high capital investment in a binding machine. For example, in the whole city of Honolulu with about 900,000 inhabitants, there is only one modern binding company, and like all monopolies, its prices are murderous. That's why University of Hawaii journals are manufactured in Asia or Ann Arbor.

So what must we do? The most radical—and most questionable—proposal came from the blue-ribbon panel put together by the old HEW in 1976 and was published by Johns Hopkins University Press as *The National Enquiry into Scholarly Communication*.[1] That august body, which included a president of the Council of Editors and Learned Journals (CELJ), predecessor to both Professor Shoaf and myself, recommended that all scholarly publication be done electronically with the gradual phasing out of hard copy. It was a proposal eagerly supported by research librarians who were running out of space and usually are at the bottom of the priority list for funding new facilities, especially for what in the eyes of live-for-today regents and legislators amounts to dead storage. The objections to going totally electronic, voiced by some, including me in 1979 were, first, that not everyone in the scholarly world—particularly in culture–rich but materially poor Third-World countries—has access to computers; second, that it is very easy to censor or sabotage the electronic highway; and, third, that it would be very expensive. Bill Gates alone has made $7 billion off the electronic revolution, enough to endow 10,000 scholarly journals in perpetuity. In fact, in 1979, Admiral Bobby Ray Inman, recently sidetracked from being secretary of defense, as reported in *The Chronicle of Higher Education*, tried to censor some freelance experiments with electronic encryption going on at Harvard, asserting that only censors could have secret codes. The censor censoring secrecy is the stuff of historical satire, but it was a real threat to the dissenting intellect.

A second possibility is to list articles in an electronic network and then send out faxed photocopies on demand. Sending out the photocopies can be time consuming for the beleaguered researcher who can now spend a fruitful three hours in a good North American research library—one of the great institutions of the modern world—with everything at hand.

A third possibility would be to have some giant E-mail setup for all scholarly articles, although without a gatekeeping function, even oceans of gigabytes could get clogged. Some smart kid whose parent bought her a new computer program instead of some Michael Jordan skywalker shoes could decide to hack up his dad's national data network.

A fourth possibility is that scholarly journals be published simultaneously in hard copy and a CD, because then the electronic storage, subject to all sorts of mischief in a bulletin board system controlled from a central location, could at least be in many hands, the next best thing to the protestants' (little "p" but doing the same thing) printed copy of scripture. But it would need a sophisticated reading machine, one that would not work in Sarajevo, where they have even run out of batteries. Two recent articles in *Scholarly Publishing* show the uses of CD from both the publishers' and librarians' viewpoint.[2] It is appropriate to remember the fate of the culminating centralized communication system of the ancient Western world, the Library at Alexandria: very centralized, very large, very rich in resources, very organized, and very destroyed.

Or look at what happened to the National Library of Cambodia when it was destroyed by the combatants. The only survivors of some materials are duplicates at the University of Hawaii library.

A final possibility for now is that consortia of scholarly publishers such as the Council of Editors of Learned Journals or the vaunted athletic conferences—limited now to the physicality of young people leaping about—could create regional co-ops to buy paper, print, bind scholarly journals, and distribute less expensively. This presumes the acceptance of the premise that hard copy is necessary not only because of electronic cost and accessibility, but also because a censor, hacker, or natural disaster could easily maim or kill a network of electronic information.

University sponsors of scholarly research and publication are now too much in cahoots with vendors who charge too much. That situation could change if there were a more cost-effective alternative by which we could compete with the economics of scale. Perhaps the production of scholarly journals is really not a matter of physicality but of that weird set of nonmaterial credits that we call finance.

What's in it for researchers to keep hard-copy scholarly media looking good at a lowered price? The approval of academic snobs (for doing the right thing for the wrong reason) and the increased number of pages available to earnest researchers. In the world of intellect, that means the critical spirit need not be fettered by the conformity of the majoritarian culture. As the former president of the University of Hawaii said, a scholarly journal is one of the most cost-effective ways to promote a developing university. Let us then look for cost effectiveness at the same time that we protect the diversity of scholarship from the megalith and megabucks of the electronic highway.

The issues raised here presume that all good public policy needs testing. Let us not forget an historical perspective on the pleasures of technology. I am well aware that Gutenberg could be considered the Bill Gates of the fifteenth century and that we should perhaps lay back and think of England. But we should also be aware that after Gutenberg and all subsequent printers were finished making their artifact, the artifact was immediately readable by a literate person. The electronic media, on the other hand, always needs the intercession of the high priests of engineering in order to administer the eucharist of the electronic byte. A final historical irony: the particularization that is at the heart of the cultural empiricism of reading marks on a piece of paper, held in the hand and beheld by the eye, is still the best way to protect the globalization of intellect from both designed and spontaneous obliteration.

NOTES

1. An early statement of the problem of library storage with a chilling recommendation to cut back on the net number of journals (p. 42) was *Scholarly Communication: The Report of the National Enquiry* (Baltimore, Md.: Johns Hopkins University Press, 1979). Significantly, no one took credit for either writing or editing the book, although Robert Lumiansky wrote the Foreword, and an eminent group called the Board of Governors is listed. Ironically, their recommendation for cutbacks coincided with a complete change yof strategy by the Conference (now Council) of Editors of Learned Journals (CELJ). Instead of an elitist watchdog group as originally envisioned by its founders in the early 1960s, starting with the presidency of Ralph Cohen in 1977, CELJ vigorously sought to include all learned journals in literature and humanities. During the 1980s, the number

grew enormously as the *MLA Directory of Periodicals* attests. CELJ enlarged its membership from about 50 to 500 from 1979 to 1994. See George Simson, "President's Message," *Editors' Notes: Bulletin of the Conference of Editors of Learned Journals* 4 (1985) 3–5.

2. James R. Raimes, "Developing a CD-ROM," *Scholarly Publishing: A Journal for Authors & Publishers* 25 (January 1994): 107–113, and Dimity S. Berkner, "CD-ROM Marketing," *Scholarly Publishing* 25 (January 1994): 113–125. The CD-ROM seems the sensible compromise between the electronic network and the paper hard copy. Although dependent on machines for both production and consumption, the individual manufactured artifact is preserved. A single hacker, censor, or natural disaster cannot destroy all copies.

13

Communities of Scholarship in the Electronic Age

Douglas Harper

BACKGROUND

This chapter briefly discusses nine years of publishing *Visual Sociology*, the official journal of the International Visual Sociology Association (IVSA). The focus is on the process through which new ideas are introduced and integrated into an academic discipline. It is hoped that these recollections will be useful for faculty members in any of several disciplines considering similar projects, or for administrators who must decide whether to commit resources to a project with such lofty goals but radical challenges.

THE CONTEXT OF A NEW JOURNAL

Knowledge exists in frames and contexts, such as scholarly books, organized in our libraries in familiar logics. Much of the knowledge that we make and consume is, of course, published in academic journals. These academic journals are not given by God to an audience of passive intellectuals. Rather, they come into existence and change in relative importance to other journals through a social process: through the dynamics of sponsorship; the competition of scholarly topics to be developed and heard; the struggle for status between journals marked in many ways throughout the publishing process; and the battle over scarce resources, which affects all aspects of journal publishing. In order to carve out a new academic area, and eventually to explore the parameters of this new area in a journal, one must understand the details of this social process as well as the lay of the intellectual landscape into which the project must fit.

In sociology, as in many other disciplines, the journals are of three types, ranked in regular and well-published lists. While it is impossible to carve these status rankings into simple categories, they do exist pretty much in the following order.

First are the journals that express the dominant theoretical and methodological paradigms. In the field of sociology, these are fewer than ten journals, published by the American Sociological Association, or sometimes by the university presses at the universities with the most prestigious graduate departments. Examples include the *American Journal of Sociology* and the *American Sociological Review*, published by the University of Chicago Press and the American Sociological Association, respectively.

Journals of a second rank express the interests of regional societies. They are generally conservative in the sense that they follow the theoretical and methodological lead of the major journals. An example is *Social Forces*, published by the Southern Sociological Society, which is ranked very highly and is traditional in orientation. At times regional journals mark a theoretical shift in the discipline. For example, *Sociological Quarterly* was established as the journal of the Midwest Sociological Association, but it also represented new disciplinary interest in symbolic interaction and related developments in theory and methods.

Finally, there remains a potpourri of journals that develop for a wide range of reasons. These might be institutional, as in the case of *Rural Sociology*, which is indirectly connected to the U.S. Department of Agriculture. Or journals develop as subject matter or theoretical orientations changed. Thus, the journal *Social Problems* came into existence when sociology became more radicalized; the journals *Symbolic Interaction* and *Qualitative Sociology* emerged when, within sociology, there developed an interest in methods other than variable analysis and logical positivism. Some of these journals are highly regarded; others exist on the fringes of the discipline. At times their role has been to overlap sister and brother disciplines, as is the case of *Human Organization*, which is inspired by parallel movements toward applied research in anthropology, sociology, and other disciplines. Most of these journals are published by smaller university presses or specialized trade publishers such as Sage Press, which combines scholarly publishing with a trade publisher's orientation. The hierarchical ranking of these journals dovetails the ranking of the other journals, with the oldest and best connected of these journals nearly equal in status to those generally considered near the top. The hierarchy reflects the pluralism of academic publishing: new ideas struggle to become part of a discipline and succeed only when the journals are accepted, that is, subscribed to, in great numbers by individuals and by libraries.

Typically, journals are extremely conservative. The editors are gatekeepers and status markers in disciplines that change very slowly. The journals are often published at universities that finance them and use them to extend their reputation. Thus the more prestigious the journal, generally the more closely it fits the disciplinary orthodoxy.

To get and keep a job at a university with a major graduate department, professors must publish in journals of first rank. Because many people share the same goal, publishing in the top rated journals is exceedingly competitive. Note that I have suggested that being published in the top rated journals is *both* an indication that the research has been done well and that its conclusions are important, and that the research fits the prevailing methodological and theoretical paradigms of the discipline. Remember, however, that much research outside of the disciplinary orthodoxy continues to be done by professors who are not in the culture of the disciplinary mainstream.

Thus, those professors who wish to advance their careers along the ascending ridgeline of the profession are is ill-advised to publish articles in journals that are experimental or that even question the assumptions guiding the research typically represented in the leading journals. The savvy professor realizes at a young age that his or her research will be marked at least as much by where it is published as by its real content. This, in turn, is a particularly thorny problem for editors of a new journal, who seek to publish research of first quality in order to establish the quality of their own projects!

These are, of course, generalizations, and they hold true in different degrees for professors at different stages of their careers. Young professors may be anxious to burst through the shackles of conservative dissertation research just to discover that to be awarded tenure it will be necessary to publish the most traditional aspects of their research in the most prestigious, and thus the most conservative, journals of their discipline. Tenured professors who continue to publish out of a commitment to their disciplines often venture into novel areas. There are those who, because of luck or stamina, are able to successfully present paradigm-breaking research to the most traditional, conservative, and exalted journals.

These are commonly accepted as the occupational constraints and conventions that influence and even control the knowledge production in academic disciplines.

FURTHER COMMENT ON DISCIPLINARY CONTEXTS

In sociology, 150 years of development drew from two epistemological streams. The first was historical relativism (historicism), which suggested that the world happened in a series of unique events and that the methods of science were not appropriate for the study of these events. This view was intellectually consolidated by the philosopher Wilhelm Dilthey and developed by the sociologist Max Weber in the late nineteenth century. The interpretive or qualitative tradition in sociology, continuing to the present, reaches to these intellectual ancestors.

The other epistemological stream drew on the assumption that sociological knowledge represented categories of experience that could be abstracted and treated experimentally. In a well-known early example, Emile Durkheim compared rates of suicide and associated them with other measurable phenomena such as religion, age and marital status. This simple experiment established the dominant model of modern sociology, which, roughly speaking, is based on the assumption that social life can be reduced to variables that can be statistically associated.

Sociology has developed within these two definitions of knowledge. For many of us this conversation was incomplete. Sociology, we believed, ought to include a new kind of epistemology: knowledge of the observed world represented in imagery rather than words. Twenty years ago we found ourselves calling this "visual sociology." As we saw it, our intent was revolutionary in an epistemological sense and in practical terms: we intended, for the first time in sociology, to present and analyze information that was primarily visual.

Thus, many of us found ourselves interested in a sociology that had not yet been developed. The choices we faced boiled down to two: we could drop our research interests and adopt a research agenda with an existing outlet, or we could develop our own publication outlet. To develop our own publication was certainly the least rational choice, measured on virtually any dimension. We would be unlikely to find a university or commercial press, certainly in the early years of our enterprise. We would be denying, or at least ignoring, the well-recognized strategies for gaining status in the profession. Not only would we be diverting our own efforts away from publishing in highly ranked journals, but we would also be establishing a journal that would initially be of so little status that it would probably not even be recognized by the majority of our colleagues. Even if we were successful at getting the project off the ground, we would gain a dubious reward of being responsible for work that we were not trained to do. The chances of really being successful—that is, establishing a journal that would attract a fine editorial board, quality submissions, adequate funding for minimal publishing, and, eventually, sponsorship by a legitimate publisher—seemed incredibly low.

We decided, however, to push on. Because we were doing something unprecedented, we lacked models. There were suggestive but incomplete models in photojournalism and documentary photography. We could certainly draw on successful experiments in visual anthropology, most of which were done several decades ago. Semiotics provided a theoretical framework for many of our questions, and the increasingly pervasive discussion of postmodernism justified, we felt, our experimentation.

We were also a group of mostly 1960s types, restless with the conventions of sociology, hoping to vitalize our discipline by nudging each other into a more direct and critical relationship with our societies. Most of us were photographers as well as sociologists, and we were predisposed to fieldwork research. To make a visual sociology was to make a place for ourselves in a discipline where we often felt we were strangers.

ESTABLISHING A SCHOLARLY CONVERSATION

Visual sociologists first began holding meetings in association with the American Sociological Association (ASA) in 1974. A seminal article, "Photography and Sociology," was published in 1974 by Howard Becker, a well-recognized sociologist often identified with unconventional disciplinary developments. During the late 1970s, visually interested sociologists in the American Sociological Association attempted to become an official "Section," which required that 200 members of the ASA needed to ask for and pay a modest fee for membership. Sectionhood would have legitimated visual sociology in the sense that presentations would be integrated into the annual sociology meetings, which attract thousands of sociologists. We could give awards to each other and entice other sociologists to attend our meetings and parties. We would be eligible for a newsletter through which we would communicate news of our developing subfield. We would, in fact, bask in the status of official acceptance by the disciplinary godmother of sociology, the ASA. In the process, we would also be rationalized into a large bureaucratic organization. This effort, however, failed in 1980 by fifteen members.

Curiously, the group did not again attempt to establish sectionhood in the following year. Rather, the group formed as the International Visual Sociology Association (IVSA) and ventured into the rocky shoals of small societyhood. This history is told in the first issue of our eventual newsletter (Curry 1986).

An immediate need arose to find a place in which to publish what we did. At the time, two journals in sociology, *Qualitative Sociology* and *Society*, published "photographic essays." While, at first glance, this development appeared to be encouraging, most of us felt that these two journals had unwittingly marginalized visual sociology by putting it in a form that few take very seriously. Visual information had never found a role within mainstream sociology journals.

In a related discipline, an outstanding journal had originated under the name of *Studies in the Anthropology of Visual Communication*. This journal, edited at Temple University, had the support of a patron family that paid for more than adequate photo reproduction, interesting design, and much better paper than is typically used for journal publication. *SAViCOM*, as it came to be known, evolved into a journal called more simply *Visual Communication*. All aspects of the journal were outstanding and groundbreaking. Unfortunately, few visual sociologists read or participated in the journal, probably (and disappointingly) because it emerged from outside of sociology. Unfortunately, the patrons eventually withdrew their support over editorial objections, and the journal ceased publication in 1986, after eleven years of publication.

Through the creation of IVSA, we had thus created the frustrating situation of identifying a new way of doing sociology without devising a way to bring it to publication. Our yearly conferences, though small, produced a steady stream of interesting work. But we had no background or experience in journal publication, scant resources, and a small membership base.

Our first attempts to solve this problem involved the sponsorship of a journal in Europe which beat its wings furiously, tried to take off, and then crashed to the ground. This journal, the *International Journal of Visual Sociology*, was a diligent effort by a small group of Europeans, supported through the extremely modest membership dues of the IVSA. It was irregularly published for three years, but it lacked such essentials as an editorial board and the necessary resources to support necessities such as copyediting. Still the journal provided a temporary home for the beginning of visual research and was published for a pittance collected through the membership dues of fifty to a hundred people.

During this period, it seemed that our best strategy was to retreat to a newsletter. This was anticipated as a modest effort, a decidedly *non*journal publication intended to encourage visual research and teaching by publishing book, video and film reviews, teaching strategies, news of the organization and related activities, and reports from the field. Knowing nothing about publishing, I reluctantly accepted the position of founding editor. The *Visual Sociology Review* was thus launched in 1986. It was a fifteen-page newsletter which we distributed widely but informally. The first two issues were printed on a dot matrix printer and pasted into a dummy the way a few of us had assembled our high school newspapers. With all the crudeness of our efforts, we were elated to have concrete evidence of our existence!

MAKING A JOURNAL

The remainder of this chapter addresses the short history of scratching ahead to our current status—a biannual refereed journal of 80, 8 1/2-by-11-inch pages, printed on 100 pound coated paper, and usually containing more than 100 illustrations. The journal, now called *Visual Sociology*, is distributed to over 500 individuals and libraries (including institutions such as the Museum of Modern Art) in more than ten countries, about half of whom, in any given year, pay their dues. We operate entirely without paid staff and still operate about 20 percent in the red. Our current small institutional subsidy, which allows our situation to continue, is tenuous at best; thus, we continue to seek sufficient subscriptions to reach a breakeven point.

There were, of course, several steps in this transition from newsletter to refereed journal, and indeed this transition is not yet complete.

The newsletter slowly evolved in length and substance. After a few issues, we were publishing at least one article per issue. These were often culled from our annual meetings. I found myself, as editor, having to ask for outstanding research reports or essays that surely could have found their way to a "real" journal. That several colleagues contributed their fine work to such a modest publication is a mark of an intellectual community. In any case, we felt like children out at play on the day of the first snowfall. We had a hard time getting the balls for the snowman rolling, and even when they started they often came apart in our hands.

During this time, I was a professor at the State University of New York at Potsdam. The *Visual Sociology Review* was smiled upon by the college president, who assigned the electronic typesetting of the newsletter to the office of publications and allowed IVSA to pay for the printing at college rates. With these arrangements I was able to edit, correct, oversee the production, and mail the newsletter for five years. The journal grew longer and more professional in appearance. The time required to make and distribute the journal, of course, increased.

The journal-butterfly emerged from a newsletter-cocoon when I accepted a position at the University of South Florida. My new dean supported the journal by purchasing for me what at the time was more than $10,000 worth of hardware and software. This included the then most powerful Macintosh computer, a rudimentary flatbed scanner, and the necessary software, Pagemaker and Photoshop. The dean also paid for the electronic pagemaking of three issues, after which we have had to do it ourselves.

IMPLICATIONS OF THE ELECTRONIC DESKTOP

This chapter can now devolve to tales of steep learning curves. Our journal is possible owing to electronic typesetting and electronic photo scanning—in a word, desktop publishing. These extraordinary inventions and advances are also a great bane to our efforts and the efforts of others trying similar processes.

First of all, producing a journal in the traditional way involves a complex division of labor. Most workers are professionals, or at least masters of very specific skills. Copyeditors may not know a whit about design, but they surely can find grammatical flaws. Designers do not really address content, but they have been trained in typography and aesthetics. And so on. Suddenly, one is armed with Pagemaker (the most common desktop publishing software) and, like a child with a welding torch, able to make extraordinary wonders or to do terrible damage. I recall, for example, making a choice about a font for the journal after looking through a font book for five minutes, and having now to live with a choice that has several decidedly funny looking characters. Each time I set out with an empty Pagemaker skeleton I certainly feel the rush of creative potential, the urge of Dr. Frankenstein. I have no formal training in design and have learned to design pages by studying other publications I admire, incorporating qualities I find successful. I receive reinforcement when our design decisions seem to work. But I also have felt the great crush of disappointment when I have made mistakes, the most gross being placing the wrong caption with a photograph in what was otherwise an outstanding article.

The great irony of Pagemaker and Photoshop is that it makes it possible to produce a journal without experts or traditional expert knowledge. Thus it makes it possible to do a very bad job—to make a monster, if I may continue my Frankenstein metaphor, a monster with a good heart—or to do an unprecedented and creative take on a new problem. In our case, electronic scanning and typesetting has been an extraordinary resource because we have been able to incorporate visual material into our journal at no additional cost. This is revolutionary in its implications. For example, my first book, published by a large university press, was limited to fifty-two photographs from the several hundred I wished to publish. These were set in galleys because the press could not afford to integrate them into the text. With Pagemaker and Photoshop, because the visual image is simply an electronic file, it can be placed on a page at no added expense.

We have thus produced a journal that does not look like any journal in sociology and that covers material not covered in any other publication. We have printed color images of postcards, enlargements of small historical photos, reproductions from the pages of magazines and books, and many original photographs and drawings. We have certainly taken sociology where it has not been before. But what has been the effect of our efforts on our parent discipline?

I began this chapter with the realization that knowledge is created in a social process. It is a painstakingly slow social process. We were naive when we assumed that the journal would take off when we began publishing an innovative and absolutely new take on sociology. Instead, our growth has been slow, though steady, at about 20 percent a year. We are increasingly cited and abstracted. We have been more and more successful at forming presentations and seminars at national meetings. We have attracted submissions of increasing quality and are currently publishing about 20 percent of our submissions. We tell ourselves that if visual sociology edges itself into a recognized position in sociology, it will be because of our efforts. All these are positive accomplishments, but they have been done at a significant cost.

The primary problem is that because desktop publishing allows the work to be done by a single individual, in this case it has evolved to be done that way. Twice a year I work around the clock for six weeks to bring another issue to life. For example, a recent issue included a single article with over seventy photographs. Simply scanning these photographs and adjusting them in the electronic darkroom of Photoshop consumed more than thirty hours. The actual hours spent making the journal—from reading manuscripts to putting completed journals in the mail—are enormous. At present the entire work of the organization falls on the shoulders of the secretary treasurer, the revolving presidents of IVSA, and myself. There is no reason why the work could not be shared, except that the skills of desktop publishing are still new, and farming tasks out to willing IVSA members is not yet practical. When it becomes possible to share these tasks further, the journal and the organization will rest on a more stable base.

IMPLICATIONS FOR COMMUNITIES OF SCHOLARSHIP

One might wonder if, after such a tale, I would recommend that other faculty undertake such a project. The answer is based entirely on the values one holds most deeply. If a scholar/professor identifies for herself the fast track, establishing a journal will only be a frustrating black hole, sucking one's time and energy into a seemingly limitless vacuum. These efforts will probably be viewed as irrational rather than professional by tenure committees at the most aggressive and self-monitored departments. Then the chances for real success in these projects are probably fairly low, which certainly casts the entire project in a questionable frame. The rewards for success—a genuinely novel contribution to a discipline—are, however, great.

For a college dean or provost the real costs of supporting such an effort are extremely low and, from my humble vantage point, well worth the risk. In an academic environment in which beginning assistant professors in the natural sciences routinely expect $50,000 labs, the $5,000 to $10,000 in initial expenses and the generally small subsidy required to keep a journal moving are small costs for a result which the university can use to its advantage. In the case of my current university, the journal has taken the name of a previously undistinguished academic department literally to several corners of the globe. Many graduate students from an enlarged national and even international pool have sought our graduate degree precisely because of the existence of the journal. Thus, the publication has helped the department improve its self-image as well as its real reputation. Because the journal is so unusual, it has attracted more than what one might expect in terms of attention and comment.

Finally, the electronic basis of the journal suggests an ironic future. Throughout this chapter, I have suggested that one of the fundamental reasons why the journal exists is because it represents a community. This community is embodied in such things as actual human contact: shared work making a journal, travel to meetings, long hours of company in crowded hotel rooms, and our fair share of conviviality. The journal has become an artifact of this community, a physical object that symbolizes and embodies our accomplishments and our intellectual vision. Ironically, because the journal is assembled on an entirely electronic form, it could be distributed through the electronic highway on the Internet. If formatted correctly and distributed through the Mosaic software, the journal would retain the journal "look" and even the photographs would appear on one's computer screen. That is, we are told, the wave of the future. Like so many futures, however, it is to be both admired and feared. Publication of our journal in a World Wide Web site would potentially increase knowledge about and participation in our intellectual movement. Presumably, this would facilitate rapidly increasing intellectual development. The pluralism of scholarly life would take place more and more efficiently, and the result would be a freeing up of a sometimes moribund process.

Distribution on the Internet, however, would have serious consequences for the movement we have founded and nourished. Access to our publication would, on the Internet, be free. Consuming our information would thus be separated from paying for its production; in an extreme situation this would, of course, cause the collapse of the entire enterprise. In addition, we would potentially replace the in-flesh community of our current organization with computer-based interaction, for our conferences would be as obsolete as our physical journal if we were all hooked together via Internet. That would save us all money, time, and the inconvenience of travel, but it would reduce yet one more life-stimulating activity to the one-dimensional drudge of robotized, though occasionally stimulating, computer play.

IMAGINED FUTURES

There are several alternative futures for IVSA and *Visual Sociology*. While the potential of electronic distribution should not be discounted, most members continue to feel that the journal needs to exist materially as well as electronically. Whether the journal is adopted by a publisher, transformed into a yearbook, or continued in its present form, spirited discussion in IVSA continues to recommit to a journal that stresses the revolutionary implications of visual sociology. We should not mimic the numerous journals that provide sufficient opportunities for publishing the full range of nonvisual sociology. Our publication should retain an experimental format and continually redefine itself as our sub-discipline continues to develop.

REFERENCES

Becker, Howard S. "Photography and Sociology." *Studies in the Anthropology of Visual Communication* 1,1 (1974): 3–26.

Boonzajer Flaes, Robert, ed. *Eyes across the Water*. Vol. 1. Amsterdam: Het Spinhuis Press, 1989.

Boonzajer Flaes, Robert, and Douglas Harper, eds. *Eyes Across the Water*. Vol. 2. Amsterdam: Het Spinhuis Press, 1993.

Curry, Tim. "A Brief History of the IVSA." *Visual Sociology Review* 1, 1 (1986): 3-5.

14

Old Solutions to New Problems: Looking to Renaissance Texts for Strategies of Hypertext Composition

Richard Smyth

The advent of media such as video and hypermedia[1] poses problems for those working and publishing in the humanities, namely, the problems of reading and writing with these media and of teaching students to do the same. The filmic and multimedia qualities of these electronic technologies offer multiple modes of communication (sound, voice, music, animation, and video in addition to text) for a denser, richer information space. Already, the new software Mosaic, a tool for browsing the World Wide Web that provides hypermedia links to visual and audio information as well as plain text, is encouraging a hypertextual form of composition within the Internet itself. My work thus involves the practical and theoretical problems involved in inventing an electronic rhetoric. As scholars exploit the resources of Internet publication, how will the practice of scholarly writing change? Despite the newness of this technology, traditions exist within classical rhetoric as well as medieval and early modern textual production that will offer models for writing within the "writing spaces" of electronic media.

One such tradition can be found in the Art of Memory. The highly visual nature of the Art of Memory, in the various ways that it was practiced from the time of antiquity to the sixteenth century, is well suited to the new technology of hypermedia, with its capacity for graphics, animation, and even video.[2] One scholar writes of the potential of drawing on this tradition: "The practitioners of mnemonics, especially Bruno and Leibnitz, had high hopes for a universal language based on spatial, visual systems. We may realize their hopes through the displays of our computers, which will spread the conventions that make language possible" (Nickerson, 1985, 390).

This chapter explores these traditions in order to discover the kinds of strategies available for composition in hypermedia. In addition, recommendations are made for how scholarly publishing will likely be transformed as a result of these changes, when scholars in the humanities begin to embrace the electronic media. It will first be necessary, however, to review the history of mnemonic practices so as to understand the various contexts in which writing with images was practiced as well as the reason for its demise. Such a review will also serve as an introduction to the kind of writing with images that may be done in the electronic media.

A BRIEF HISTORY OF MNEMONICS

Originating in classical Greece and perpetuated via institutional practices until the sixteenth century, the Art of Memory enabled individuals to perform spectacular feats of mnemonic aptitude. Latin rhetorics, primarily the anonymous *Ad Herrenium* but also Cicero's *De inventione* and Quintilian's *Institutio oratoria,* direct the student to establish a set of *loci,* or "places," which usually are set in a place well known to the student, such as his or her garden or house. Within these *loci,* students place images, selected for their affinity to the subject matter of the speech to be memorized, in the preestablished memory places. Then, to recall the topics of the speech in the process of speaking, they are advised to walk through the house in order to encounter the mnemonic images that are meant to stimulate their memories (Yates, 1966, 1-26).

The manuscript culture of the Middle Ages adapted this system into written forms of memorial practices. These hybrid practices facilitated the monks' task of memorizing books and account for much of the ornamental marginalia and illuminated imagery of the books produced during that period. Manuscripts frequently contained images painted within the margins, images that sometimes made puns on certain words or themes of the text, while occasionally these images developed over a number of pages as a narrative. "Such images, it seems to me, are not iconographical, nor do they illustrate or explain the content of a particular text. They serve the basic function of all page decoration, to make each page memorable" (Carruthers, 1990, 247).

Bestiaries, common in the Middle Ages, also served to fulfill the mnemonic function of making the page memorable. Descriptions of the beasts and birds were graphic enough to make them likely candidates for images to be placed in a person's *loci.* "Indeed, the bestiary may have owed its popularity in part to the facility with which it might be remembered. For here were the *imagines agentes,* each one in its place and with its accustomed rubric that externalized the rhetorician's chambers of memory" (Rowland, 1989, 20).

Allegory itself, of which bestiaries were one manifestation, was part of this tradition. The structure of allegory suggests the mnemonic procedure inherent in placing images in places to trigger the memory. Craig Owens states that, in allegory, "the image is a hieroglyph; an allegory is a rebus—writing composed of concrete images" (1984, 209). This procedure of writing with concrete images is precisely what the Art of Memory cultivated in its practice of "speaking other" (*allos agoreuei*). Examples of such practices include the fabrication of personified abstractions of graces or sins, which served as memory images for traveling friars trying to preach to commonfolk (Yates, 96). The dream-vision, too, with its catalogues of mythic and historic personages orderly painted on the walls or columns of significant buildings, was also a locus of such practice.

The sixteenth century was a period of transition in terms of its mnemonic practices, part of which is attributable to the Protestant Reformation. With the increasing antagonism being displayed toward icons, all that was associated with images came under attack. One debate between a Ramist (an adherent of Peter Ramus) and a Brunian (a follower of Giordano Bruno) centered on the opposing arts of memory, one the traditional art of building memory palaces that had been practiced for centuries and the other a new method devoid of images that Ramus had developed. The debate, Yates writes, was "at bottom a religious controversy" (267), and she explains "why Ramism was so popular with the Puritans. The dialectical method [of Ramus] was emotionally aseptic" (275). Ramus cleansed memory of those allegorical images—often of questionable moral content—one had to use in the practice of building memory palaces. Information comes to be stored on the two-dimensional surface of the page, and spatial arrangements of the information become significant. Although Mary Carruthers takes issue with Walter Ong on this point, saying that this practice of spatial arrangement already existed in the Middle Ages, there is one difference: during the Middle Ages the mnemotists used images, whereas during the Reformation Ramus did not.[3] This elimination of images defines the primary distinction of information storage in the age of print, such that, until the twentieth century, the image was secondary as a resource for remembering.

This state of affairs no longer exists. With the proliferation of video cameras and VCRs on the one hand and flatbed scanners, desktop video editing, and CD-ROM laserdisks on the other, writing with images has returned with a vengeance. And the presence of technologies such as hypertext and virtual reality, which are three-dimensional (or, in the case of cyberspace, n-dimensional) in terms of their "writing space" (as Jay David Bolter would call it), challenges current scholars in the humanities to theorize compositional strategies for storing information in these new media.

One area of exploration that I will now take up in fuller detail is the memory palace as a manifestation of the Art of Memory. With this in mind, I turn to one example of how the idea of the memory palace helped me structure a hypertext composition.

THE GENETIC CELL AS MEMORY P(A)LACE

From the memory palace tradition, I derived a structure for a hypertext that I composed entitled "Genetis: A Rhizography."[4] The title suggests the structural metaphor of genetics, the "natural" medium for information storage,[5] and also hints at its contents, which on one level proposes genetics as a metaphor for generic invention. Since the current biological term cell comes from the Latin word *cella* meaning "storeroom," it only made sense that a hypertext composed of "cella," or storerooms, be modeled after the cells of the body. DNA inhabits every cell of the body in the same way that images or words are stored in the *loci* of the memory palace tradition.

The hypertext program I employed, called "Storyspace," lends itself to this kind of metaphor. Its interface for authoring consists of the "writing space," which appears on the screen as a box with a title bar. Clicking with a mouse on the title bar allows an author to write within the space, storing whatever information desired—text, graphic, quick-time video, and/or sound. Clicking within the writing space opens up the space to allow the author to store more boxes on the inside, providing the effect of "Chinese boxes." The author then is able to provide links between these boxes, thereby creating the multilinear effect of hypertext. Jay David Bolter, one of the creators of Storyspace, has himself employed the term cell to describe these writing spaces and has compared the Storyspace environment to that of exploring a dungeon or castle: "Any book can be thought of as a dungeon, a receptacle of treasures and dangers. A printed book is a dungeon whose walls are solid. In an electronic book the walls of each cell may give way to the touch. Hidden passages may transport the reader across many levels of the structure" (*Writing Space*, Storyspace document). His description is significant, especially for a project such as mine which is attempting to find in the memory palace tradition a model for storing information in a hypertext environment.[6]

Choosing to use DNA as a specific aspect of cellular composition offers a number of advantages. First, it provides a three-dimensional model for the problem of structuring a text composed in hypertext, a medium that can be conceived as a three-dimensional writing space. With its helical structure and its linked pairs of purines and pyrimidines structured in a ladder-like fashion, DNA furnishes a visual schema for the deployment of information in a three-dimensional space.

Second, DNA provides an allegorical model for invention. DNA, as the basis for the generation of new life, supplies the guidelines for inventing hybrid forms or mutations of preexisting entities, be they animal species or literary forms. In *Teletheory: Grammatology in the Age of Video* (1989) and *Heuretics: The Logic of Invention* (1994), Gregory Ulmer creates the genre of "mystory" for videography (a genre that emphasizes the need for situating one's own experience in relation to the experience of the broader culture) and "chorography" for hypermedia composition (a genre that incorporates Jacques Derrida's philosophical and theoretical reconceptualization of place as "chora" rather than "locus"[7]), thus providing two exemplars of such inventive practice. Such generic invention stems from the close etymological association of genre and genetics and suggests a general model of procedure in the electronic realm, especially during the embryonic formation of electronic genres. I subtitle my hypertext "A

Rhizography" to indicate a variant genre specific to the electronic environment within which I composed my text.

Finally, DNA provides a conceptual model for organizing information in a three-dimensional space as well. This conceptual model can be seen in the spatially organized feature of DNA molecular structures. These structures have four levels of organization:

> *Primary structure* is the linear sequence of amino acids in apolypeptide. *Secondary structure* refers to certain repeatingconformation patterns. *Tertiary structure* refers to the overall polypeptide conformation. No clear distinction can be made between secondary and tertiary structure. *Quaternary structure* refers to the spatial relationships between subunits in proteins that consist of two or more polypeptides. (Wood et al., 1974, 75)

The emphasis on patterns here is significant insofar as electronic rhetoric will be a rhetoric of patterns.[8] Readers will need to become adept at detecting patterns encoded within the information to fully realize the potential inherent in visual representations of knowledge: "Features (patterns of meaning and characteristics of content) can be extracted at a glance, once the reader becomes attuned to the new 'rhetoric' and the new definition of 'sight' reading" (Carlson and Gonzalez, 1993, 30). Composers of three-dimensional texts will have to consider this visual potential for the conveyance of meaning.

In my hypertext, I attempted to incorporate such structures into the disposition of my Storyspace boxes by establishing five plateaus, each of which had its own primary structure of a strictly linear narrative (taking the cellular phenomenon of "H-bonds," in that they are "linear and therefore maximally stable" [Wood et al., 75], as a parallel to the maximal stability that linear narrative provides and has provided in both oral and literate cultures). I then tried to incorporate secondary/tertiary structures of patterns by repeating themes and motifs in each plateau rather than having each plateau deal with only one subject. I also conceived of a helical spire twisting downward through the plateaus, similar to the strands connecting the base pairs constituting the DNA molecule. While this was not an actual structure within the three-dimensional authoring environment of Storyspace, working with such a visual conception allowed me to organize some of the cells in an alternative pathway that amounts to a tour of the text. DNA, therefore, came to provide both a literal and a metaphoric model for organizing my hypertext.

CONCLUSIONS AND RECOMMENDATIONS: THE WAYS SCHOLARLY WRITING WILL CHANGE

Based on the above described experience of working within one hypertext environment and upon my research of medieval and Renaissance mnemonic practices, which offer guidelines and models for writing with images, I believe that the processes of scholarly writing, as well as the kinds of topics we will be teaching under the rubric of "English composition," will change in the following ways:

1. Writers will begin to increase the incorporation of imagery and video into their writing. Writing will truly become not just hypertextual but hypermedial as the cost of graphics programs, multimedia computers, and desktop editing software decreases and as programs become easier to use. Increased use of voice and sound will also characterize electronic texts.

2. As writers begin to write visually, a fusion of writing and image reminiscent of the emblem book will come about, and the kinds of practices engaged in by emblem book readers and writers will become more frequent. Images from one context will be appropriated and used in different contexts, their meanings determined by the surrounding text. Daniel Russell illuminates such emblem book practices:

> But however an emblem is constructed, any emblem picture taken alone could accommodate other texts that would, effectively, turn it into a different emblem according to the will of an active,interpreting viewer, be he the author of another emblem book or simply the reader who changes the text he has just read or who physically attaches the picture to another text, perhaps in another book, as was done from time to time. (1985, 174)

Such a description reminds one of the postmodern artistic practices of appropriation and collage in that "the emblematic processing of traditional materials" consists of "the fragmentation of well-known allegorical works or traditional sign systems and the subsequent recombination of fragmented elements of them into new and striking signifying units" (Russell, 164). In this "age of mechanical reproduction," in which some individuals now have laser printers and scanners in their homes as well as the capacity to manipulate video imagery in desktop editing programs, the kind of appropriation once confined to clipping images from an emblem book becomes digitized, and the kind of active reading inaugurated in the sixteenth century becomes the norm.

3. Because of the new emphasis on what is visually communicated in writing, the need for "visual literacy" has emerged. As one scholar writes, "Teachers and students alike can only benefit from being made more perceptive of what I would describe as the *visual editing* of any piece of written matter that they may be handling as reader and as writer. It should no longer be considered as a matter of professional, specialized training. Today it is a matter of general literacy" (Baudin, 1984, 86). Thus, graphic design is a form of visual literacy that will become the province of scholars as part of the composing and publishing process.

4. Given the above possibilities, scholarly writing might become more "literary," in the Derridean sense of the term. As Hillis Miller writes, "To turn

whatever is written 'on' into literature might even be said to be the deconstructive move par excellence. Deconstruction, it can be said, if there is such a thing, is the exposure of the literary in every utterance, writing, or graphic mark. But this exposure can only be performed through literature" (1994, 20). Because writing will incorporate imagery, a return of "picto-ideo-phonographic" writing will occur, "a double-valued writing, ideographic and phonetic at once, which puts speech back in its place in relation to nonphonetic elements" (Ulmer, 1985, 98). In providing the potential to fulfill Derrida's desire "to restore to writing the balance between design and symbol it had in hieroglyphics" (Ulmer, 46), electronic writing will foster a more allegorical or ironic bent. If scholars learn to exploit the allegorical potential in typography[9] and rebus-writing, then people may read scholarly writing the way they once read literature, as these two categories collapse into one.

5. Interdisciplinary collaboration and research will become more frequent. George Landow has already commented on the ways in which large hypertext "webs" require collaborative working relationships among experts in different fields (1992, 88-100). Aside from this new configuration of disciplinary relations, interdisciplinary research will become necessary, so that the study of biochemistry, for instance, may have something to offer the electronic composer.

6. My experience of composing in hypertext leads me to conclude that what occurs in hypertext is a kind of generic "meltdown." Hypertext swallows all other genres into itself, such that essay and poem, history and autobiography, inhabit the same textual space. I have written elsewhere (Smyth, 1994) that this textual phenomenon should be called "rhizography" insofar as the texts that can be created in Storyspace are reminiscent of the rhizome not only in their web-like form but also in the potential for a nomadic wandering of meaning and a crossing of generic boundaries. Whatever text is composed in Storyspace, if it exploits the potential within this electronic medium, will inhabit the space of the "between," which is the space of the rhizome.

NOTES

1. George Landow defines the terms *hypertext* and *hypermedia* in the following ways: "Hypertext denotes text composed of blocks of text—what Roland Barthes terms a *lexia*—and the electronic links that join them. *Hypermedia* simply extends the notion of text in hypertext by including visual information, sound, animation, and other forms of data. Since hypertext, which links a passage of verbal discourse to images, maps, diagrams, and sound as easily as to another verbal passage, expands the notion of text beyond the solely verbal, I do not distinguish between hypertext and hypermedia" (1992, 4). Like Landow, I use the terms interchangeably throughout this chapter.

2. In his video entitled *Virtual Play: The Double-Direct Monkey Wrench in Black's Machinery* (1984), Steve Fagin acknowledges the potential of using the Art of Memory by directly alluding to the memory palace.

3. "My study will make it clear that from the earliest times medieval educators had as visual and spatial an idea of *locus* as any Ramist had, which they inherited continuously from antiquity, and indeed that concern for the layout of memory governed much in medieval education designed to aid the mind in forming and maintaining heuristic formats that are both spatial and visualizable" (Carruthers, 1990, 32).

4. This has been published in disk form in *Perforations* 5, a multimedia publication that includes text, computer disks, audio tapes, and video.

5. Biochemistry employs the metaphor of language to describe the processes of genetic reproduction. Wood et al., for instance, write that "most biomolecules are built from 30 small-molecule precursors, sometimes called the alphabet of biochemistry" (1974, 7) and that "The genetic code is the relationship between twenty-letter language of the proteins to the four-letter language of the nucleic acids" (462). R. C. Lewontin, a leading geneticist, compares the information that DNA provides with words in a language, which require a particular context to determine meaning: "A deep reason for the difficulty in devising causal information from DNA messages is that the same 'words' have different meanings in different contexts and multiple functions in a given context, as in any complex language" (1992, 66). Eric Havelock examines this metaphor and derives from it a model of cultural inheritance to explain how an oral culture preserves its identity: "The term 'information' [used by biologist Ernst Mayr in his discussion of genetics] embodies a metaphor borrowed from the idiom of human culture and applied backwards to the genetic process" (1986, 55).

6. The recent Internet phenomena called MUDs (Multi-User Dungeon) and MOOs (MUD-Object-Oriented) also invoke the architectural as a way of conceptualizing the organization of electronic information spaces. One MOO even calls itself the "Hypertext Hotel," in which a user starts in a "foyer" and can choose to go into different "rooms" hypertextually linked to the foyer. MOOs are interesting in that one can encounter another virtual person in any given room (who could be logged on from a computer somewhere across the world), converse with that person in real time, and interact with "objects" in the rooms.

7. Ulmer writes in *Heuretics*, "In order for rhetoric to become electronic, the term and concept of *topic* or *topos* must be replaced by *chora* (the notion of 'place' found in Plato's *Timaeus*). That is what I learned from Derrida. For now a dictionary definition must suffice: *chora* is 'an area in which genesis takes place'" (48).

8. Ulmer writes, "There are three ways to organize the release of information, which are used across all media: narrative, exposition, and pattern. The three modes are not mutually exclusive; on the contrary, all three are present in any work, with one dominant, and the other two subordinate. Narrative is the native form of oral culture, exposition is the native form of alphabetic literacy (in the sense that scientific writing is the privileged discourse of the print apparatus), and collage pattern is the native form of electronics" (1985, 160, 163).

9. Tom Conley writes of the allegorical nature of letters and this awareness as manifest in the sixteenth century: "If perspectival, calligraphic, or hieroglyphic properties of the visible letter were used to structure literature of the time, its decipherment also offered poets and artists other avenues for transcoding meanings. A piece of type could become a landscape, a chimera, it could turn into what it was not—into a monogram, a cipher, a number, a vocable from a foreign tongue—all the while remaining a letter" (1992, 12).

REFERENCES

Baudin, Fernand. "The Visual Editing of Texts." *Visible Language* 18 (1984): 81-86. 22-36.

Bolter, Jay David. *Writing Space: The Computer, Hypertext, and the History of Writing.* Storyspace hypertext document, 1990.

——. *Writing Space: The Computer, Hypertext, and the History of Writing.* Hillsdale, N.J.: Lawrence Erlbaum Associates, 1991.

Carlson, Patricia A., and George Gonzalez. "When Books Become Environments: Virtual Reality and the Technology of Text." Post-Literate. Special issue of *Felix: A Journal of Media Arts and Communication* 1, 3 (1993): 24-31.

Carruthers, Mary. *The Book of Memory: A Study of Memory in Medieval Culture.* Cambridge: Cambridge University Press, 1990.

Conley, Tom. *The Graphic Unconscious in Early Modern French Writing.* Cambridge: Cambridge University Press, 1992.

Havelock, Eric A. *The Muse Learns to Write: Reflections on Orality and Literacy from Antiquity to the Present.* New Haven, Conn., and London: Yale University Press, 1986.

Landow, George P. *Hypertext: The Convergence of Contemporary Critical Theory and Technology.* Baltimore and London: Johns Hopkins University Press, 1992.

Lewontin, R. C. *Biology as Ideology: The Doctrine of DNA.* New York: Harper Perennial, 1992.

Miller, J. Hillis. "Derrida's Topographies." *South Atlantic Review* 59 (1994): 1-25.

Nickerson, Jeff. "The Mind's Eye and the CRT Terminal: Towards a Diagrammatic Interface." *Visible Language* 19 (1985): 387-400.

Ong, Walter J. *Ramus, Method, and the Decay of Dialogue: From the Art of Discourse to the Art of Reason.* Cambridge, Mass.: Harvard University Press, 1958.

Owens, Craig. "The Allegorical Impulse: Toward a Theory of Postmodernism." *Art after Modernism: Rethinking Representation.* Ed. Brian Wallis. New York: New Museum of Contemporary Art, 1984. 203-235.

Rowland, Beryl. "The Art of Memory and the Bestiary." *Beasts and Birds of the Middle Ages: The Bestiary and Its Legacy.* Eds. Willene B. Clark and Meradith T. McMunn. Philadelphia: University of Philadelphia Press, 1989. 12-25.

Russell, Daniel S. *The Emblem and Device in France.* Lexington, Ky.: French Forum Publishers, 1985.

Smyth, Richard. "Genetis: A Rhizography." *Perforations* 5 (1994). Storyspace hypertext document.

——. "The Rhizography: Manifesto for Hypertext Composition." Proceedings from the Southern Humanities Conference. Forthcoming.

Ulmer, Gregory L. *Applied Grammatology: Post(e)-Pedagogy from Jacques Derrida to Joseph Beuys.* Baltimore and London: Johns Hopkins University Press, 1985.

——. "Grammatology (in the Stacks) of Hypermedia, a Simulation: or, When Does a Pile Become a Heap?" *Post Modern Culture,* 1, 2 (1991). Report in *Literacy Online.* Ed. Myron Tuman. Pittsburgh: University of Pittsburgh Press, 1992.

——. *Heuretics: The Logic of Invention.* Baltimore and London: Johns Hopkins University Press, 1994.

——. *Teletheory: Grammatology in the Age of Video.* New York and London: Routledge, 1989.

Wood, William B., et al. *Biochemistry: A Problem Approach.* Media Park, Calif.: W. A.
    Benjamin, 1974.
Yates, Frances A. *The Art of Memory.* Chicago: University of Chicago Press, 1966.

PART III

INITIATIVES FOR PROMOTING GRANT WRITING

15

Developing and Supporting Faculty Grant Success: Building Research Capacity at Medium-Size Colleges and Universities

Sandra Featherman

Increasing successful external grants activity at colleges and universities becomes more difficult for a number of reasons. Competition for federal funds from agencies such as the National Science Foundation (NSF) and the National Institutes on Health (NIH) is growing. Both privately and publicly funded institutions, which have faced serious budget constraints over the last several years, have sought to enhance budget flexibility by adding externally generated grant dollars. Grant requests from private-sector funders such as foundations compete with requests by civic and charitable organizations to fill gaps in budgets caused by governmental cuts in social welfare funding.

Colleges and universities whose external funding for research will grow in such difficult times will be those that carefully plan and improve their programs and grants-generating activities in effective and synergistic ways. While the major elements leading to grant success will continue to be the quality of proposals and the reputation and performance of individual principal investigators, institutions can take a number of steps that can help to increase the grants-achieving effectiveness of their given configuration of faculty and staff. Some of the effective ways that will be explored to increase sponsored research include sharpening institutional focus, investing in grants-generating activities, building appropriate departments and programs with requisite faculty strengths, linking internal resource allocation to planning and outcomes, building more collaborative research efforts, promoting cross-disciplinary projects, building effective outreach, and enhancing research capacity overall.

OVERVIEW

Universities have sought external funds to support or enhance their research enterprises for many reasons. One major reason involves institutional reputation. The amount and type of federal research support provided to universities constitutes an important external verification of both the quality of work produced at an institution and the presence of faculty on the research cutting edge, particularly where peer-reviewed projects are awarded by such agencies as the NSF or the NIH.

Prestige in the academy is awarded largely on the basis of two factors: the selectivity of the student body, and the scholarly reputations of the faculty as generally demonstrated by their publication and grants activities. For selective liberal arts colleges, low student-to-faculty ratios are another frequently accepted measure of quality. For universities, the prize status is to be designated a Research "A" university. According to the Carnegie Foundation modified ranking system, a Research University "A" provides a full range of baccalaureate programs, awards at least fifty Ph.D. degrees each year, and received at least $90 million in research support in 1990–1991. A Research "B" University met the same standards, except that the total support for research in 1990–1991 was less than $90 million.[1]

Another benefit of external research grants is that grants dollars may provide support for graduate students to work on the projects, allowing institutions to offer aid packages that can attract high-quality students. In addition, government programs that fund research generally cover not just direct costs but institutional indirect costs as well. The indirect costs that universities may add to the direct costs of projects are set by the federal government for each institution, based on the share of a university's overhead which supports its research mission. This is the institutional cost recovery (ICR) rate.

The ICR-generated dollars attached to grants are intended to reimburse universities for the indirect costs of supporting their research environment infrastructures. Indirect cost recovery allows institutions that are successful in gaining grants to use the indirect recovery dollars to help maintain and enhance parts of the research enterprise such as libraries, laboratories, and grant management offices. At the same time, the ICR funds brought in by grants may also provide budget flexibility for institutions, which might not otherwise by available. The ICR dollars may provide for journal subscriptions, graduate student aid, equipment setup costs for new faculty, and other expenditures that can help enhance institutional research infrastructure and performance.

As budgets have tightened across the academy, colleges and universities have increasingly sought external research grants as a budget enhancer. Costs of higher education have risen faster than inflation over the last two decades. Higher education is not, by and large, an efficiency-improving sector. Unlike industry, higher education has not been able to make productivity gains through better engineering. We do not value larger classes as better classes, any more than we accept the playing of a composition for a quartet by a trio as an efficiency improvement. Higher education is human resource intensive, and people are expensive.

Recently, some academic institutions have attempted to achieve efficiencies through process improvement techniques, such as continuous quality improvement (CQI).[2] Mostly, however, efforts to meet expanding needs and tight budgets have turned outward, looking at research dollar potential as one of the possible palliatives. Generating research awards requires investment in a research support infrastructure, however, the costs of which will be addressed later.

RESEARCH ACTIVITY NATIONALLY: WHO GETS THE DOLLARS

University and college expenditures for research have increased dramatically over the last four decades. In 1953, for example, universities spent $255 million on research and development in science and engineering. By 1993, expenditures had grown to nearly $19 billion.[3] Federal support, which provided 59 percent of the funds for university research in 1992, has also grown steadily over the last four decades. In 1953, the federal government spent $138 million on research and development at colleges and universities. By 1992, this sum had increased more than 8000 percent, to more than $11 billion.[4] Other major funders are state and local government and industry.

Of these federal research dollars, 84 percent were awarded to projects at 100 universities and colleges. In fact, 48 percent of the federal support went to just thirty universities; ten of those thirty were responsible for nearly a quarter of the federal obligations for university research and development in 1992.[5] One university, Johns Hopkins, accounted for 6 percent of all federally financed research expenditures.[6]

With such substantial sums of money available, it is not surprising that universities sometimes compete aggressively for the researchers who can generate federal and other research dollars for their projects. Grants success has become one of the criteria by which faculty are assessed. Persons hired on research lines, rather than as faculty, generally must support their positions through the grants they bring in.

A number of universities have become known as "wannabes." These are institutions that aspire to be major research centers, but have not quite made it into the Research "A" category or the top fifty universities in either federal or total external grants dollars generation. This second tier of research institutions is growing in its share of total research expenditures. A recent study of academic research growth and dispersion by Irwin Feller and Roger Geiger found that "dispersion is evident in the loss of research share by the largest or most highly rated performers and gains by mid-level, smaller, or less distinguished institutions" (1993, 6). While all but three of the 200 top-ranked university research performers in 1979–1980 experienced growth in research expenditures over the decade of the 1980s, the decline in share of the largest ten performers from 20.2

to 17.9 percent represented "a shift of funding to other institutions of approximately $368 million in end-year current dollars" (8).

The study also pointed out that during the 1980s the federal proportion of support "declined from 67.3 to 58.8 percent, the industry proportion rose from 3.8 to 6.7 percent, and research costs supported by the universities' own funds increased from 13.7 to 18.7 percent" (7).

INSTITUTIONAL ANALYSIS OF POSITIONING

In order to increase or even maintain a particular level of institutional grants activity, it is useful to analyze an institution's strengths and challenges. Institutional self-studies enable issues to be framed and funding trends to be examined. In addition, a self-study can focus on specific problems confronting the institution, at a given time.

Recently, the University of Minnesota completed a study focused on maintaining and enhancing its relative position.[7] Temple University took a different approach in its study, which explored various models of growth, to answer the question posed by the university's president, "Whither research at Temple University?" (Liacouras, 1989, 3). In the case of the University of Minnesota, the study was spurred by the realization that, despite the university's historical successes, "there is evidence that we will not be able to maintain our high status without decisive action in response to trends at both the national and state levels" (*Enhancing Research*, 1994, 1). The university, which ranked sixth nationally in total research expenditures in 1992 and sixth among universities in patents on new discoveries, has begun to recognize that its present position will be difficult to maintain and that it was experiencing a slight decline in relative position as well as in total awards dollars.[8] In fact, in 1991, the University of Minnesota had ranked third in total research expenditures.[9] In addition, the university had been hit with several investigations over alleged conflicts of interest and grants mismanagement by principal investigators. There were other concerns, too, about potentially eroding the quality of graduate programs as a result of cutbacks in the level of state support for the university. In 1993, the University of Minnesota had nearly $219 million in sponsored research expenditures, $171 million which was from federal monies.[10]

Vice president for research Anne Petersen set up a Strategic Planning Committee for Research and Postbaccalaureate Education. The committee decided to adopt a SWOT approach to its planning task, assessing strengths (S) and weaknesses (W) in the internal environment, and opportunities (O) and threats (T) in the external environment.[11] The committee set forth a vision for the university to "achieve national and international eminence as one of the top ten research universities" (*Enhancing Research*, 1994, 3).

The committee proposed four strategic activities: evaluate quality, develop the faculty, implement strategic initiatives, and communicate the significance of contributions to society by faculty and students. All postbaccalaureate programs and academic units should develop qualitative and quantitative indicators of performance, with results used to guide planning. Procedures should be implemented to assist departments with improving faculty quality, including recognition programs. Strategic initiatives to be undertaken include improving funding mechanisms for postbaccalaureate students, fostering interdisciplinary research, and promoting external collaborations that share information with industry, government, and other universities in the Upper Midwest.

Temple University explored its research potential in 1989. The provost, Barbara L. Brownstein, pointed out that Temple, a "major urban senior comprehensive public research university," was not receiving the same level of federal research and development funding as the leading research universities, or its own peers in Pennsylvania, nor was it keeping pace with "rapidly-developing research universities" (1989, A2). Temple's fear was that it wasn't where it needed to be and was in danger of falling even further behind.

One reason stated for the need to expand the research efforts was that for Temple to continue to assure that its diverse student body obtained full opportunities, the institution needed to provide opportunities for high-quality graduate and professional education taught by "a faculty of thinkers, creators, inventors and doers" (A3). A second reason given was that the university, in its competition for faculty, needed to remain an attractive option for scholars. Third, "while the cost of building a top research university will be great, ultimate financial position and budgetary flexibility must rely on external funding" (A3). Another reason was that the ability to attract major gifts was seen as frequently depending on recognition as a major research university.

Temple's provost offered three models for discussion and examined the resource investments that would be required for each. Model I involved continuing along the present path, but doing it a little better. An opposite approach was argued in Model II, becoming one of the top twenty research universities. A compromise position, Model III, proposed targeted growth, moving Temple from ninetieth to seventieth in grants funding within five years, and to fiftieth within ten years.

The draft document explored what it would take to dramatically increase research productivity. Increased faculty strength would be needed to enlarge small departments, particularly in the bench sciences, where much of the research dollars are generated. Other substantial investments would need to be made in substantially increasing graduate assistantships, finding space for the new researchers (estimated at 1,000 square feet per new faculty member), providing new core research facilities, instrumentation, equipment, and library research materials.[12]

None of the models was ever adopted. The price tags on Models II and III were prohibitive for Temple, particularly in the face of political demands in Pennsylvania for an emphasis on undergraduate programs and teaching. Temple continued what it was doing but fell out of the top 100, much as had been predicted. Nonetheless, it dramatically increased its external dollars for research from 1987–1988 to 1992–1993, according to its associate vice president for research. In 1987–1988, the year before the study draft was circulated, Temple brought in nearly $34 million in external funds for research. By 1992–1993, it brought in $57 million.[13]

PLANNING FOR GROWTH IN EXTERNAL GRANTS

Three basic approaches may be used to increase grants activities intentionally. The first strategy is to take advantage of opportunity by investing in individual researchers with promise who are already on campus. A second strategy is to lure researchers with established reputations and funding. The third way is to build capacity across an institution, by increasing support for graduate assistants and by gaining agreement that research activity will be an increasingly important factor in tenure and promotion decisions and that open faculty lines will be used to attract faculty with research potential.

In one version of this model, institutional support can be provided across all departments and programs. In another version, investment and emphasis areas are targeted by analyzing the institution, agreeing on its strengths and areas of potential growth, and focusing on those areas to build capacity.

The first strategy allows institutions to move into research growth without any extraordinary effort, by capitalizing on potential that already exists within the institution. This may occur when researchers become more entrepreneurial and approach their deans or provosts with proposals asking for support for new centers or institutes, or other investments in their research.

The second approach, luring a successful investigator from another campus, offers universities a fast track to an established funding stream and recognized area of capability. The up side is that the operation can start immediately, that it brings a reputation with it, and that it can frequently grow, with appropriate internal investments. The down side is that many universities have made large investments to bring an established research star onto campus, only to find the person being lured away by yet another institution, leaving a sunk investment in an infrastructure that may have been specifically developed for that star. One example of this occurred in a large eastern university that lured a scientist by promising him a substantial part of a large research building. Several years into the remodeling of this older facility, the star left for a third university, which custom designed a new facility for him.

The third strategy, a general enhancement of capacity, offers the greatest potential for success, particularly for small to midsized institutions, for colleges and universities changing their mission from a teaching emphasis to a richer mix of teaching and research, and for larger institutions seeking major growth in funded research.

As institutions and academic leaders have discovered, increasing sponsored research activity generally requires internal commitments first. Policies need to be in place to reduce teaching loads and to enable salary and merit awards for grants-productive faculty. Faculty development opportunities must also be available in order to help prospective principal investigators learn how to develop successful grant applications.

John Mishler, who has written several articles on increasing sponsored research at small and midsized colleges and universities, stresses that institutions must set clear long-term goals about their expectations for growth in external research funding.[14] In addition, he states that central offices must provide a pool of graduate research assistantships, adequate laboratory space, state-of-the-art equipment, monies to implement grant programs, and support from nonacademic units, such as computing. Colleges and universities must also develop research administration offices and venture capital funds.[15]

All of these approaches are clearly desirable and frequently necessary in expanding external research funds. Just how important they are has been attested to by Gerald Stahler and William Tash, in their study of factors predicting success at the fastest growing research universities.[16] Their interviews of chief research administrators at those fastest growing research universities suggest that among the most significant perceived factors in generating growth are having presidents, provosts, deans, and department chairpersons setting research as a high priority.

Other important factors include hiring new research faculty in selected fields, supplying new research space, providing rewards for productive researchers, such as release time, tenure, and promotion, and giving appropriate start-up support to new faculty.[17]

All of these cost a lot of money. Generating new dollars externally requires investing internal funds up front, as lots of colleges and universities have discovered.

PRIORITIZING AND TARGETING INVESTMENT

Because it costs a lot to increase the level of research grants at a university, some thought needs to be given to the appropriate level of investment and the anticipated payoff. Temple University's planning model for a move into the top twenty research institutions was estimated to require an investment of at least $185 to $215 million, much of it in recurring costs, with an additional cost of $1 to $2 million just for staying in place.[18] Targeted investment can help keep costs more manageable.

At the University of Minnesota, Duluth (UMD), a long-term plan, Vision 2000, was developed through a broadly participatory planning process. A campuswide committee, that worked on the plan for several years, received input from the entire campus, through circulating drafts, holding hearings, and getting feedback from units. After the Campus Assembly approved the overall plan, academic and noncollegiate units developed unit plans.

A working group of senior administrators then sought to cull from the unit plans a set of several strategic priorities for the campus, based on mission, strengths, and opportunities. Some conflict initially developed over the particular priorities selected (or more likely because so few were selected), because, as members of the Campus Planning Committee pointed out, people realized that they now had to pay attention to plans and priorities, since funding decisions were being tied to planning. The conflict was resolved by sending the proposals back to the Committee for some modifications.

One of the two academic areas stressed as a priority was fresh-water research. At UMD, there already was a very successful Center for Water and Environment which was part of the Natural Resources Research Institute (NRRI). NRRI provides applied research on the environment, technology enhancement, and economic development. The Institute has grown substantially since its formation less than a decade ago, and it now brings in more than $6 million a year in federal-, state-, and industry-supported research funds.

In addition to the NRRI, many faculty in biology, chemistry, geology, chemical engineering, and medical school departments bring in fresh-water-related federally funded research grants. Furthermore, UMD enjoys a good working relationship with the EPA Fresh Water Laboratory in Duluth.

UMD was originally a teachers college. It became part of the University of Minnesota in 1948, and over the last two decades it has become increasingly research oriented. It is now considered the second research university in Minnesota (although it is clearly overshadowed by the Twin Cities campus, which was sixth in the nation in research expenditures in fiscal year 1992, with $317 million).[19]

Over the last three years, the Office of the Vice Chancellor for Academic Affairs has sought to convince University of Minnesota system officers of the appropriateness of building a focus on fresh-water research at UMD. Two key opportunities for expansion existed. First, a legislative committee had given the system a $400,000 grant, spread out over two years, to develop a research institute focused on Lake Superior, with the expectation that the system would then provide ongoing funds. Several years of budget cuts had reduced the system's enthusiasm for the project, however. Concurrently, an effort was made to relocate the Minnesota Sea Grant offices (part of the national Sea Grant Program) from the Twin Cities campus to the Duluth campus. A political battle opposing the move was waged by some of the Twin Cities faculty, alleging that the UMD research enterprise was not developed enough to support Sea Grant.

For UMD, the sharp focus on water research as an area of targeted strength paid off. UMD demonstrated how much strength it already had in water research and its geographic accessibility to Lake Superior. One of its strongest departments, geology, committed itself to a focus on hydrogeology, and the Office of the Vice Chancellor committed itself to providing one-third of the operating costs for the new institute, as well as four faculty positions in addition to the director.

The Regents of the University voted to relocate Sea Grant at UMD. Several months later, the president of the university as well as two vice presidents agreed to support the new institute, the Large Lakes Observatory, by providing several additional faculty positions, operating dollars, and start-up funds. An internationally recognized scholar who had taught at UMD earlier in his career was hired as director. He is bringing large grants with him.

The Duluth campus now has a critical mass of outstanding researchers specializing in fresh-water research, with six more to be hired by the Large Lakes Observatory over the next few years. The reinforcing presence of several highly focused water projects should help each of the three water-related centers and institutes at UMD attract additional grants. Top faculty and researchers should also be attracted to UMD, in water-related disciplines. We already have begun international research efforts with Canadian, Russian, Chinese, and now African large-lake researchers. We expect both our reputation and our external funding in this area to grow.

Another effort to enhance funded research at UMD involved investing in training and grants support activities. The university system has a grants officer working on the UMD campus. Although he and his assistant provide high-quality service in the processing of grants, they lack the time to generate much grants activity. To do this, the vice chancellor's office hired a half-time grants developer to work with faculty and deans, particularly with faculty who have little grants experience and who are engaged in cross-disciplinary projects. Several million dollars in new grants are presently pending as a result of this investment.

In addition, the grants-writing specialist, along with the grants officer and the associate vice chancellor, presented a series of workshops on grant writing, open to all staff. These were very well attended. The four workshops offered in 1993–1994 covered university policies and procedures on externally funded projects, proposal writing and budget preparation, tips from successful researchers, and a discussion by representatives of funding agencies about their criteria for funding.

Funded research has been increasing at UMD. We have experienced dramatic growth over the last decade and in just the last four years have doubled the overhead recovery dollars we generate. We cannot invest everywhere, however. In fact, there were formidable pressures against any investments, for UMD took

2 to 3 percent retrenchments in each of the last four budget years. Nonetheless, even in the worst of times, it is important to set priorities and move forward. Targeted investment, in areas of strength and opportunity, make sense under such scenarios.

At UMD this has been done by developing a sharp focus on areas of specialization, capitalizing on areas of strength, linking resources to planning priorities, and building collaborative efforts. We have invested in grants-generating activities and in the general enhancement of our research capacity. We have increased our external funding, and external reviewers tell us that we have the potential to further enhance several already strong departments as research-productive new faculty join our staff.

NOTES

1. *State Profiles: Financing Public Higher Education, 1978 to 1993* (Washington, D.C.: Research Associates of Washington, 1993), 247. (As of April 1994, the standards for research university designation have been changed.)

2. Sandra Featherman and Valerie Broughton, "Allocating Faculty Lines with CQI," *Continuous Quality Improvement: Making the Transition to Higher Education*, ed. Dean L. Hubbard (Maryville, Mo.: Prescott Publishing, 1993).

3. "R&D Expenditures at Universities and Colleges by Source of Funds: Fiscal Years 1953–91," *Selected Data on Academic Science and Engineering R & D Expenditures: Fiscal Year 1992* (Washington, D.C.: NSF 94–303, 1994), 5.

4. *Selected Data*, "R&D Expenditures at Universities and Colleges, by Source of Funds and Science and Engineering Field: Fiscal Years 1985–91," 6.

5. *Selected Data*, "Table 12. Federally Financed R&D Expenditures at Universities and Colleges: Fiscal Years 1985–92," 17.

6. Ibid.

7. Report of the Strategic Planning Committee for Research and Postbaccalaureate Education, Office of the Vice President for Research and Dean of the Graduate School, *Enhancing Research Effectiveness: The Foundation for Learning and Teaching in the 21st Century* (Minneapolis: University of Minnesota, 1994).

8. Office of Research and Technology Transfer, *Levels and Trends in Sponsored Programs* (Minneapolis: University of Minnesota, 1994), 29.

9. "Fact File: Top 100 Institutions in Total Research–and–Development Spending, Fiscal Year 1991," *The Chronicle of Higher Education*, December 9, 1992.

10. *Levels and Trends in Sponsored Programs*, Appendix, 31.

11. John Bryson, "Strategic Planning for Public Institutions," unpublished outline (University of Minnesota, 1992).

12. Barbara L. Brownstein, *Research at Temple University: How Much Further to Invest: Three Models for the Future* (Philadelphia: Temple University, 1989), A5.

13. William Tash, Associate Vice President for Research, telephone conversation (Temple University, March 10, 1994).

14. John H. Mishler, "Enhancing the Prospects for Acquisition of Sponsored Funds at Small to Mid-Level Colleges and Universities: A Guide for Program Development," *Research Management Review* 2 (1988): 17–31.

15. Ibid., 19.

16. Gerald J. Stahler and William R. Tash, "Success in External Funding at the Fastest Growing Research Universities: Contributory Factors and Impediments," *Research Management Review* Vol. 6, 1 (Spring 1992): 14–24.

17. Ibid., 1, 5.

18. Brownstein, *Research at Temple University.* A5, A6.

19. *Selected Data on Academic R&D Expenditures*, NSF 94–303, 15.

REFERENCES

Brownstein, Barbara L. *Research at Temple University: How Much Further to Invest: Three Models for the Future.* Philadelphia: Temple University, 1989. A2, A3.

"Executive Summary." *Enhancing Research Effectiveness: The Foundation for Learning and Teaching in the 21st Century.* Report of the Strategic Planning Committee for Research and Postbaccalaureate Education. Minneapolis: University of Minnesota, 1994. ES1–3.

Feller, Irwin, and Roger Geiger. "The Dispersion of Academic Research during the 1980's: A Report to the Andrew W. Mellon Foundation." Institute for Policy Research and Evaluation, Graduate School of Public Policy and Administration: Pennsylvania State University, 1993. 6, 7, 8.

Liacouras, Peter J. "Cover Letter." In *Research at Temple University: How Much Further to Invest: Three Models for the Future.* Draft for discussion. Barbara L. Brownstein. Philadelphia: Temple University, 1989. 3.

16

Publishing, Proposing, and Progressing

W. A. Sibley

INTRODUCTION

It is commonly assumed that the role of a modern research university is to generate and disseminate knowledge. But it is also known that the purpose of any university is to educate students to compete at their highest level of ability after completing their prescribed programs of study. Graduates of our institutions must become productive members of society by obtaining meaningful positions from which they can contribute. For this to happen, a university must develop and maintain an outstanding reputation that will help graduating students compete for and obtain positions of merit, whether volunteer or paid. Universities can meet these obligations and opportunities only by maintaining a comprehensive program of scholarly creative activities and teaching. Research and teaching are essential parts of the fabric of the education cloth. It is very important for university administrators, from the president to the departmental chairperson, to be knowledgeable about and involved in the development of faculty careers by encouraging faculty to aspire to excellence in teaching and by helping faculty in publications and grantsmanship. This chapter provides an outline that promotes discussion of the interpenetration and need for creative activities and instruction as they pertain to faculty growth and progress.

NEW WINE AND OLD WINESKINS

Some observers believe that the university scene is changing with the demise of the Cold War and the advent of multiple communication possibilities.[1] Universities have done a magnificent job in accomplishing their mission over the last several decades. The United States possesses the best all-around graduate education programs in the world. The universities have supplied both undergraduates and graduates who have helped make this country the economic envy of the world. In addition, new ideas and technology have enabled the United States to remain strong and more advanced than most nations in military preparedness. The government has provided much needed funding to the institutions of higher learning for these benefits. Now times are changing, and the enthusiastic support of the population has waned as the funding for research based on military needs appears to be ebbing. The new information infrastructure, with the development of relatively inexpensive two-way interactive television learning, is putting pressure on some schools. How will the higher education institutions cope?

Lately, a common theme on many campuses is that the research expenditures at these institutions must double if they are to remain in the forefront. If this attitude prevails, great pressure will be placed on faculty, some of whom are already spending too much time away from undergraduate teaching, to do more research, more publishing, more proposing, and less teaching in the classroom. As pointed out earlier, this will not lead to progress in meeting the basic imperatives of the universities.

When the doubling of the research base of any university is contemplated, certain important elements must be considered. Table 16.1 illustrates the federally financed R&D expenditures at universities and colleges for the years 1987–1992.[2] It should be noted that the top forty schools expend 56 percent of all federally financed funds. There have not been many changes in the top forty over the past eight years. The dollars shown in the table are in thousands. Since the top twenty schools expend 38 percent of these available funds and are excellent research institutions, it is not likely, with federal research funds increasing more slowly in the next several years, that schools outside this group will make any inroads. Perhaps industrial support for research will be the answer for some schools.

In 1991, industry support in funding amounted to 12 percent compared with that of the United States government. Charles Larson of the Industrial Research Institute (IRI) reports that "Industrial R&D in the United States is a creative, productive enterprise, but aggregate funding is growing at an extremely slow pace. The pattern of funding and organization of industrial R&D is changing from corporate/centralized to business unit/decentralized, respectively, for many companies" (1994, 35). The future will bring a new situation and opportunity for many universities, but old attitudes about fundamental or basic research will have to change. If effective university/industry alliances are to be made, there will have to be a profit line somewhere in the equation. Figure 16.1, which illustrates the responses of 158 member companies of the IRI, is informative for future projections in this area.

As in the story of the blind men and the elephant, each person may view the situation in a somewhat different way. Nonetheless, most would state that education is in a new situation. Some things, however, will not change. It still will be necessary for universities to introduce students to state-of-the-art equipment in all fields from journalism to engineering if they are to provide the

Table 16.1
Federally Financed R&D Expenditures at Universities. (Dollars in thousands)

Institution Ranking	1992	1991	1990	1989	1988	1987
Total All Institutions	11,087,032	10,226,104	9,637,485	8,996,808	8,191,521	7,341,570
1. Johns Hopkins University	666,696	641,239	599,851	590,184	509,009	476,290
2. Stanford University	265,687	243,219	255,821	238,650	232,572	204,386
3. University of Washington	257,840	221,124	203,353	182,453	160,261	145,184
4. Mass. Inst. of Technology	237,972	237,667	233,813	215,140	210,419	206,785
5. University of Michigan	223,452	206,276	180,456	174,875	160,854	137,558
6. Univ. of California, San Diego	219,843	200,451	182,555	171,479	159,778	142,751
7. Univ. of California, San Francisco	202,283	190,936	175,257	159,906	137,747	117,302
8. Univ. of Wisconsin, Madison	199,816	183,652	178,862	169,452	162,384	149,665
9. Univ. of California, Los Angeles	180,743	167,885	164,442	159,002	146,946	130,763
10. Cornell University	180,361	173,478	171,249	157,984	153,662	144,604
Total First 10 Institutions	2,634,693	2,465,927	2,345,659	2,219,125	2,033,632	1,855,288
11. Columbia University	174,777	163,651	156,270	146,712	139,558	133,018
12. Harvard University	174,632	156,014	154,090	143,451	133,003	119,955
13. University of Minnesota	165,926	164,887	143,810	132,880	119,789	109,003
14. University of Pennsylvania	159,574	144,451	133,747	123,810	115,080	111,185
15. Yale University	157,345	149,506	144,962	138,835	132,952	116,943
16. Pennsylvania State University	151,877	146,212	136,656	114,646	106,020	93,200
17. Univ. of California, Berkeley	148,954	140,261	131,717	123,371	116,565	108,828
18. Univ. of Southern California	141,713	132,230	123,714	119,005	112,615	101,749
19. University of Colorado	129,987	119,068	116,394	109,145	96,041	83,144
20. University of Illinois, Urbana	129,086	118,748	117,168	114,398	109,633	104,420
Total First 20 Institutions	4,168,471	3,900,865	3,704,187	3,486,378	3,214,888	2,936,733

Table 16.1, continued

Institution Ranking	1992	1991	1990	1989	1988	1987
21.Duke University	125,742	114,879	106,053	99,036	86,240	67,925
22.Univ. of Texas, Austin	124,614	113,192	109,593	94,311	89,982	88,395
23.Washington University	123,863	112,475	105,759	96,829	88,843	77,757
24.University of Pittsburgh	121,077	99,932	90,700	81,217	72,462	62,060
25.Univ. of North Carolina, Chapel Hill	113,774	103,485	92,468	93,280	82,723	72,529
26.Texas A&M University	112,918	97,727	93,001	93,584	90,163	75,432
27.University of Rochester	110,413	106,874	105,644	101,049	92,533	80,322
28.University of Arizona	105,912	101,818	92,920	80,533	73,309	65,024
29.Georgia Inst. of Technology	101,295	101,476	94,842	98,048	78,798	63,132
30.California Inst. of Technology	99,198	100,820	90,577	84,167	78,750	71,086
Total First 30 Institutions	5,307,277	4,953,543	4,685,744	4,408,432	4,048,691	3,660,395
31.Ohio State University	97,940	88,542	78,878	75,484	69,135	58,555
32.University of Chicago	97,182	93,683	96,327	90,459	80,967	75,889
33.Univ. of California, Davis	91,319	79,961	77,424	72,718	63,435	56,622
34.University of Iowa	88,360	81,007	79,046	74,271	64,370	57,159
35.New York University	87,081	81,896	80,756	81,143	77,746	76,126
36.Baylor College of Medicine	85,734	78,752	75,793	69,336	60,825	49,834
37.Case Western Reserve Univ.	83,387	76,390	70,515	68,632	59,078	53,580
38.Univ. of Maryland, College Park	82,469	77,866	66,410	58,924	55,365	55,194
39.University of Alabama, Birmingham	82,392	76,317	74,486	68,204	62,369	54,534
40.Vanderbilt University	79,594	71,021	66,747	56,151	44,646	31,343

Figure 16.1
R&D Trends Forecast: 1988–1993 (In % of Respondents)

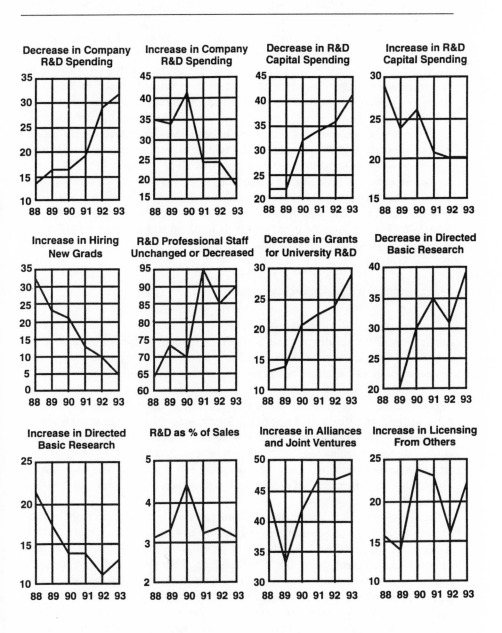

desired outstanding education. Faculty must continue to be up-to-date and share new ideas and information with the students. Facilities must be renovated and improved. It is not likely that the funds for all of these endeavors will come from tuition and state resources. University faculty will still have to compete for grants and contracts to ensure that these necessities are available. In the Christian literature, there is the story of putting new wine in old wineskins, with the ultimate loss of both the wine and the skins. As universities move into the new era, it will be necessary for administrators and faculty to develop new wineskins. For university faculty to compete at the level that will be required in the future, strong interdisciplinary teams must be formed and equipped. Administrators will have to select "niches" in which the school can compete with the very best and leave some areas uncovered. Faculty will have to be more applied in outlook and willing to work with others. This will require a new theme of cooperation. Schools may need to form a network that will allow students in a geographic region to obtain a broad-based education from several participating partner schools. Universities, national laboratories, and industry will have to form teams in a far more realistic way than in the past. The new wine will require new wineskins, but the ingredients of excellent teaching and creative activities that include publishing and proposing will remain the same.

PUBLISHING AND PROPOSING

One payoff for the creative activities of both faculty and students is the publication of the results of these activities. This allows the information to be used by others and promotes funding for future projects. Publication is important, but counting publications is not a measure of the quality of a faculty member. The essence of faculty activity is the development of new ideas and the dissemination of information that will help others. Since faculty come in all sizes, shapes, and forms, it is necessary for the leadership to assist each faculty member in facilitating the publication of results. This is done through the availability of modern technology, personal interaction, peer review and suggestions, and professional contacts. Administrators at all levels must seek to help faculty, especially young faculty, find the appropriate channels for the exposition of their results.

Grant writing is a different and difficult game. It is very important for most careers. Faculty must be excellent researchers if they are to stimulate creative thinking by students and keep abreast of new thrusts. In addition, faculty must be excellent researchers in order to compete for grants, and they must be effective communicators of good, innovative ideas. Even outstanding ideas must be presented with enthusiasm and clarity. Only through the attainment of external funds can faculty in some career disciplines make progress at a rate acceptable to their peers and thus gain tenure. Yet, the proposal award rates at most federal agencies are extremely low.[3] For example, at the National Science Foundation for the years 1988 to 1993, the funding rate in the Mathematical Sciences Division was about 42 percent. In 1993, action was taken on 1,680 proposals, with the number of awards being 684. In 1993, the Chemistry Division acted on 1,143 proposals with 425 funded, for an award rate of 37 percent. For the Division of Materials Research and for the Engineering Directorate the award rates for these years were in the range of 25 to 35 percent as illustrated in Table 16.2. Of course, the size of the awards varies greatly between the divisions, accounting for some of the differences in award rates. In Mathematical Sciences, for instance, the annualized median award is about $30,000, whereas for Materials Research it is $85,000. Nonetheless, it is evident that, when experienced researchers who have outstanding refunding records are considered, the award-winning rate for a new proposer is about 15 to 20 percent. This suggests that experienced administrators and faculty can be of great assistance to new faculty.

In addition to a local environment conducive to career development, a regional or national network of interacting individuals is becoming necessary in order to compete well. Multidisciplinary activities are important. As multidisciplinary research activities grow, the need to access people, facilities, and equipment on other campuses also increases. It has already been noted that the administration must make available state-of-the-art equipment and facilities and develop an environment of cooperative peers and mentors. These elements are necessary to help faculty achieve the goal of producing excellent proposals.

Table 16.2
NSF Proposal Success Rate

Unit	Fiscal Year							
	80	85	86	88	90	91	92	93
Mathematical Science	43%	48%	48%	44%	38%	44%	43%	41%
Chemistry	30%	36%	35%	27%	38%	40%	38%	37%
Materials Research	53%	36%	33%	26%	29%	39%	31%	32%
Engineering				23%	24%	28%	28%	22%

The present national proposal success rate of less than 40 percent means that a proposer can expect failure the first time or two. Persistence and technology are needed to succeed. Some of the characteristics of good proposals are portrayed in Figure 16.2.

Proposals should be on computer disks so that the reviewers' comments can be incorporated and the proposal returned rapidly to the agency for another review. At the University of Alabama at Birmingham, a computer disk is available to each faculty member on which all of the "boiler plate" information is listed for the university, such as the mainframe computer capability, library holdings, and special programs. This same proposal format is also available on the university-wide electronic bulletin board. A budget format is included with

Figure 16.2
The Characteristics of a Good Proposal

- The proposed activity is clearly established through the use of data and experience.
- Important ideas are highlighted and *repeated* in the abstract and the text.
- Objectives are provided in detail.
- A detailed schedule of project activities and a complete project schedule are included.
- Collaboration with all interested groups in the planning of the proposed project is evident in the proposal; joint publications with collaborators are noted.
- Project staff and consultants are known to have agreed to participate in the project: this is indicated in the proposal.
- All the directions given in the proposal guidelines have been followed carefully.
- The budget and proposal narrative are consistent; the budget explanations provide an adequate basis for the figures used in building the budget.
- Appendices are used for detailed and lengthy materials that the reviewers may not want to read but are useful as evidence of careful planning or previous experience.
- There is a clear statement of commitment to continue the project after external funding ends.
- Qualifications of project personnel are clearly communicated.
- Assessment, assessment, assessment.

---

the appropriate indirect costs and fringe benefit amounts. Faculty can use or delete this information and concentrate on the work they wish to present. Computer availability of the draft proposal allows the faculty member to insert comments from fellow faculty most effectively. This provides opportunity for an "in house" review by peers, the value of which cannot be overemphasized. It is important that "red flags" be found internally before the agencies start a review of the final proposal.

Proposals are so well prepared today and the competition is so keen that reviewers sometimes base ratings on negatives. For example, in an equipment proposal a reviewer might give great importance to the fact that the proposer understood the system well enough to obtain large discount prices on the equipment. It is a red flag if the proposer did not. The principal investigator needs a track record to illustrate that the requested funds will be well spent, since the work will be done on state-of-the-art equipment and with outstanding graduate students. However, young faculty must be encouraged to submit proposals while developing a track record. The reviewer comments are very helpful in providing insight and direction. The proposer needs to be persistent in contacting federal agency program directors. It is important that the person reviewing a proposal know the qualifications and capability of the proposer.

In the present peer review system, a program officer at a federal agency will generally have many more excellent reviews of proposals than can be funded. When this happens, the program officer must make the best decision possible concerning which institution can provide the best research value. For this reason, the proposer needs to communicate the capabilities that exist to accomplish the goals of the proposal with the program officer. In many cases, the decisions of program officers in the federal agencies are reviewed by an external audit team of peer reviewers. This implies that the program officer needs to know the proposer's capabilities and have a good feeling about the prospects of accomplishing the proposal goals. There is no doubt that program officers have a great workload. In addition to handling a large number of proposals, they must have knowledge of the field and a concept of what is needed for the future. In the mission-oriented agencies, the program officers must play a major role in establishing future research goals. Nevertheless, most of these individuals would like to talk to investigators on the telephone or in person, and every effort should be made to make contact.

PROGRESSING

Ultimately, a university is judged by its faculty, staff, and students. Therefore, faculty excellence and growth are of prime importance to the university. As Figure 16.3 illustrates, environment is important for faculty and university development. The constituents of this environment are the faculty, colleagues, cooperation between groups, good students, the technical staff, and the quality of facilities and equipment available for state-of-the-art performance. Because of funding constraints at many institutions, new faculty positions are scarce and career development requires even more attention. University administrators need to make sure their faculty are so good that they are receiving offers from other institutions, and they must provide such a productive and harmonious environment that the faculty want to stay. Interest in faculty growth through research and instruction must be shown at the highest level of the university. This interest must be demonstrated in a significant fashion and not just in talk. It is important that the faculty who participate in creative activities be given verbal and written encouragement. Awards also are an incentive to those who are successful, but it is more important that the infrastructure be provided for a productive environment. State-of-the-art communication, including electronic mail, electronic bulletin boards, and international connections, the latest state-of-the-art equipment, and good students are required for faculty career progress.

The president and vice president for academic affairs, or provost, must provide the academic leadership for progress. There must be clear communication that creative activities and instruction intermesh and that both are important. They must allocate resources to meet both infrastructure and faculty salary needs. Of course, there will be times when infrastructure purchases compete with faculty priorities such as salary increases. But the administration must keep in mind that without the appropriate instrumentation and facilities and the cooperative spirit

Figure 16.3
Environment for Faculty and University Development

that must exist between faculty and students, progress toward educational excellence is unlikely. Funds also must be available for faculty development seminars, for faculty opportunities to take advantage of sabbaticals, and for leaves without pay to enable faculty to achieve expertise in certain professional areas. The administration must encourage these types of activities, including consulting, at all levels.

A key player in faculty development is the department chair which must act as coach or team leader. Each faculty member is unique. In any particular year, one faculty member may need to teach more and another focus more on creative activities. The department chair must balance the departmental load and develop cooperation between faculty. There must be a clearly communicated plan for departmental development, and each faculty team member must be rewarded for his or her role. It is important that upper administration, when assessing performance, evaluate the unit and not just individuals. This allows the department chair to form a team that meets expected goals. Such goals should be established with administrative support and assist in achieving the goals of the university.

SUMMARY

As noted earlier, the growth of faculty and student expertise and capability must be comprehensive and compatible. In the fabric of faculty progress, many individual patterns can be woven, but the fabric itself is an appropriate mix of teaching and creative research activities. Students remain the reason for the universities' existence and the joy of most faculty. They must be exposed to the latest ideas and equipment. Most of all, students must have a feeling of accomplishment and pride. If a university is to meet the objectives of obtaining and maintaining an outstanding reputation and providing excellent education, it must meet these student and faculty needs.

In order to accomplish this goal the administration must

- Make faculty development a high priority
- Treasure student involvement
- Delineate expectations of the faculty clearly
- Reward good teaching and good research
- Build an infrastructure that supports faculty growth and assists with publication and proposal preparation
- Educate young faculty on the proposal game

In the latter case, a good proposal will include

- An executive summary or introduction that clearly highlights the need and objectives of the proposal
- A detailed schedule of activities and timelines
- Evidence of alliances and collaboration with others where applicable
- Attention to budget so that it clearly is related to the needs of the project
- Budget expenditures in the text as well as in the budget
- Evidence of assessment and continuation of the project even after the agency or foundation support ends
- A thorough in-house review to remove red flags

The future of higher education in this country is bright, but changes will take place. As competition for so-called research funds increases, each university must develop a strategic plan for the future. This plan must be disseminated to the faculty, and then every effort must be made to assist the faculty in achieving the goals of the plan.

NOTES

1. E. A. Lynton and S. E. Elman, "New Priorities for the University" (San Francisco: Jossey-Bass, 1987). A. W. Astin, "Achieving Educational Excellence" (San Francisco: Jossey-Bass, 1985). R. Gates, "Can Colleges be Reengineered?" *Across the Road* (New York, March 1994), 16.

2. *Selected Data on Academic Science and Engineering R&D Expenditures: Fiscal Year 1992* (Washington, D.C.: NSF 94-303, 1994), 5.

3. Private Communication: National Science Foundation, Washington, D.C., February 23, 1994.

REFERENCE

Larson, C. F. "R&D in Industry." *AAAS Report XIX: R&D FY 1995*. Washington, D.C.: AAAS, 1994.

17

Characteristics of Successful Institutional Grants

Robert A. Lucas

When academics think of proposals, they usually picture something like a National Science Foundation or a National Institutes of Health grant for basic research. Yet as much as a third of all grants awarded to colleges and universities across the country are not for research but for activities that are directly supportive of the instructional mission. These grants are for curriculum improvement, training activities, service, and facility development. Campuses use the awards to mount new majors and minors, to develop new courses and programs, to train their own students and other adult populations, to provide special services for both their students and the community at large, and to improve teaching facilities and laboratory equipment.

Instructional grants can be of two types: model and local. Model instructional grants are intended to create and test new ways of teaching that will be emulated nationally. Local grants are awards whose impact is felt primarily at the campus level. Their purpose is not to improve teaching in the discipline as a whole but rather the immediate teaching environment of a single campus. Local grants are often called institutional grants.

SIMILARITY BETWEEN MODEL GRANTS AND RESEARCH GRANTS

Like research grants, the goal of a model grant is to create new knowledge, in this case about pedagogy, that will have an impact on the discipline. The trickle-down theory of models states that change begins with a few proven experimental programs and spreads. One example is the TRIO programs of the U.S. Department of Education: Talent Search, Upward Bound, and Student Special Services. These programs began as pedagogical experiments which, once their worth was proven, were implemented through a series of replication grants now funded at hundreds of colleges and universities throughout the country.

Proposals for model grants require many of the same qualities that are necessary for success in a basic research grant application: established reputation, cutting-edge presence, and strong supportive institutional infrastructure. Because the model will function in a national context, grant makers prefer those who are in leadership positions in their disciplines to propose ideas. A successful proposal cannot be written by someone who does not know the trends in the discipline. Indeed, it is expected that the writer of the grant will be the person creating the trends. As a result, the halo effect counts. When sponsors weigh proposals for model grants of substantially equal merit, they favor those from high-profile institutions rather than those from regional or comprehensive universities.

The good news is that because sponsors want to solve a pedagogical problem for the discipline as a whole rather than just for the local campus, they will pay for all the costs of developing and testing the model, and for disseminating results. Model grant budgets are regularly three to four times the size of institutional grant budgets, and cost-sharing requirements, the bane of the institutional proposal, are minimal.[1]

REQUIREMENTS FOR SUCCESSFUL INSTITUTIONAL GRANTS

If you're going to write a proposal to improve the instructional program and haven't written one before, avoid starting with the model grant. The competition is too stiff for someone who has not done a lot of research and published on the topic previously.[2] Try writing an application for a program whose purpose is to improve the local institution. To be successful, you will need neither a national reputation nor a unique idea. Your main challenge will be to show that you have the competence to effect a greater improvement in instruction—say, teach more students better science—than similar campuses can with a similar size grant and similar institutional needs. Also, once your grant is completed, you will not have to demonstrate, as you will in a model grant, that your innovative system has been incorporated into teaching practices across the country. Rather, your primary responsibility will be to prove that you have met your campus goals in terms of the number of students recruited, served, retained, and graduated.

The following often characterizes successful institutional proposals: (1) the problem is significant at the campus level and recognized as such; (2) the proposed activity is an improvement over local practice; (3) the potential impact on the host institution is well documented; (4) the evidence of broad involvement in planning is clear; (5) the likelihood of success is strong; (6) the plans for institutionalizing the finished grant are plausible; and (7) cost sharing by the campus is significant.

Who funds institutional grants? The National Science Foundation and state councils for the humanities have some programs and local foundations and corporate foundations have others.[3] Even friends of the university support projects by making gifts through the alumni or development office. For example, one faculty member whose proposal to the Fund for the Improvement of Post Secondary Education (FIPSE) was turned down because it was not innovative enough, took it to the development office on her campus. A staff member there wrote letters on her behalf to several alumni describing the proposal to improve student writing. Three alumni made gifts of $75,000 each, giving the project director over $200,000 to fund the first eighteen months of her program.

What kind of local needs will agencies support? Sponsors look for new initiatives rather than requests to pick up continuing expenses for ongoing programs. It often helps if the idea is novel in the region as well. The bias toward the new and untried can be frustrating since many campuses have a serious and enduring need for core programs such as professional development and equipment, which are often neglected by the state or university endowment. Fortunately, the situation is not totally hopeless. The *Directory of Operating Grants* chronicles 640 foundations that will accept proposals for operating grants.[4]

To get a feel for the differences between model and institutional grants, it will be useful to consider two examples.

Model Grant Case Study: Uri Treisman

A program developed by Uri Treisman at the University of California, Berkeley, makes a good case study. It has the key elements of a model grant: FIPSE funded a person with a national reputation to develop and validate a major new model for mathematics instruction which was later widely disseminated.[5]

In the late 1970s, Treisman discovered that African Americans and Hispanics who were failing freshman calculus learned better when they studied in groups, a practice that most successful Anglo students followed. This information led him to propose a new model for a mathematics workshop. In it, whenever students asked teaching assistants questions, they were not given answers. Rather, their questions were consciously fed back to them, forcing them to look to each other as learning resources. That simple practice promoted active learning among the students and increased their comprehension significantly.

The results were astonishing. Fifty-six percent of blacks and Hispanics who studied in small groups earned a B- or better in calculus as opposed to 21 percent of those who continued to study alone or who worked only with tutors. Only 3 percent of those in the experimental group dropped calculus, compared to 25 percent in the control group, and more than four times as many students in the mathematics workshop eventually pursued math-based majors. Treisman's study showed that when African Americans and Hispanics worked in small groups, they achieved remarkable progress without active tutoring or intervention.

FIPSE was so enthused about the results that it funded twenty projects to test this concept, to validate its success, and to extend its range of applicability to a variety of settings. These projects then served as patterns for replication in many regions throughout the country.[6]

Institutional Grant Case Study: Barbara London

An institutional proposal does not require the same kind of potential national impact as Uri Treisman's to be successful. A good example is a proposal written by Barbara London of San Diego State University.[7] Shortly after she became assistant dean for community development, London was assigned to write a proposal for a newly established China Institute. But she was not a China scholar; she had no experience writing proposals; and the deadline was only three weeks away. Her approach offers a handy guide to survival and illustrates that even under stressful circumstances, an academic without a leading reputation in the field can achieve success with an institutional grant proposal.

London began by thoroughly studying the guidelines for the International Program at the U.S. Department of Education. Then she called the program officer at the agency to ask for sample proposals to study. In addition to these, she received abstracts of all grants made by the program in the previous year. She read proposals for other grants the University had received in international education. Using some as models and others for grist, she interviewed widely on campus and began drafting.

The proposal was well grounded in the San Diego State experience. She described in detail the planning that led to the establishment of the institute; she reviewed the contributions of the two current China scholars; and she named professors in allied fields and outlined how some of their related courses would be modified through the grant. She explained why the local environment was a rich field in which to plant the seed. Most importantly, she described why even though the setting was perfect, the institute could not succeed—at least in a timely fashion—without the infusion of external dollars.

It is important not to underestimate this last task. The most difficult challenge in making a compelling case to your sponsor is to convince it that, even though you are good enough to receive a grant, you are not so good that you would succeed if you didn't receive the grant. Dr. London met this challenge head on. Her argument ran like this: faculty at her institution had a four-course teaching load each term; the general campus fund provided no resources for new course development; all new offerings had to be developed as an overload; and once a new course was taught, it took two years for new funding to show up in the general budget. Thus, if the campus did not receive a grant, it could easily take the institute three to four more years to become viable, and an important Pacific Rim university would lose valuable time preparing graduates to compete internationally. Her argument was successful and won her college a significant grant the first time around. Her experience demonstrates some basic grant strategies: (1) start by reading the guidelines carefully; (2) contact the sponsor's program officer; (3) seek clarification and learn the current interests of the sponsor; and (4) keep in touch with key people on campus and with the sponsor.

Your best guide to writing a proposal is, of course, the sponsor's guidelines. In the event the sponsor gives no directions for developing the narrative of an application, you can use the following format for an institutional grant request. It covers what you need to say in the introductory sections, the statement of approach, the description of resources, and the final sections, including budget and appendices.

COMPONENTS OF AN INSTITUTIONAL PROPOSAL

The Title Page

Besides title of the proposal, address of the applicant institution, and amount requested, the title page carries the signatures of the project director and the authorized institutional representative. For research proposals, the signature of the vice president for research or academic affairs is often *pro forma* because research projects are considered the personal property of the principal investigator. This is not the case for an institutional proposal. Here the signature means that the campus makes a commitment to carry on the project even if the project director leaves the campus. In other words, an institutional proposal carries an institutional commitment. As a result, local impact proposals are scrutinized more carefully than research proposals before they are submitted to the sponsor.

Abstract

The proposal begins with an abstract or executive summary. Use lay terms and complete the summary in about 250 words. The abstract summarizes the whole proposal, not just the significance of the activity to the campus. Many beginners make the mistake of lifting the first two paragraphs of their narrative for the abstract. The difficulty is that those paragraphs usually summarize only the need and significance of the project; they say nothing about the approach to be taken, which must be included in the abstract. Summarize the whole proposal, not just the introductory sections.

Even though the abstract does not receive a score on the rating sheet, the abstract makes a deep impression on the reviewer by being both his or her first, and often last, impression of the proposal. Don't slight it, no matter how tempting it might be to hurry through the final major writing task of your proposal.

The Introduction

The introduction begins with a clear statement of need and what it is you propose to do. It is important to document the need. For instance, a major proposal to a corporate sponsor for professional development will do more than simply state a need for travel funds because the institutional allocation is inadequate. Rather, the character of the request will flow persuasively from the statement of need and will address such questions as, Are all faculty in need of more contact with industry? Do some need opportunities or released time for research? Do others need to attend professional courses, seminars, or graduate work to complete a degree? Has a survey been done? How likely is it that, if offered, faculty will accept a year's assignment at a remote location? What industries have shown interest? Is there an advisory group? A steering group? A taskforce appointed by the provost? A systemwide report or context?

The more convincing the statement of need, the more likely it is you will find interested sponsors. They look for projects that will have a demonstrable impact in their area of funding priorities. Even so, don't overdo the need statement. There is a delicate balance between stating a need in a compelling fashion and sounding desperate. Few sponsors are interested in saving a sinking ship. Your need must convey a sense that although the situation is in need of attention, it is also remediable through the infusion of outside funds.

The Background

Even if your grant will have only local impact, don't limit your background statement to the local situation. Place your project in the context of what's happening nationally. What is known now, for instance, about the most effective configuration for professional development programs? Does the one you propose follow an established model, an innovative model, a promising model?

Once you have sketched the national context, describe the campus scene that led to your proposal. You should have plenty to cite here in terms of what the campus taskforce did with surveys they conducted and the reviews of practices that isolated problems. If you have nothing to say here but rather have planned to spend the grant for this part of your project, your proposal stands a poor chance of funding. Sponsors expect you to know exactly what you need to do to be successful. Many use this section to gauge how well their grant will be spent. Poor planning leads to poor implementation, and conversely, careful preparation augurs a well-run project. If you haven't planned carefully, you will probably lose out to an aggressive competitor who has done a meticulous job of it.

Objectives

This is where the vague goals of the proposal—say, to improve professional development opportunities for faculty—become clarified in specific objectives. The best way to convince your reviewers that your goals are achievable is to reduce them to manageable activities by quantifying them and placing them in a time frame. For instance, to achieve the ultimate goal of broadening the base of experience for science faculty, one objective might be to place a total of five faculty members from the school of science and mathematics in industry for a six-month period over the next three years.

Objectives such as that give reviewers a picture to consider and a base for comparison. Reviewers either implicitly or explicitly compare proposals with one another for extent of impact per dollar spent. Given equally strong proposals, the one with the greater impact in terms of population served will get the nod. If they cannot calculate the impact because they have no quantitative data, reviewers will likely ignore the whole proposal. Therefore, resist the temptation to be vague so that you can't be pinned down to a specific program of action later. Reviewers want specificity, and they will read proposals until they find it.

Program Methodology

The section on methods or procedures is the heart of the proposal. It describes how the elements of the project fit together to achieve success. If you are proposing a comprehensive professional development program for your department, interdisciplinary group, or school, for instance, you should explain the plan here.

Beginning proposal writers often resist going into detail about procedures because it requires a great deal of effort. The evidence is abundant, however, that vague methodologies don't generate enthusiasm among reviewers. The most frequently quoted reason for rejecting proposals is not that the idea is unattractive, but that the approach or method is inadequate or faulty.[8] One expert proposal writer and reviewer goes so far as to recommend that you spend two-thirds of your writing time on the methods section.[9]

Start by making sure your objectives are specific. Then approach each objective as a task and generate a timetable for the steps you will take to accomplish the task. As you define objectives in time, you will notice that it's a lot easier to itemize the resources you will need to reach your objectives. This in turn will help you simplify the task of developing an adequate budget.

Thus, if you're proposing a new course or program, give ample information about your proposed design. List the courses to be offered, the interrelationship of parts, and the program leading to certification or a degree. Discuss where the student or participants will come from and how they will be selected. Detail plans for faculty orientation retreats, negotiations with cooperating institutions and companies, and release time for developing laboratory experiments.

Don't pad the section by reprinting material from past courses or programs. Such things belong in the appendixes. Concentrate here on the material for the new initiative. If after a few paragraphs you find yourself without much to say, you're probably not far enough along to write a full proposal yet. You need to do more work before you can continue writing. Sponsors expect this section to be right when you send the proposal in. Sponsors may call you to negotiate your budget before they make an award, but they never give you a chance to fine-tune your program description. They're more inclined to say the project fell outside their priorities, or there were too many worthy projects and too few funds, than to wait for you to get it right.

The methods section is a key element in your proposal because it serves several important purposes: (1) it convinces the sponsor of the soundness of your design; (2) it demonstrates that your goals and objectives are achievable; (3) it explains to others in your department, group, or school how your project will work; and (4) it serves as an internal contract after you receive a grant about how the money will be spent. Since success draws attention, people whom you could not interest in the planning stage will suddenly become intensely engaged in helping you spend your money once you get your grant. When this happens, you will be grateful that you can point to an explicit approach in the proposal and remind the meddler that this is the plan the sponsor bought.

Evaluation

For a research grant, evaluation is straightforward; if you publish the results in a refereed journal, the project is a success. The case for evaluation in an institutional grant is not so simple.

All proposals for instructional awards must have an evaluation section, and it must be explicit. Despite the fact that most writers of institutional grants spend their daily lives teaching and improving curriculum, few are skilled in evaluating its impact. But evaluation is a necessary component of a proposal. FIPSE is so insistent about its importance that it makes a three-page bibliography available to proposal writers on how to go about doing it.[10]

If you don't know the difference between formative and summative evaluation, contact a colleague in the school of education and ask him or her to serve as a consultant in the planning and evaluation stages of your project. Look for someone who respects the fact that you have limited time at the conclusion of the project to determine its impact. If his or her design stretches into a longitudinal study that will follow the subjects into their retirement, engage someone else to help.[11]

Institutional Commitment

Of special importance in instructional programs is the section on institutional commitment. Here you detail agreements that your own department, related departments, and cooperating units have made to support the project while the grant is being run. The sponsor needs to be assured that its funds will not be wasted on a campus that has jumped at a funding opportunity without reflecting soberly on its responsibilities to assure success of the venture. It is essential that you can satisfy the curiosity of the reviewers by describing the steps taken to involve the academic leadership in your program. These administrators should document that commitment in letters, which you will reproduce in the appendix.

Future Funding

In this section you discuss plans for picking up any continuing costs once funding has expired. These costs typically include maintenance agreements for significant equipment purchases and salaries for new hires. Your plans must be explicit. A simple sentence stating that following conclusion of the grant you will seek further funding from local foundations will leave your sponsor cold.[12] Agreements to continue the program after termination of funding should be noted, with clear indications about how personnel and resources will be funded. This is no place to taper off into vague statements. Describe your plans for cost sharing explicitly.

The ideal project is one that can be continued without incremental funding other than that which additional user fees (e.g., tuition) provide. Grant-makers particularly like grants that examine current practice, take it apart, keep what works, reenergize what doesn't, and reassemble the parts in a renewed form.

Institutional Resources

Here you concentrate on a review of resources that were not introduced in earlier sections. For instance, if the request is for a new educational program, you will describe departmental resources, the computer center, the library, special collections and archives, research facilities, local environmental characteristics, and other relevant facilities whose descriptions were not appropriate to the methodology section. Copies of related curricula should be kept for the appendix.

Personnel

The section on personnel contains a written summary of key people and two-to three-page resumes for each. If running the project will involve complex administration, describe in greater detail the organization that may have only been alluded to in the procedures section. The resumes of the project director and colleagues will demonstrate their ability to perform the work proposed.

For research and model curriculum proposals, the principal investigators must have a national reputation. In a local impact proposal, however, national recognition is less important. Here, campus experience and past service count. But if once you've listed your qualifications, you wish your resume to appear stronger, you can enhance the appeal of the proposal by engaging better qualified colleagues from campus or elsewhere to serve on an advisory committee and by inserting their resumes in the appendix.

Budget

Budgeting an instructional proposal involves most of the same considerations that budgeting a research proposal does.[13] A budget is a restatement in monetary terms of what has already been covered in the description of procedures. If your explanation in the procedures section is detailed, it will be easy to isolate the resources needed to run the project and cost them out.

When you reach the budget section, the only question you should have is how much it costs to hire a half-time administrative assistant, staff benefits and all, for six months, not whether or not you need one. Too many questions about resources at this stage indicates that your methods section isn't clear. One solution is to go back to the methods section, pretend you just received the grant, plot your activities over the next twelve or eighteen months, and describe the steps.

A major difference between a budget for an institutional proposal and one for a research proposal is the attention given to cost sharing. For research proposals or model grants, you can expect to receive full support for your project from the sponsor. But for institutional proposals, significant cost sharing is expected. Sponsors are suspect of proposals in which the college is so uninvolved that it won't provide significant real resources. As a rule of thumb, the budget of institutional proposals, either through in-kind or hard dollar matches, should show contributions of a third to a half of the cost of the grant.

Appendix

Use the appendix for letters of cooperation and endorsement, unpublished articles, course descriptions past and future, stock descriptions of institutional facilities, and resumes of advisory groups. Do not use the appendix to pad the proposal in an attempt to provide an appearance of substance that you fear the proposal itself may not convey. Sponsors are unimpressed with this ploy. Indeed, some, like the National Science Foundation, are considering banning the use of appendixes altogether because of dismay with their misuse. So resist temptation and use the appendix section sparingly.

Final Review

Once you have completed your proposal, reread the guidelines. If they include criteria for making awards, have these in hand as you reread your proposal. Then check specifically for how well what you say corresponds to what the sponsor wants and score yourself for each criterion. If the guidelines rate an item about which you have said nothing, this is a good time to add something on that topic.[14]

Check to be sure that you have used the sponsor's words to describe common phenomena at least half as often as you have used your own favorite terms. Then underline, use *italics*, and print in **bold** key statements and phrases that tie your proposal directly to issues of importance to the sponsor. Don't overuse special formatting techniques, but don't neglect them either.

Beginning proposal writers can achieve success if they start small and slowly raise their sights to larger targets. One or two successful institutional grants followed by a smattering of publications can set the stage for a larger, model project and recognition as a leader in the field. To ensure you are off to a good start, be sure your institutional proposal has the following: (1) documented evidence of substantial consultation with the department, chair, and dean about the proposed program; (2) evidence of significant planning with key faculty in the department and college; (3) evidence that the campus is willing to support the project, usually demonstrated through a monetary commitment to cost share in the project; (4) a convincing approach to carrying the objectives into action; (5) a strategy for evaluating the impact of the grant; and (6) a viable plan for continuing the activity once the award expires.

NOTES

1. Garrison Keillor, "Jack Schmidt on the Burning Sands," in *Happy to Be Here* (New York: Penguin, 1983), pp. 84–101.

2. The main exception to this rule is the Fund for the Improvement of Post Secondary Education (FIPSE), which encourages applicants from all types of postsecondary institutions to apply for model grants. See FIPSE, *The Comprehensive Program Application for Grants Fiscal Year 1995* (Washington, D.C.: U.S. Department of Education, 1994), p. 2.

3. Dorin Schumacher, "Strategies for Helping Your Faculty Get More Grants from Companies," *Research Management Review* 7, no. 1 (1994): 37–52. For an excellent discussion of how to modify a proposal written for a federal sponsor to meet the requirements of a foundation, see Jane C. Geever and Patricia McNeill, *The Foundation Center's to Proposal Writing* (New York: Foundation Center, 1993).

4. Andrew J. Grant and Suzy D. Sonenberg, Loxahatchee, Fla., Research Grants Guides, Inc., 1993.

5. Dora Marcus, Eulalia B. Cobb, and Robert E. Shoenberg, *Lessons Learned from FIPSE Projects II* (Washington, D.C.: U.S. Department of Education, 1993), pp. 67–75.

6. Ibid., p. 73.

7. Frea E. Sladek, "Before You Begin to Write," *Grants Magazine*, 12, no. 2 (1989): 97–115.

8. Janet M. Cuca and William J. McLoughlin, *Cancer Investigation* 5, no. 1 (1987): 55–58.

9. John E. Niederhuber, "Writing a Successful Grant Application," *Journal of Surgical Research* 39 (1985): 277–284.

10. FIPSE, *Comprehensive Program Application*, p. 17.

11. An excellent resource for doing your own evaluation is contained in the chapter on evaluation in Norton J. Kiritz, *Program Planning and Proposal Writing* (Los Angeles: Grantsmanship Center, 1980), pp. 28–32.

12. Robert A. Lucas and Thomas R. Harvey, "Successful Strategies for Institutionalizing Grants," *Grants Magazine* 7, no. 1 (1984): 19–24.

13. The classic guide to constructing a budget remains that done by Frea E. Sladek and Eugene L. Stein, *Grant Budgeting and Finance* (New York: Plenum Press, 1981).

14. For a review of the typical criteria that sponsors use to evaluate proposals, see Robert Lefferts, *Getting a Grant in the 1990s* (New York: Prentice Hall, 1990), pp. 14–24.

PART IV

INITIATIVES FOR PROMOTING SCHOLARLY PUBLISHING

18

Adam Smith's Rules for Writers

Robert Boice

> The man who works so moderately as to be able to work constantly, not only preserves his health the longest, but in the course of the year, executes the greatest amount of work.
>
> —Adam Smith, *Wealth of Nations*

When I began helping blocked writers some twenty-five years ago, I had few clues to what lay ahead. There were no useful precedents in the literature apparent to me then. The best known therapist on writing blocks, Edmund Bergler, attributed their cause to a symbolic rejection of mother's milk and claimed that the alternative, writing fluently, was also neurotic. I could tell that the usual advice ("put your manuscript away in a drawer until you are in the mood to write") would not work for writers whose silence had lasted for years (e.g., Mack and Skjei, 1979).

I learned far more from writers themselves and from the few people who have taken the trouble to know how writers work (e.g., Hayes and Flower, 1986; Murray, 1994; Tremmel, 1989; Zirinsky, 1993). In my own writing programs, some of them for academics and some for real-life writers, what my groups and I found most useful got expressed as rules (Boice, 1994). We liked having maxims as reminders of how to change our ways. With each new rule we congratulated ourselves on another clever invention.

The first rule to find wide currency was this: Wait (while patiently preparing to do the writing task well). Later, we found that one of our heroes, Donald Murray (1978), had not only been using it for a long while but he had also borrowed it from Franz Kafka (over whose writing desk hung a sign that said "WAIT"). No doubt, we were resurrecting ideas we had once seen but had consciously forgotten. No matter, the rules proved to be one of the most successful components of our writing (and teaching) programs.

Only recently, however, did I begin to make sense of these rules. Without an unplanned break I might never have seen the light. It came suddenly, when a rock-climbing accident forced me into a period of quiet reflectiveness. The unimaginable had happened: I could no longer speak to the writers I had scheduled for individual and small-group therapies. At first, I luxuriated in self-pity, but then I noticed some benefits from my malady. Because I could talk very little, I was at long last becoming a better listener and observer. My timeout from injury let me resee what I had been doing (Boice, 1994). The real insight came when I compared my accounts of how writers progress to similar accounts of how newcomers to the professoriate learn to become teachers (Boice, 1992). I realized that the most effective rules derived from each domain were simply about economies; no more, no less. Just then, one of those lucky accidents came my way, the sort that emerges in reading things on the far boundaries of one's own work. I had been perusing Adam Smith's classic, *Wealth of Nations*, as a bedtime soporific, and I was roused to see a conclusion of his that summarized my programs for writers and teachers. I quote it at the beginning of this chapter.

What Smith had called constancy, I had been advocating as a way of finding more productivity by working at writing in brief, daily sessions. What he meant by the moderation that promotes health is what I had encouraged as working at a reflective, relaxing pace. Once I saw this simplicity, I felt impelled to rearrange and clarify the twenty-five or so rules that had been so central to my work. Given the economies of what emerged, I was not surprised to see that the resulting ten rules (all of them derived from Adam Smith's Rule), applied equally well to writing and teaching. By adjusting each rule to fit both domains, the result became even more economical.

Adam Smith's Rules, as I now use them with writers in my classes and programs, are presented below in bold type for good reason. Each has struck most of its readers as bold, even preposterous. So I ask you, the reader, to bear something in mind as you consider these rules. The writers (and teachers) who fare best with them treat them playfully, irreverently, flexibly. I encourage you to do the same. Knowledge of something else may encourage tolerance for these counterintuitive admonitions: They work.

ADAM SMITH'S RULES

Each of these rules was selected for two reasons. First, the practice of each had proven to be a distinguishing characteristic of young academics who make quick, exemplary starts as scholarly writers (and as teachers). Second, each rule has proven effective in reshaping the habits, attitudes, and successes of uncomfortable and dysfluent writers (Boice, 1994, 1995). Here, I present each of Adam Smith's Rules as a brief bit of advice, in terms of how writers appreciate and practice them, and (occasionally) as related to effective practices in improving teaching. Where useful, I draw parallels between the rules and far-flung literatures on writing dysfluencies, teaching, psychotherapy, the psychology of work, and other foreign sources. A glance will suggest what makes this writerly (and teacherly) advice different from counsel usually given. Adam Smith's Rules are more about the efficiencies and economies of writing than about issues of content or form. They are more about how than about what to write. First things first, as old Adam liked to say.

Rule 1. Wait

This rule is about patience. It means waiting actively and delaying closure. It does *not* mean waiting passively—for the Muses, magic, or deadlines.

This first rule is about enhancing motivation and direction by waiting to uncover something that is worth saying, to decide on the right problem to solve. It means not rushing, impulsively, into writing without first making preparations and plans. It means expecting to find the most enduring motivation in unrushed work. It means finding the most compelling ideas and discoveries by slowing down and taking more time to prewrite (Murray, 1978), to collect and arrange (Mills, 1959), to notice and connect (Perkins, 1981).

How the Wait Rule is put into practice. Waiting is more than not being impulsive; it is also a matter of pacing and pausing. Writers who master waiting work in comfort (contrasted to the strained seating and writing positions displayed by impatient writers). They work with relaxation (e.g., by stretching and breathing meditatively before, during, and after sessions); with a rhythm of working and resting that moderates fatigue (and the errors that symptomize it); with regular involvement in preparations for writing (e.g., brief, scheduled sessions of collecting and noting).

First results. Writers in the program report finding motivation and patience after, not before, regular involvement in acts that lead to formal prose. The most effective kind of regular involvement is daily practice.

What makes the Wait Rule difficult. Waiting is the most demanding and pivotal of all these rules because most writers have learned to work impatiently. They put off writing, and they wait passively while impatiently turning to easier tasks. They hope inspiration and other kinds of magic will eventually impel them to write. Then, as deadlines near, they rush into action, they work in marathon sessions, and they ride the euphoria and excitement of working under pressure until they are finished and exhausted. Woe be to anyone who disturbs them.

The problem with bingeing at writing, beyond its proven costs in long-term productivity (Boice, 1993), is that it means working beyond the point of diminishing returns. Writing gets rushed and too-little edited or revised. Quality and satisfaction suffer.

The effects of rushing can be seen all too clearly among teachers. With hurried, binged preparations comes an excess of lecture material. Once in class, teachers who have not learned to wait do all the wrong things: they hurry, confuse, and distance students. They pause too rarely to check on student comprehension, and they delay only milliseconds before answering their own questions. They speak quickly, and they often leave classes floundering in their wake. Impatient teachers strike students as unfriendly, unfair, and incompetent (Boice, 1991).

Why do so few of us manage patience on our own? We would all prefer to have motivation and inspiration at hand before beginning to write. But in reality we usually have to build them as we go, something few of us have been taught. When we choose, usually unconsciously, to wait passively for magic, we end up having to force ourselves to work under deadlines and in great binges that take on a momentum and motivation of their own. Each time we manage a completion under such duress we reinforce the short-term benefits of impatience: the excitement, the seeming freedom of not having to face difficult tasks well in advance, the apparent accomplishment of having completed a project quickly, and the chance of at last catching up. What happens in the long run is less noticeable, at least to the writer: an increasing tendency to busy-ness, to rushing, and to always being behind schedule (Boice, 1989).

Patience is difficult because it is a seeming contradiction. On one hand, it demands waiting; on the other it requires a leap of faith (see Rule 2).

Rule 2. Begin Before Feeling Ready

Oddly, this second rule often precedes the first. There is no clear linearity or separation in Adam Smith's Rules.

The second rule means getting started before feeling fully prepared to write. It requires a leap of faith in launching a project before feeling fully prepared. It even demands getting to work well before ideal conditions arise. Without this rule, writers may passively await the great blocks of free, undisrupted time necessary to the sort of writing that can only come to people of legendary genius and leisure: whole weekends, vacations, sabbaticals, retirements, reincarnations.

How the Begin Early Rule is practiced. It is scheduled and rehearsed as playful, tolerant preliminaries to writing—as what Murray (1978) calls pre-writing. Writers in the program begin to find imagination and momentum by way of interactive reading and notetaking where they carry on dialogues with authors and anticipated audiences in the margins (i.e., writerly reading and writerly notetaking). They find it in systematic work at filing and rearranging notes and outlines that presage what they write (Mills, 1959). And, throughout, when they need momentum or clarification of what they want to say, they free write—that is, they write without listening to their internal critics, without worrying about finding the perfect word for the moment (Elbow, 1973). Most important (according to the data about what practices make a difference in helping writers find comfort and fluency), they share preliminary work early with friendly and helpful critics, while the work is still formative and still open to change.

Other results of the Begin Early Rule. Early beginnings delight writers by enhancing creativity (because prewriting encourages extra noticing and re-arranging while preparing to write), easier transitions to formal prose (with proper preliminaries, writing becomes little more than rewriting), less pressured work (with slowed, relaxed pacing writers feel more freedom), and, most crucial to participants, timely completions (because projects are started early and worked at daily).

What makes the Begin Early Rule difficult. The main inhibition is impatience. Once writers begin, their feeling that they have too little time for preliminaries can impel them to rush into formal prose.

Rule 3. Work in Brief, Daily Sessions (bds)

This third rule means working at things like writing (i.e., tasks easily procrastinated) in bds, not in occasional bursts. It means giving up cherished habits of waiting for big blocks of undisrupted time. Why? Because ideal conditions for writing may be long in coming. Because, as every book on procrastination points out, large tasks are more likely to be completed in timely fashion if they are broken into small, manageable bits of work.

How the bds Rule is practiced. Writers in the program, even those with busy schedules, find and use small openings that usually seem insufficient to do good writing. They establish the regular habit of bds, regardless of mood. And temporarily, only until the habit is established, they use contingencies to make themselves work on schedule (e.g., they earn access to the day's newspapers by first completing their scheduled bds).

Results. Writers who practice bds report automatic, painless writing. They emphasize the growing feeling of becoming *real* writers as they work at writing regularly, as their writing stays fresh in mind from day to day (Tremmel, 1989). And they particularly value another thing they hadn't expected: with bds they find more free time. My own measures of their progress include clear evidence that bds lead to greatly increased productivity over prior habits of spontaneous bursts of writing (Boice, 1993).

Difficulties. Nothing in my writing programs strikes writers as more un-believable than the notion that bds can produce sufficient outputs (at least until they try bds). Consider four of the reasons why. First, impatience and busy-ness incline writers to suppose that once they write, they need at last to catch up on overdue projects. When they realize how much they have to do, they wait for bigger, more ideal blocks of time. Second, habits of working in long and intense sessions carry short-term benefits of euphoria and excitement. Third, many writers believe they need more time than the half-hour or so usually allotted for an entire bds just to warm up properly. Fourth, the writers who have the most trouble immersing themselves in practicing bds are the least sure that my writing programs (or any writing programs) will help. Their lack of faith reminds me of what best predicts fluency (cf. blocking) in writers: Hypnotic susceptibility, that willingness to go along and try things (Bowers, 1979).

Rule 4. Stop

This means pausing and stopping in timely fashion (when breaks are needed or when enough has been done for the day). It means moving onto other things including rest.

How the Stop Rule is practiced. Writers in the program make a habit of calming and slowing before work. They begin to set and maintain a moderate, relaxing pace as early as awakening, when they sit on the edges of their beds to breathe meditatively. They work more deliberately, with an eye to timely stopping. They keep records of their success at pausing during writing sessions to rest and reflect. They stop a bit early, often without completing entire sentences, paragraphs, thoughts (because stopping in the midst of things makes them easier to resume the next day; because timely stopping means that writers will have time to move on to other things, even to exercise and to social lives; because timely stopping means leaving writing before diminishing returns set in).

Results. Practice of the Stop Rule is difficult but rewarding. Its results include more free time and better quality writing. Other outcomes might not seem so predictable. Writers who learn to stop make their writing sessions less fatiguing, less aversive, less onerous to resume. And writers who stop in timely ways actually get more done in the long run (as Adam Smith might have predicted).

Difficulties of the Stop Rule. Stopping is more difficult and more important than starting. Why? When we are on a roll, we hate to lose momentum and the euphoria of easy fluency. We may suppose that momentum will never come again. And stopping requires patience, something foreign to the ways we learned to write. Stopping, as we have just seen, requires faith.

Difficulties of the First Four Rules

The first four of Adam Smith's Rules are the most burdensome for most writers I have known. Once writers master these, the rest come relatively easily. To help writers who are still struggling with these basics, I often draw parallels to other difficult changes that require mastery of the same four rules. My favorite, because writers so often require help in this domain, is insomnia.

Consider how treatment for insomnia proceeds at some of the most prestigious, research-oriented sleep centers (Perl, 1994): The first step is to wait before going to bed, until truly tired (in contrast to the usual, impatient tendency of hoping to catch up on lost sleep in a single night by going to bed early). The second step is to begin preparing for sleep well before bedtime. This means calming and slowing toward day's end. It also means proper diet and exercise. The next, third step strikes insomniacs as most incredible: It admonishes patients to sleep in briefer sessions. This means not going to bed or staying in bed except to sleep. It means getting up early, at regular times and regardless of felt readiness. It means getting more from less—by spending time in bed getting more of the deep sleep that provides rest and recovery. The result of this regimen is being able to go to sleep readily, to spend less time in bed and in sleep, and to feel more rested.

Rule 5. Balance Preliminaries with Writing

This rule had its origins in observations of exemplary writers and teachers. Both spend only moderate amounts of time preparing (prewriting or preteaching), and both spend no more time in preliminaries than in formal presentation (prose or lecturing). Odd as this rule may seem, it has clear precedents. The most productive, cited writers in academe spend only modest amounts of time writing, and they spend as much time socializing about writing as doing it (Creswell, 1985). The most effective mentors fall at the middle of the continuum in terms of how involved they become with their apprentices (Pascarella, Terenzini and Hibel, 1978). They find the balance between doing too little and too much.

How practiced. Writers in the program rehearse the Balance Rule by scheduling preset periods of productive delay before moving to prose. They not only collect, file, organize, and outline, but they also make and revise conceptual outlines that more and more closely approximate the prose that comes next. This way, when they write prose, they rewrite from conceptual outlines. This way, they balance writing with rewriting.

Usual resistance. Until writers have practiced the Balance Rule regularly, they react to it with incredulity (much as they first did to the bds Rule). They cannot believe that exemplars spend as much on time on preliminaries or that, if they do, the same practice would work for them. And, as with the bds Rule, writers often feel they have too little time, too many pressing deadlines to practice it now.

Results. When writers do practice this balance, the outcomes are uniformly positive because it simply harmonizes the economies already underway: learning to wait, to begin early, and to stop. Writers balance excitement with patience, certainty with tolerance.

Rule 6. Supplant Self-Defeating Thinking Habits

This rule is about positive thinking, a topic usually skirted in manuscripts of advice for writers (but not in books for salespeople). It means noticing, in patient and systematic fashion, the thoughts and attitudes that commonly hinder or block writing. One common example is the pessimistic, self-downing cognitions that lead to depression and its inaction (Seligman, 1991). Another example: self-defeating styles of shyness that leave writers reluctant to write when public scrutiny is a possibility (Baumeister and Scher, 1988).

How practiced. Correctives for scripts of pessimism and self-defeat are well-established in psychotherapy but light years distant from writing books. The strategies that writers like and use most successfully in my programs begin with the economy of habitually monitoring their thoughts, especially at writing times, for negative self-talk (e.g., "I was thinking that I could write my heart out, but it will just be rejected again"). Next comes replacement of negativities with more optimistic thinking (e.g., "Once I put these irrational worries aside and get to work, I will begin to enjoy the writing"). Then, writers work in longer term ways to spot and correct self-defeating styles (e.g., "I finally noticed that I set perfectionistic, unrealistic goals for my writing that end up defeating me before I even get underway").

Results. Writers who practice this rule report (and test) as less depressed and pessimistic about writing. They demonstrate fewer delays, interruptions, and blocks as writers. They find writing an easier, happier experience.

Difficulties. One usual objection to this sixth rule comes as reservations from nonpsychologists about practicing psychotherapies on themselves. They feel unqualified. But when these writers immerse themselves in popular books of self-help like Ellis and Knaus's *Overcoming Procrastination* (1977), they see why those writings are perennial best-sellers: Nearly anyone can use them with profit. Another objection is harder to overcome. Some writers simply dislike psychology and psychologists and want nothing to do with their offerings.

Rule 7. Manage Emotions

This rule, like the sixth, is about self-control but more about the affective, emotional side of writing (see Brand, 1989). This rule means noticing and managing the emotions that help or hinder writing. It means looking in particular for the emotion that accompanies rushing and time pressures: hypomania (that less-than-manic state of euphoria, impulsivity, and grandiosity that usually leads to exhaustion and depression—American Psychiatric Association; Boice, 1994). We saw its mention presaged in our discussion of bingeing at writing.

How practiced. Writers learn this sort of moderation of emotions by re-inforcing things they have already been practicing: lessening excessive reliance on rushing and bingeing at writing. They add new practices too. They work more at varying their pace by punctuating it with occasional bursts of excitement and speed that do not prevent getting back to moderate gaits. Just as important, they work with more of the mood of mild happiness (often with a small smile). The latter is hardest for native New Yorkers.

Results. More than anywhere else in the program, writers begin this step with displays of resentment. They dislike being pressured to give up their beloved habits of making writing hypomanic—like manics who resist taking their medication (lithium) for fear that it will undermine their creativity (it doesn't). Similarly, hypomanic writers suppose that writing will be less imaginative and fun without the excitement of rushing and without the euphoria of ready fluency (it isn't). Still, the outcomes of practicing this seventh rule are much like the third (bds) and fourth (Stop): Writers who moderate their emotions report and display less fatigue; more productivity and quality of prewriting and writing in the long run; greater self-confidence and sense of freedom. They even come to realize what is crucial to these accomplishments: moderation and variation (but not suppression) of emotions in writing.

Rule 8. Moderate Attachments and Reactions

The eighth rule follows naturally from the seventh and sixth. Its meaning can be appreciated in an old maxim repeated by composition teachers (North, 1987): *The worse the writer, the greater the attachment to the writing.* It means that as we become too invested in the content and format of our writing, we grow less able to change it or improve it. An interesting parallel appears in novice teachers. The more locked-in they are to what they have prepared, the less often they see what works and what doesn't. (Our rule for writers can be restated for teachers: *The worse the teacher, the greater the attachment to the content of the course.*)

Practice and results. In everyday use, the Moderate Attachment Rule takes on two characteristic styles. In one, writers work to moderate their attachments to content (e.g., by finding ways to humorize about it). In the other, writers practice ways of tempering their reactions to distractions that come from surprises and criticisms. To help with the first style, they make a habit of noticing signs of overattachment to content and to work itself: (1) a pronounced reluctance to pause or stop; (2) feelings, early on, that the writing is brilliant and must be flawless; and (3) a reluctance to share unfinished work. To economize on the second kind of overinvestment, the kind that makes criticism intolerable, they move to the ninth rule.

Rule 9. Let Others Do Some of the Work, Even Critics

This rule is about letting go, which is no easy task for writers who hurry to demonstrate their genius. It is about accepting help, which is no easy matter for writers who overvalue their autonomy. It means delegating some of the responsibility for good writing to early readers (who can suggest alternative sources and directions), to occasional collaborators (who can share the load and increase the likelihood of publication), to critics (who, whether reasonable or not, can always be seen as providing useful information about how some readers will respond, about where unnecessary confusions can be minimized).

How practiced. Writers in the program work together on exercises pertaining to the toughest component of this ninth rule. They make social contracts with each other for early sharing of prewriting and writing. This sharing includes preliminary praise (at least some, of a specific sort, is obligatory) and criticism. And, most crucially, the interactions include practice at the social skills of eliciting, listening to, and accepting criticism (Boice, 1992). Examples: asking a critic to comment on a passage that seems worrisome ("What point do you think that paragraph makes?"); taking written notes of what a harsh critic is saying (and interrupting, calmly, for clarification: "So is this what you you're saying?"); finding ways to agree with even the most deflating of criticisms ("I can see how you might find it boring. I felt excited about it, but maybe I didn't communicate that somehow, do you think?"); and eliciting specific suggestions for improvement ("So how can I better communicate my enthusiasm in my paper and make it less boring?").

Results of the Eighth and Ninth Rules

Both exercises in letting go are more difficult than writers expect; both occasion more relapses than elsewhere; but both bring some of the strongest results of the program. Self-ratings of patience at last reach acceptable levels. So do ratings, both mine and writers', of tolerance for disruptions (e.g., distracting noises, disasters, deflating criticisms) while writing. And so do recorded instances of seeking, accepting, and using criticism. The surprise for writers in these outcomes is the greater sense of audience they finally begin to acquire. They talk about feeling a part of the conversation of real writers and what that means in terms of knowing who is in the conversation and what the key topics of discussion are or could be (Bruffee, 1984; Olson, 1992). Here, more than ever before, they begin to mention "getting more from less." Adam Smith and economies at last enter our own conversations spontaneously.

Difficulties

You may anticipate these: a reluctance to let go and show trust; a perfectionistic fear of sharing work early, before it is perfect; an understandable dislike for criticism. A more general difficulty, writers tell me, is giving up so many old, familiar, and partially successful habits. Not until writers see the payoffs of productive constancy and healthy moderation (the stuff of Adam Smith) do they say they are hooked on the rules. Does hooked mean overattached? Usually not. For the most successful program participants, rules get adopted with playful adaptations to individual needs. Said one writer: *The worse the participant, the greater the attachment to these rules.*

Rule 10. Limit Wasted Effort

In my oral, more scintillating version of this chapter at Joe Moxley and Lagretta Lenker's conference,[1] I had occasion to demonstrate this tenth rule on the scene. By this point, the audience seemed to tire (mysteriously). So I paused and demonstrated what I generally do in my writing classes and groups (something probably unsuited to the decorum of a keynote address): I stood away from the podium and stretched, I even encouraged the audience to join me. (Some of the distinguished writers, researchers, editors, and publishers in the audience did, and some didn't.) Then, with everyone more or less refreshed, I moved back to make the point. Just at the moment when I was tempted to rush (because I sensed my own impatience and the audience's for me to finish), I slowed down to make my final thoughts clearer, less rushed. To have rushed would have wasted effort.

Another point followed from that one. The reason for learning to work in less wasteful ways goes beyond economies such as improved productivity, quality, and enjoyment. It also includes resilience (what Adam Smith called constancy with health).

This tenth rule is about resilience and can be appreciated by way of another old maxim: *The less the wasted effort, the greater the resilience.* In fact, writers who show the greatest constancy and moderation in these programs evidence the most reliable and pleasurable output as writers over the long run. They persist through roadblocks, traumas, illnesses, rejections, and other things that usually derail writers from their newly established habits.

How practiced. Methods used in this tenth step are hardest to describe because here writers adopt individualistic strategies. Still, there are commonalities. Now, writers who had not yet made writing a daily habit see the need for constant bds when they compare their own records of resilience with those of habitual writers. And here, writers make a new habit. They work (together and alone) to monitor for inefficiencies, especially the fruits of impatience and intolerance (e.g., rushing to start a new project; overreacting to a disturbance during an intense writing session).

Results. In the year that followed the year of systematic meetings and exercises, writers continued to track and share their resilience with fellow graduates and with me. Continued progress toward fluency and comfort appeared for all but a few writers. It came slowly but surely. And almost all instances of progress, at least in our eyes, were economies. Writing was reportedly becoming easier and quicker, even while writers maintained a maddeningly slow, nonfatiguing pace. Far more manuscripts were being finished, submitted for editorial review, and accepted for publication (Boice, 1995).

Resistance to the Economy Rule. Perhaps because writers, including me, are natural grumblers, even the most successful of my participants continued to express resistance toward Adam Smith's Rules and practices. At times all of them said they still wanted to write without a schedule (although they later admitted, as would addicted exercisers, that they missed their daily "fixes" of writing when they took vacations). Occasionally, every writer wished aloud for magic: "I still fantasize that *some* of my writing, I'm not asking for all of it, could just come to me all of a sudden. I would look up and realize that I had just written a masterpiece." (But by this point, writers recognized such wishes as pleasant, unlikely, and harmless.) And eventually all of us, me included, were more devastated by criticisms than we later wished we had been. What had changed was the speed with which we recovered, readjusted, and got back on track. That too is a way of indexing resilience.

SOME GENERAL LESSONS

Academicians in the program taught me a special lesson about the usefulness of Adam Smith's Rules. These writers, as new faculty members, struggled to teach while they tried to publish enough. And they, once settling in as comfortable and fluent writers, noticed that they could use the same rules as teachers. This is worth mentioning here because the subgroups of new faculty who followed their stint at writing with a similar program in teaching improvement showed the biggest gains, overall, as writers (Boice, 1995).

With that benefit of applying the rules more broadly came others. Rules used in both contexts, writing and teaching, could be expressed more succinctly and more concretely by new faculty. Practice with the rules in both domains led to more application of basics to complex skills such as learning the writing style of, say, Strunk and White (1979) and the critical thinking methods for teachers advocated by J. G. Kurfiss (1988). They led to more reports of transferring ideas from writing to teaching and vice versa; to more charted constancy in writing and to higher teaching ratings on a standardized form; to the highest rates of editorial acceptance in journals and other outlets valued by departments; and to the clearest progress toward satisfying the expectations of retention/tenure committees (Boice, 1995).

Later, as I spent those quiet, nonspeaking days looking over my notes and records, I realized that my nonacademic writers had also benefited in generalizing their rules. Those who applied the rules to other endeavors, like overcoming insomnia or time management as executives, showed the greatest gains as writers among their peers. Why? When I asked my writers (some of them economists) this question, they encouraged me to take a closer look at the master. Adam Smith's own enduring fame came in applying his advice for nations to himself (or was it the other way around?).

NOTE

1. "The Politics and Processes of Scholarly Publishing," a conference held at the University of South Florida, St. Petersburg Campus, March 12–14, 1994.

REFERENCES

American Psychiatric Association. *Diagnostic and Statistical Manual of Mental Disorders*. Washington, D.C.: 1994.

Baumeister, R. F. and S. F. Sher. "Self-defeating Behaviors among Normal Individuals." *Psychological Review* 104 (1988): 3–22.

Bergler, E. *The Writer and Psychoanalysis*. New York: Doubleday, 1950.

Boice, R. "Developing Writing, Then Teaching Amongst New Faculty." *Research in Higher Education*. Forthcoming, 1995.

——. *How Writers Journey to Comfort and Fluency: A Psychological Adventure*. Westport, Conn.: Praeger, 1994.

——. "New Faculty as Teachers." *Journal of Higher Education* 62 (1991): 150–173.

——. *The New Faculty Member*. San Francisco: Jossey-Bass, 1992.

——. "Procrastination, Busyness, and Bingeing." *Behaviour Research and Therapy* 27 (1989): 605–611.

——. "Tacit Knowledge and Writing Blocks." *Journal of Higher Education*, 64 (1993): 19–54.

Bowers, P. "Hypnosis and Creativity: The Search for the Missing Link." *Journal of Abnormal Psychology* 88 (1979): 564–572.

Brand, A. G. *The Psychology of Writing: The Affective Experience*. Westport, Conn.: Greenwood Press, 1989.

Bruffee, K. A. "Collaborative Learning and the Conversation of Mankind." *College English* 53 (1984): 123–135.

Creswell, J. W. *Faculty Research Performance*. Washington, D.C.: Association for the Study of Higher Education, 1985.

Elbow, P. *Writing Without Teachers*. New York: Oxford University Press, 1973.

Ellis, A. and W. J. Knaus. *Overcoming Procrastination*. New York: Institute for Rational Living, 1977.

Hayes, J. C. and L. Flower. "Writing Research and Psychology." *American Psychologist* 41 (1986): 1106–1113.

Kurfiss, J. G. *Critical Thinking: Theory, Research, and Possibilities*. Washington, D.C.: Association for the Study of Higher Education, 1988.

Mack, K. and E. Skjei. *Overcoming Writing Blocks*. Los Angeles: J. P. Tarcher, 1979.

Mills, C. W. *The Sociological Imagination*. New York: Grove Press, 1959.

Moxley, J. *Publish, Don't Perish*. Westport, Conn.: Praeger, 1992.

Murray, D. M. "How to Get the Writing Done." *The Subject Is Writing*. Ed. W. Bishop. Portsmouth: Boynton/Cook, 1994. 213–216.

——. "Write before Writing." *College Composition and Communication*, 29 (1978): 375–381.

North, S. *The Making of Knowledge in Composition*. Upper Montclair, N.J.: Boynton/Cook, 1987.

Olson, G. A. "Publishing Scholarship in Humanistic Disciplines: Joining the Conversation."*Writing and Publishing*. Ed. J. Moxley. New York: University Press of America, 1992. 49–69.

Pascarella, E., P. Terenzini, and J. Hibel. "Student-Faculty Interactional Settings and Their Relationship to Predicted Academic Performance." *Journal of Higher Education* 57 (1978): 155–175.

Perkins, D. N. *The Mind's Best Work*. Cambridge, Mass.: Harvard University Press, 1981.

Perl, J. *Sleep Right in Five Nights*. New York: William Morrow, 1994.

Seligman, M. E. P. *Learned Optimism*. New York: A. A. Knopf, 1991.

Strunk, W., and E. B. White. *The Elements of Style*. New York: Macmillan, 1979.

Tremmel, R. "Investigating Productivity and Other Factors in the Writer's Practice" *Freshman English News* 17, 2 (1989): 19–25.

Zirinsky, D. "Mucking about in Language, I Save My Soul: An Interview with Donald Murray." *Writing on the Edge* 4, 2 (1993): 11–23.

19

The Role of the Scholarly Editor

Brian J. Thompson

My contributions to this debate on the role of scholarship and publishing at our colleges and universities will be from the editor's point of view, but more precisely as a provost who is an editor and who is deeply interested in faculty development and institutional educational commitment. As faculty members, our role is to be educators at all levels from freshman to the highest level that our individual institutions reach, which for some of us is postdoctoral education. Our personal scholarship and research must be an integral part of that educational mission and must not be viewed as a self-indulgent solitary activity.

AN EDITOR'S ROLE

There are many views about editors. Let me start with W. B. Yeats's words from his poem, "The Scholars."[1]

> Bald heads, forgetful of their sins,
> Old, learned, respectable bald heads
> Edit and annotate the lines,
> That young men tossing on their beds,
> Rhymed out in love's despair
> To flatter beauty's ignorant ear.

On the other hand, the layperson views the editor as "the person who makes a long story short!"

Consultation with a dictionary[2] results in reading that "to edit" means "to prepare an edition" or "to alter, adapt or refine especially to bring about conformity to a standard or to suit a particular purpose." The real question is: conformity to whose standard and whose particular purpose?

The editor is certainly a key player in the lives of authors. It is my belief that as an editor it is my responsibility to help the author get his or her material published consistent with the standard set for the particular journal or book and to be an interface between the reviewers and the authors to assist and often insist on the revisions being made.

THE EDITOR AND THE AUTHORS

The editor serves as the gatekeeper or, more precisely, as the keeper of many gates. That is, the authors submit their work to the editor—that is the first gate. Traditionally, in my field submission of a paper or manuscript to a journal is made exclusively to that journal. Many journals actually ask the author to certify that "this manuscript contains new content not previously published or submitted elsewhere for simultaneous consideration."[3] I confess that I leave it to the author's professional integrity to follow the rules. But you can be burned. Recently, a reviewer alerted me to the fact that essentially the same paper had recently been reviewed for another journal and was in the process of being revised for publication in that journal. After an editor-to-editor conversation, we asked the authors for an explanation. I hope to get this issue resolved soon.

In another incident, a paper was submitted and reviewed. Based on the reviewers' reports, the paper was not accepted, but I suggested that the author could submit a revised version for further review. After a routine followup with the author, I discovered that the paper had been accepted for another journal for a special section devoted to the topic of the paper. The author believed that he was free to do that since I had not accepted his paper. True, I suppose, but he should have formally withdrawn the paper before submitting it elsewhere. However, that is not the end of the story. One of my reviewers who had significant negative comments about the paper and many suggestions for revisions turned out to be the guest editor for the special section of the other journal—but only I know that!

When I took over the editorship of *Optical Engineering*, I had the opportunity to write an editorial for each issue. To my own amazement, I have taken that opportunity. I am even more amazed that these editorials appear to be read. Hence, I recently wrote an editorial with the title, "Advice to Authors." I thought that I would share that editorial with you as part of this chapter.

> I know that this sounds like a very portentous title and I didn't really mean it to be. However, I wanted a title that would allow me to comment on the preparation of manuscripts—comments that may sound obvious. I have now looked at more than a thousand manuscripts since I became your editor and I can assure you that it isn't obvious to me that these comments are obvious!

Authors have a responsibility to themselves to prepare the best possible paper they can that describes their work. The more significant the technical content, the more important it is to present it clearly and concisely for the reader. I naively assume that the authors wish to make sure that every reader understands the importance and the context of the work that is being reported and its value to other workers in the field. Scientific and technical progress is made by many people working on problems with as much interconnection as possible; this interconnection is most often provided by conferences, conference proceedings, and journal articles.

My advice to those preparing manuscripts is to make sure that the concepts are conveyed clearly. Put yourself at the reader's desk as you write. Make the paper look good too! A good-looking manuscript with clear figures and well-presented data in graph and tabular form makes an excellent impression not only on your editor, but more importantly on the reviewers.

The opposite is even more true; a manuscript that looks thrown together will create the impression that the work that is reported was conducted in the same manner.

My second piece of advice is to follow the format set forth for the journal as closely as possible, even if some of the requests seem odd. Following the format set forth in those guidelines makes your editor's life much easier and helps the manuscript move more easily through the review and publication process. One of my pet peeves as an editor and as a reader is an inadequate set of references that contains serious errors in page number, or volume number or even gives the wrong journal. These errors are very difficult to spot, of course, although reviewers will often notice some of them just from their own familiarity with the field, so it really is an important author responsibility.

The bottom line of this discussion is that, as you can well imagine, I am not very sympathetic when an author has not prepared a good manuscript. I very often get papers that "will be rewritten after the review process" if the material and the content is judged suitable for the journal. If I accepted that idea, I would end up going to reviewers twice! Another example is the author who sends in a report "that could be turned into a paper if." Finally, there is the draft manuscript that arrives with a statement such as "thank you for your consideration of the preliminary version of a (possible) future manuscript." (1993, 3005)

THE EDITOR AND THE REVIEWERS

A healthy tension exists between the reviewers and the authors. In my world, the reviewers are anonymous, but the authors are not. Generally, I find that authors are receptive to reviewers' comments and more often than not genuinely believe that the reviewers' comments have improved the manuscript. There are, of course, moments of humor and moments of serious tension. In the humor department, I offer you this response from an author when I queried him about the revisions. The response was, "I am hardly working on my revisions and will have the revised paper to you very soon!" At the other end of the spectrum are the authors who believe they have been defamed by the reviewers' comments. I have such a case at this very moment. Clearly, one editing task that an editor must not take on is to edit the reviewers' comments!

The interface with the reviewers is not always easy. I often track down reviewers by telephone; thus, on one occasion recently I was speaking to a distinguished colleague about his delinquency. He was not sure where the paper was and said, "We have a system here that is designed to lose any manuscript." It turned out in the end that our paper was no exception.

The choice of reviewers is certainly serious business. An unethical editor can determine the outcome of the review process. We all know colleagues who would reject any work because it is not original, is original but is a trivial extension of known ideas, and so on; and we all know reviewers who will recommend anything for publication. Being too kind is not better than being too harsh. I believe in choosing reviewers specifically for the particular paper rather than using a roster of reviewers and taking them in turn.

I do not subscribe to Samuel Taylor Coleridge's view of reviewers expressed in his *Seven Lectures on Shakespeare and Milton*:

> The crying sin of modern criticism is that it is overloaded with personality. If an author commit an error, there is no wish to set him right for the sake of truth, but for the sake of triumph—that the reviewer may show how much wiser, or how much abler he is than the writer. Reviewers are usually people who would have been poets, historians, biographers, etc., if they could; they have tried their talents at one or at the other, and have failed; therefore they turn critics, and, like the Roman emperor, a critic most hates those who excel in the particular department in which he, the critic, has notoriously been defeated. Reviewers should be very productive scholars in their own right.[4]

As editors, we must avoid those reviewers who subscribe to the view that "I never read a book before reviewing it, it prejudices a man so."[5] This was, of course, a joke to poke fun at Sidney Smith's good friend, Francis Horner (Pearson, 1934).

THE EDITOR AND THE PUBLISHER

The working relationship between the editor and the publisher is perhaps the most critical part of the "politics and processes of scholarly publishing." While we may have been able to dilute the publish or perish solution to faculty promotion, for the publisher it is still publish or perish. The scholar needs to publish highly regarded peer-reviewed material as opposed to publishing anything anywhere to up the publication count. The publisher needs to publish highly regarded material but only as long as it can be done profitably—the profit margin required is different for professional and scholarly society publication programs than for commercial publishers. Societies and university presses continue to be able to publish, amongst other works, the shorter print run items of high-quality material aimed at a limited audience.

I must say that I have been very pleased indeed with my relationship with the variety of publishers I am associated with. These relationships work, I am convinced, because of the careful definition of the scope, intent and processes for each project area. Finally, they work because of the infrastructure, both personnel and systems, that is available to the editor at his or her location (institutional support) and at the publisher's location. It might be trite to say it, but, indeed, dedicated teamwork is the essential ingredient.

SOME EDITORIAL ISSUES

There are many editorial issues of policy, style, responses to changes in academic life and expectations, responses to public perception of academics, and responses to technological change. A few of these issues are covered in this chapter.

Unreviewed Material

In many disciplines, conferences are an important part of the scholarly interchange. It has become popular, and often valuable, to publish proceedings of these conferences. Generally, these proceedings contain the papers presented by the authors and are completely unrefereed or edited (since they are usually camera ready supplied by the authors). In a real sense, these proceedings volumes are a record of the conference. Since the papers are unreviewed and have a limited circulation, (but parenthetically, they are part of the open literature with ISBN numbers), the question is whether some of the material in these conference papers could or should appear in the archival literature. I have had to face the issue in my own editorial work. My initial statement after consultation with the publications committee was that we (i.e., the professional society that I represent with one of my editorial hats) have "available a large body of knowledge developed by a wide range of competent workers. . . . At present, that material is published in (conference) proceedings. As editor, I would like to capture some of that knowledge into the archival literature"[6] for wider dissemination.

Later, in another editorial I stated:

Some believe that this process is double publication and, hence, clutters the literature. However, I believe that proceedings and journals fulfill important yet different roles, and that it is acceptable, on occasion, to have basically the same material appear in both places. Of course, there will always be some difference between the two publications of the material dictated by format, author revisions, and the review process. Nevertheless, I expect this to be a continuing area of debate.[7]

But clearly that is not a specific enough statement, so in my next editorial I stated:

Let me try to be more specific about the guidelines that I believe are in place based on discussions with the Publications Committee of the Society:
- A modified version of a proceedings paper may be submitted to *Optical Engineering* as a regular or special section paper. The paper should meet the guidelines set forth in the "Information for Contributors" that is published in each issue of *Optical Engineering*.
- The paper for *Optical Engineering* cannot be identical to the paper in a proceedings. Just a format change is not sufficient. As a guideline, we expect about 25 percent of the paper to be different—these differences will certainly be in the actual text but may also be in the figures.
- Authors should clearly identify that the paper submitted to *Optical Engineering* is a revised version of a paper presented at an SPIE conference. Details of the proceedings publication should be added including volume number, page number (a paper number if not yet published), conference title, and location with date.
- Papers submitted will go through the standard review process used by the journal.
This means that authors need to think carefully about the preparation of papers for proceedings and for the journal and not be mislead into writing one paper for both. The time to plan both papers is before either is finalized.[8]

Well, the jury is out on this issue, but it is working well so far.

Copyright and Dissemination

Today, in most situations, the copyright is owned by the publisher and not by the author or the author's institution. The type of wording used indicates that, as of the date of acceptance of a work for publication, the authors transfer to the publisher full ownership throughout the world of all rights, titles, and interests, including copyrights and renewals and extensions thereof to the work. Fundamentally, there should not be any particular issue with these "copyright transfer agreements" as they are called. For many journals the author's work is published in that journal, and the work is then disseminated to the readers of that journal. In addition to the transfer of copyright, authors or their institutions are often asked to pay page charges to help defray the cost of publication; average charges are perhaps $100 a printed page in the scientific fields. We need to remember that one of the missions of a scholarly society is to disseminate information in the field they represent. In particular, they are charged with the dissemination of papers and articles through their publications. They should be acting on behalf of the authors to make sure that the author's work is as widely available as possible.

So, what is the issue? The issue is that as part of the copyright transfer agreement the publisher has the right to grant permission to other parties to republish the author's work (sometimes with and sometimes without the author's permission). However, the original publisher has the sole right to charge either a fee or a royalty for the reprint rights. This income is retained by the original publisher. In the last four years these charges, which are supposed to be "reasonable," have been increasing rather rapidly and are making it impossible, in some cases, to reprint the author's work in anthologies or collected works on a particular subject. I am, of course, reporting first-hand experience here through my work as general editor of the Milestone Series of Selected Reprints. One particular case on my desk at the moment involves $10,000 of republication fees for a volume that contains about 100 articles from the world's literature. Remember the copyright owner incurs no cost in this transaction. Since we are talking about short print runs of 500 copies, the cost per volume is $20 before we start. Finally, I note two things. First, the original author does not share in those republication fees, and second, what happened to the concept that the professional society has a responsibility to help disseminate the author's work?

Publishing Formats

Of course, we publish in many formats; working papers (which are popular in the academic business school world); research reports (which are often required by government contracts and grants); refereed and unrefereed conference proceedings; progress series that consist of a few lengthy review articles; research monographs that are either single or multiauthored; scholarly texts and anthologies; and finally, textbooks—but only a highly selected portion of the knowledge gets into the textbook.

The big discussion today is about electronic publishing. There are two thrusts. The first is to do some or all the things in the above list in electronic rather than in paper form. Here we will be debating the issues of ease of access, ease of browsing, and the like. The second thrust is to use electronic publishing to have a scholarly exchange of ideas in a different mode that could replace the need for scholarly gatherings and conferences. There is at least one problem with that idea, and it is simply that when scholars get together hallway interactions prove as valuable as the formal sessions.

The most profound effect of publishing in the communication age is the effect on our university libraries. The role of libraries must change from that of collection, cataloging, and maintenance of books to that of dissemination of information. For the user, access is the important attribute. Can we see and read what we need in a relatively short period of time? Answering that need does not mean that each and every library must have the material on its own shelves. Clearly, we have a long way to go before we achieve that kind of access.

CONCLUSION

As scholars, we are all very fond of books in whatever form, and we sometimes even enjoy and appreciate the contents. Let me close with Benjamin Franklin's epitaph for himself:

> The Body of
> Benjamin Franklin, printer,
> (Like the cover of an old book,
> Its content worn out,
> And stript of its lettering and gilding)
> Lies here, food for worms!
> Yet the work itself shall not be lost,
> For it will, as he believed, appear once more
> In a new
> And more beautiful edition
> Corrected and amended
> By its author.[9]

Despite his experiments with electricity, Franklin probably didn't imagine that the "more beautiful edition corrected and amended" might be electronic.

NOTES

1. W. B. Yeats, "The Scholars," (in, *Selected Poems and Three Plays of William Butler Yeats*, ed. M. L. Rosenthal (New York: Collier Books, 1915).

2. *Webster's New Collegiate Dictionary* (Springfield, Mass.: Merriam, 1974).

3. Applied Optics (Optical Society of America), Manuscript Submission form.

4. S. T. Coleridge, "The First Lecture." *Seven Lectures on Shakespeare and Milton*, ed. J. P. Collier (London: Chapman Hall, 1856), 4.

5. H. Pearson, *The Smith of Smiths Being the Life, Wit and Humour of Sydney Smith* (New York: Harper and Brothers, 1934), 54.

6. Brian J. Thompson, "Editorial." *Optical Engineering* 30 (1991): 4.

7. Brian J. Thompson, "Publication of Proceedings Paper—Revisited." *Optical Engineering* 31 (1992): 1141.

8. Brian J. Thompson, "Publication of Proceedings Paper in Optical Engineering: A Topic Revisited—Again!" *Optical Engineering* 32 (1993): 2021.

9. Benjamin Franklin. "Epitaph for Himself." *Oxford Dictionary of Quotations*, 3rd ed. (New York: Oxford University Press, 1980).

REFERENCES

Applied Optics (Optical Society of America). Manuscript Submission Form.

Coleridge, Samuel Taylor. *Seven Lectures on Shakespeare and Milton.* Ed. J. P. Collier. London: Chapman Hall, 1856. 4.

Franklin, Benjamin. "Epitaph for Himself." *Oxford Dictionary of Quotations.* 3rd ed. New York: Oxford University Press, 1980.

Kelley, D. R., ed. *The History of Ideas: Canon and Variations.* Vol. 1 of *Library of the History of Ideas.* New York: University of Rochester Press, 1990.

Pearson, H. *The Smith of Smiths Being the Life, Wit and Humour of Sydney Smith.* New York: Harper and Brothers, 1934. 54.

Thompson, Brian J., ed. "Advice to Authors." *Optical Engineering* 32 (1993): 3005.

—. "Editorial." *Optical Engineering* 30 (1991): 4.

—. *Milestone Series of Selected Papers.* Vols. 1–90 and continuing. Bellingham, Wa.: SPIE—International Society for Optical Engineering, 1985–present.

—. "Publication of Proceedings Papers in Optical Engineering: A Topic Revisited—Again!" *Optical Engineering* 32 (1993): 2021.

—. "Publication of Proceedings Paper—Revisited." *Optical Engineering* 31 (1992): 1141.

—. *Research Reports of the Link Energy Fellows.* Vols. 1–9 and continuing. New York: University of Rochester Press, 1985–present.

Webster's New Collegiate Dictionary. Springfield, Mass.: Merriam, 1974.

Yeats, W. B. "The Scholars." *Selected Poems and Three Plays of William Butler Yeats.* Ed. M. L. Rosenthal. New York: Collier Books, 1915.

20

Active Mentorship in Scholarly Publishing: Why, What, Who, How

Terri Frongia

The pressure to publish has been steadily increasing throughout the academic profession. Indeed, as one august faculty member at a well-known research university remarked to a graduate student: "When I began my career, it was: 'publish and prosper.' Then the truism became: 'publish or perish.' Now I seem to hear: 'publish, publish, publish—and perhaps perish anyway.'"

At many institutions, the key to obtaining tenure and promotion is publication. Increasingly, it has also become the key to obtaining the tenure-track job in the first place. As Cezar M. Ornatowski observes, the "trickle-down effect" doesn't end there: "While a few years ago it was relatively rare for Ph.D. students to publish in major refereed journals, today more students publish earlier in their careers, raising the ante for others. (Recently, I even reviewed an application to an M.A. program in literature from an undergraduate who already had published in an edited collection from a major university press)" (1994, 29).

But professional advancement is only one force behind the impetus to "publish, publish, publish." Yet another—more beneficent, perhaps, but equally compelling—is that of intellectual survival. Rapid change has marked virtually every area of study during the last twenty years or so. Now even dramatically different disciplines—mathematics and literature, for example, which find common conceptual territory in chaos theory—provoke transformation in one another.

How is it possible then to fulfill the various demands of personal preference, discipline, and career within the realm of scholarly publication in an intelligent, time- and resource-efficient manner? The answer is through active mentorship, an integrated, systematic approach to the process of scholarly publishing.

WHY ACTIVE MENTORSHIP IN SCHOLARLY PUBLISHING?

The highest levels of higher education have long been pervaded by an unquestioning belief in—or at least passive acceptance of—the efficacy of *osmosis* as an instructional device. As Jack Schuster points out, "graduate education succeeds admirably in training would-be professors in the ways of doing research and by providing, largely by osmosis, models of what professors actually do in their many-faceted professional lives" (1993, 30).

Recently, however, institutions, faculty, and, most particularly, students, have become acutely aware of the deficiencies and dangers inherent in relying on osmosis as a means of instruction, particularly in regards to preparing faculty for the complex contemporary realities of the academic's professional life.

Institutions have particularly been exposed to pressures both external and internal. Movements either to supplement or diminish the traditional reliance on osmosis in both teaching and research have steadily gained support. To give but one example of pressure from without: In the state of California, taxpayers began to complain to legislators that their University of California-enrolled offspring were being taught by graduate students who were ignorant of the craft of teaching. The legislators, in turn, took those complaints to the president of the nine-campus UC system. As a result, training in their pedagogic duties became mandatory for all graduate student instructors (i.e., teaching assistants) through-out the UC system.

And an example of pressure from within? In 1988, graduate students aiming at academic careers and intolerant of osmotic practice petitioned the University of California, Riverside, Department of Literatures and Languages, for a "Research and Publication" seminar. They requested that their department provide them with both an experienced, knowledgeable faculty member and a unit-bearing course that would systematically and comprehensively introduce them to the multiplicitous world of academic research and publication. The department, recognizing the value of such a course to the aspiring professionals in its charge, granted the petition. Their positive response led to the creation not only of a graduate course but also of a kind of self-help mentor, *The Grad Student's Guide to Getting Published*, coauthored/edited by two of the graduate student activists. So-called nontraditional students—those who may have families, outside jobs, and a few more years than most of their colleagues—in particular have little time or energy to expend negotiating the maze of osmotic practice. Of course, both these students and their "traditional" peers are susceptible to the sometimes overwhelming pressures of finding gainful employment in a "downsized" academic market. Both recognize early publication credits as a way to stand out from the overstocked pool of fellow applicants.

Faculty, too, feel the pinch in this high-demand environment. Expanded teaching loads, increasing numbers of students in each class, more and more committees to serve on, exponentially exploding "cutting-edge" scholarship, review committee upon review committee demanding greater and greater levels of performance: the clock ticks and precious time to dedicate to research, thinking, and writing slips away from their grasp as they sit, solitary and forlorn, in their office cubicle.

Time, tools, strategies, connection, community—whether formally and institutionally organized or informally and individually provided, active mentorship
alone offers this full array of skills and techniques to enhance achievement in the
arena of scholarly publishing.

WHAT IS ACTIVE MENTORSHIP IN SCHOLARLY PUBLISHING?

Scholarly publishing may be defined as the end result of the full process of
scholarly activity—query, investigation (research), cogitation, application, form-
ulation/expression (writing), submission/review, and acceptance (publication)—
which makes its full, "public" appearance in a scholarly forum (preferably a
blind, peer-reviewed, readily recognized, academic or professional journal).

Of course, the term also refers to the larger environment of that forum. This
environment embraces a large variety of distinct but related areas of intellectual
endeavor and territory. It includes, for example, the whole range of opinion and
dialogue on what constitutes "real" or "significant" scholarship, and why. It also
includes the entire apparatus of publishing itself, such as the scope or mission of
a publication (that is, how it defines and contributes to the discipline it
represents); its criteria for submission and review (how it performs its function
as "gatekeeper"); the forms and kinds of editorial intervention it may make (the
intellectual space and relationships it constructs for its authors, readers,
subscribers, and advertisers); and its "weight" or "rank" in the profession (the
history and vicissitudes of its status).

Clearly, the realm of scholarly publishing encompasses not only this broad,
complex territory—what could be termed the academic publishing macrocosm—but also the narrower confines of individual practice—that is, the
scholarly microcosm. Since the stakes have become so high and the terrain so
difficult to negotiate, it is all the more imperative that both practitioners and
institutions supplant their traditional reliance on osmosis as *passe-partout* to the
realm of scholarly publishing with explicit initiation—that is, formal instruction—into its language, expectations, politics, and realities. The term I use for
just such a clear, structured, straightforward approach to this facet of professional
endeavor is *active mentorship*.

Depending on need, the practice of active mentorship may address the entire
gamut of the process of scholarly production (research, writing, and publication),
or it may treat only the placement of the scholarly product (submission and
publication). The mentorship may be provided by peers, colleagues, departments,
colleges, faculty development offices, professional institutes, or independent
consultants. It may also take the form of seminars, workshops, informal support
groups, individual consultations, or self-help initiatives.

WHO SHOULD BE INVOLVED IN ACTIVE MENTORSHIP?

There are as many answers to this question as there are possible forms of active mentorship in scholarly publishing. It makes the most sense, however, to begin at the beginning, for, as Robert Boice notes: "While we might readily suppose that new hires come to campus without proper grounding as teachers, my studies indicate similar deficits in managing writing and publishing. Not only did new faculty fail to find time, support, and ideas for writing; they often lacked a clear conception of how to format and prepare manuscripts for publication" (1992, xi).

Or, to view the situation from a different perspective, the most fundamental problem is this: Graduate schools are not providing their graduate students—our future faculty—with even the basic tools required to succeed in their chosen profession as academics. In *The Grad Student's Guide to Getting Published*, a new faculty member shared his graduate experiences with the interviewers. When asked whether he had received any practical or formal training in publishing, his answer was negative—and he had never heard of any such programs offered by other departments either. Furthermore, when asked whether there were expectations that he would somehow publish anyway, he responded:

> Yes and no. Although professors recognized the importance of publication in one's professional life, many seemed to feel that the "how to" of publishing is something best learned on one's own—something any suitably motivated graduate student could figure out for himself. Their main objective was to train you as a philosopher and get you through the program. If you felt the work you produced while under their supervision was good enough for publication, then, I suppose, you would submit it yourself. But there was never any instruction in how this should be done. (51–52)

Whether present on the individual, departmental, or institutional level, reliance on osmosis as the method of choice (or merely of default) in professional preparation and development is clearly miscalculated and counterproductive. Utilization of this method clearly promulgates the insensitive, potentially debilitating environment Joseph Moxley identifies in *Publish, Don't Perish*, for "the implicit message that scholars, institutions, and professional organizations give about scholarly publishing is sink or swim, publish or perish" (xvii). Clearly, each level of faculty is at risk in its own way and so would benefit from at least some form of active mentorship in this area. Without clear instruction in the requirements of academic research, writing, and marketing, graduate students and freshly minted Ph.D.s may stand little chance of landing that all-important first job. New faculty require not only the tools provided by such instruction, but also a certain measure of success in order to obtain much-desired tenure.[1]

Finally, as Boice mentions in *Professors as Writers*, even established faculty may require stimulation through active mentorship, either because they have lost habits and mindsets conducive to writing, or because they continue to write and yet become "blocked" or disillusioned by their lack of success in placing and publishing their work. (Boice also shares an astounding discovery, which bears repeating here: "Estimates typically attribute some 85 percent of publications to some 15 percent of those who could potentially write them.")[2] Without active intervention, too many scholarly voices will be lost to us. Can the contemporary academy afford that loss? Can our future?

Although Boice indicates that over the twenty-odd years of his career the wall of silence protecting the arcane mysteries of scholarly publishing has been steadily eroding, Moxley observes that even today "most institutions and professional organizations have failed to provide guidance or support for scholarly publishing. Few institutions provide workshops in writing and marketing scholarly manuscripts" (xvi).

The need is evident. Tools and information abound.

How do we move from the current state of professional breakdown brought about by an unexamined faith in osmosis, an unhealthy acceptance of inertia, and the stress provoked by high anxiety over the steady increase in the academic publications ante?

HOW CAN *YOU* ENGAGE IN AND ENCOURAGE ACTIVE MENTORSHIP?

There are two basic ways to take your own initial steps toward active mentorship. The first follows the easiest, most economical, and most rudimentary path: that of self-help. Dozens of volumes exist which can guide you through any number of issues involving research, writing, editing, and publishing. (See Bruce Speck's Annotated Bibliography of Academic Publishing Sources.) After you've familiarized yourself with the territory and what it has—or doesn't have—to offer, you may decide to move further outward in your search. This is when you should turn to your own campus resources for assistance: the information, materials, and programs you need may already be at your fingertips, just waiting for you to discover and take advantage of them.[3]

As we have seen, however, the kind of active mentorship by which you would profit most is probably not readily available. That brings us to the second path, the path taken by those graduate students mentioned earlier at the University of California, Riverside: the path of active initiative and collaborative effort.

Several strategies are available for taking the initiative, regardless of whether your intent is principally to benefit yourself or to assist others. The strategies you choose, however, depend in large part on what your particular needs seem to be, how comfortable you are in revealing those needs, and what kind of climate exists at your department or institution. Because it is easier to achieve one's goals with a plan or template of action and to modify it as you go, several suggestions for initiating active mentorship are offered below. Furthermore, with proper modification the models provided may be molded to suit various target audiences—for example, graduate students, junior or established faculty, emeriti, or professionals new to academia. They can also be designed for implementation by individuals, teams, departments, colleges, faculty development offices, or consortiums of educators.

As mentioned earlier, the process of scholarly publishing consists of three phases or activities: research, writing, and placement (publishing). While much has been written about the first two, it seems that the last is the least explored and thus the most deeply affected by the tradition of osmotic practice. This area, then, will be the focal point for the models presented. Before offering these models, however, I would like to reiterate a few useful techniques or tools for enhancing research and writing.

If the part of the scholarly process on which you would most like to work is research, then you may want to consider participating in a library\informational technologies orientation or workshop. Or you may want to join an organized research center or institute working in your discipline. (If none is available, you could facilitate the formation of an informal research group within your department or college.)[4] Although it takes additional effort and commitment, collaborating with a faculty or student colleague(s) may bring you the kind of results you desire. (After all, the sciences do this all the time!)

If writing is the professional obligation you find most difficult to negotiate, you could begin with a solid program like the ones offered by Boice in *Professors as Writers* (1990) and Moxley in *Publish, Don't Perish* (1992). Locate or form a group of others with similar needs in the areas of time management, drafting, composition, editing, or whatever. Several sets of eyes and ears will help clarify lines of thought and smooth out rough spots in expression and style. (Regular meetings also force you to keep up with production; both I and a colleague completed the writing of our dissertations in just a few months, mainly because we met regularly to read our writing to each other.) You'll find that sharing inspiring success stories and effective coping strategies is useful in charting your own progress. Be sure also to identify those people on your campus who are editors, readers, and reviewers, or organizers for professional conferences, and invite them to share some of their expertise with your group. Most are delighted to take the time to help demystify the scholarly publishing process, and all will no doubt provide truly useful gems of wisdom. An example of one such gem is the following, which was volunteered by Professor Max Neiman, a reader for several journals in the field of political science, to an inquiring group of graduate students:

> It is essential for you to understand that the vast majority of submissions—even papers submitted by experienced or well-known people—don't get accepted the first time. In fact, as a reader I generally accept about no more than maybe one out of every seven or eight manuscripts I read. But that doesn't mean that I think

only one out of seven should get published. I would say that at least half of them are ultimately publishable. Of all the things I myself have published, maybe only two or three of them hit the first time. You can't expect a manuscript to just go there and score a direct hit.[5]

Dr. Neiman's remark provides not only insight into the process of scholarly publishing from the "other side" (that is, from the perspective of the peer reviewer or editor); it also identifies where the unmapped territory of active mentorship in scholarly publishing lies—that is, in the netherworld of "marketing," submission, editorial decision, and publication. It is in this all-important territory of professional success and personal validation that many academics lack compass and tools. While some of the tools, techniques, and formats offered in the three models below may be familiar to some, experience in the field indicates that they will be a revelation to most.

MODEL I

This model represents a very timely graduate-level course that approaches the issue of scholarly publishing in a holistic—and supremely pragmatic—manner. Developed by UC Riverside faculty Stephanie Hammer, associate professor of comparative literature and German, and acting associate director of the Center for Ideas and Society, the 10-week (thirty-hour) course seeks to offer graduates strategies for career initiation. Since one of the most important strategies for success is self-marketing, the course requires the preparation, delivery, and videotaping of a short conference paper delivered by the student. This paper is then reviewed for submission, with specific journals identified as likely "homes" for the piece. The course syllabus follows:

Research, Publication, and "Getting Ahead"

Week 1: **Library Visit: Research Orientation**

—Guest speaker: Grad students and scholarly publishing
—Tools for research, traditional and technological
—Bibliography-building

Week 2: **Reports and Bibliographies**

—5–minute concise report on paper[*] and its argument
—More bibliography-building/critically reading materials

Week 3: **Paper Proposals and Professional Conferences**

—Write 2-3 page proposal based on paper
—Start developing 15-minute-long paper for mock conference

Week 4: **Giving and Getting Good Conferences**

—Mock conference planning and scheduling
—Completion of 15-minute-long paper

Week 5: **Mock Conference**

—Delivery of papers to invited guests
—Videotaping of conference for self-critique

Week 6: **Conference Postmortem and Videotape Discussion**

—Debriefing of conference experience
—Reworking your piece into a publishable article
—Targeting your piece: sample journals

Week 7: **Reports on 2–3 Targeted Journals**

—Oral reports about targeted journals
—Guest speakers: "How I got published" roundtable
—Continued work on the article
—Preparing an annotated bibliography of the article

Week 8: **Looking Ahead**

—Dissertation prospecti
—Grant proposals

Week 9: **The Big Time**

—Dealing with university presses

Week 10: **Conclusion: Nitty-Gritty Vocational Matters**

—Cover letters
—C.V.s
—Job interviews
—Guest lectures

* Guidelines for choosing a paper for development: (1) A graduate paper you have already written and for which you have received no less than an "A-"; (2) an essay you feel passionate about (probably your best work to date); (3) and—ideally—the professor for whom you wrote the paper would be willing to discuss and reread it as it progresses. (Next best choice: a more advanced peer.)

MODEL II

Dr. George Slusser, director of the comparative literature program and curator of the Eaton Collection of Science Fiction and Fantasy at UC Riverside, developed the second model. It represents the template of the course, "Introduction to Scholarly Publishing," for which graduate students in the Department of Literatures and Languages petitioned in 1988. Slusser expressed his goals for the course in "Gates of Ivory and Gates of Horn: Teaching the Craft and the Art of Scholarly Publishing in the University," one of the twenty-six contributions in *The Grad Student's Guide to Getting Published*: "The entire thrust of the graduate course in scholarly publishing is that even when the realities of publication, as graduate student or as fully sanctioned academic, are faced head on, there still remains a possibility of combining craft and art, of making pragmatism and idealism function together in order to create new avenues of scholarly discourse" (1993, 4).

As the syllabus reveals, his approach was to take "a pragmatic look at the different areas of scholarly publishing" (5). Because this approach is focused on the various genres, "givens," opportunities, biases, and ethics of scholarly publishing, it offers a simple yet productive forum for encouraging faculty dialogue and production.

Introduction to Scholarly Publishing

Week 1: **Articles and Essays**

(Introduction to the stacks; individual consultations)

Week 2: **Articles and Essays**

(Guest: Editor/ Reader, *French Review*; *French Forum*)

Week 3: **Dissertations**

(Individual consultations)

Week 4: **Books**

(Guest: Editor/ Reviewer, *Studies in Modern Philology*)

Week 5: **Books**

(Guest: Editor, University of California Press)

Week 6: **Journals**

(Visit to the stacks; individual consultations)

Week 7: **Editing**

(Guests: Editor, Dryden Project; Editor, *Eighteenth Century Studies*)

Week 8: **Translations; Desktop Publishing**

(Guests: Multilingual academic translator; Reviewer, Borgo Press)

Week 9: **Book Reviews**

(Individual presentations: projects)

Week 10: **Conclusion**

(Individual presentations: targeted placement of projects,
with rationale for selection)

Although the structure of this model is that of a basic introduction to the topic, it is carefully orchestrated to provide insight into pragmatic issues like "staking out" scholarly territory (such as genres, specialties, hierarchies) as well as to offer the opportunity for intense interaction with a broad range of guest speakers representing a variety of disciplines, institutions, functions, and measures of scholarly acceptance or success. Conceived in such dynamic terms, it is no surprise that the course may take unexpected directions, as Slusser points out when he reminisces about his own experience: "[class discussion] gradually evolved into a very cogent mixture of cultural analysis and ethical self-examination. As possibilities for publication unfolded, so did assumptions about and prejudices toward certain kinds of scholarly endeavors; students began to see the academic world for what it is. They came to articulate its hidden assumptions, and by doing so learned to seek out its broad opportunities for creative expression" (5).

One tangible outcome of both the course and this search for creative expression was, as indicated earlier, *The Grad Student's Guide to Getting Published*, which recreates, at least in part, some of the conversation and flavor of that course.[6]

MODEL III

The third and last model grew out of Alida Allison's and my work on the *Guide*, as well as our subsequent "lived experience" as teachers, mentors, and publishing scholars. It is, in a sense, yet more pragmatic and restricted than the other two, for it focuses very much on acquiring (and imparting) basic tools for successful shaping, placement, and promotion of one's scholarly work.

As the title suggests, this model is designed to be not a course in the subject, but a free-standing module in a series of workshops on scholarly publishing. The goal of this module is to help break reliance on osmotic practice by providing participants—through interactive participation such as hands-on practice, discussion, and collaborative techniques—with a more informed understanding of the *specific* demands and requirements of academic publishing. This understanding, along with the techniques and materials utilized, is in turn intended to create a foundation not only for enlightened personal practice, but for a concrete plan of action for actively mentoring others as well.

Introductory Workshop on Scholarly Publishing*

I. The Situation: Scholarly Publishing

What is it? What is it for? Who needs it?

Using a worksheet, participants answer each of these questions. Subsequent discussion should reveal not only where each individual is "at" in their understanding of scholarly publishing, but should also provide direction for broadening their understanding of, as well as dialogue about, the topic. For example, responses to "What is it?" should include reference to various *types* (contributing source: *Scholarship Reconsidered*), *genres* (contributing sources: *Publish, Don't Perish, Persist and Publish, Grad Student's Guide to Getting Published*), *criteria* (research, citations, peer review, etc.), and so forth.

II. The Language of Scholarly Publishing

Fundamental Terms
Essential Instruments

Here participants are presented with definitions of key terms like "multiple submission," "blind submission," "referees," and "style sheets." Besides mastery, this segment results in discussion of important issues like "What's wrong with multiple submissions?," and leads to assessments of *why* certain editorial policies exist, *who* they benefit and *how*, and what the *consequences* may be for not following them.

In the second segment participants are presented with definitions of critical instruments like cover letters, letters of inquiry, abstracts, and "introductory cv's." Models or templates may be shared and analyzed. A second worksheet on compiling submission packets for inquiries as well as for actual submissions may also be prepared for/by participants.

III. The Game: Gathering Information

Using Directories of Periodicals
Using Journals and Assessment Sheets

In the first segment, participants are introduced to that essential but ill-known tool, the Directory of Periodicals. Sample entries are analyzed for the critical information they offer. This information is then interpreted for what it may communicate about the macrocosm of scholarly publishing, as well as what it "says" to the reader/scholarly author. In either group or individual activity, participants may be invited to "place" a work by being given the abstract, an outline, and several entries from various journals; results can be compared and analyzed for further discussion. Broad strategies may then be defined and articulated, based on desired outcome (e.g., query, feedback, publication).

The second segment continues the first by introducing the "primary" or "hard" evidence—that is, the journals themselves. Not only are actual journals perused and analyzed, but an "Assessment Sheet" (source: *The Grad Student's Guide to Getting Published*) is provided to assist in the process of "reading" and thus "targeting" likely journals for the "marketing" of participants' work.

IV. The Work: Doing Your Best and Finding the Fit

Assessing the Writing
Assessing *Your* Writing
Preparing the Manuscript

Participants are given excerpts of *published* writing to respond to and discuss. The goals of this exercise are to see writing through the eyes of the reviewer/editor and to illustrate that not all scholarly writing—even successfully published writing—is perfect, polished, or eloquent.

Depending on amount of time allotted and final results desired from the workshop, participants may either be given guidelines for assessing the quality of their own writing, or they may participate in small peer review sessions for the second segment.

In the final segment, participants are given general yet concrete guidelines for submitting their work (sources: *Publishing in the Academy* and/or *Grad Student's Guide to Getting Published*).

V. The Strategy: Playing the Game

Plans of Action/ Keeping Records
Coping With Rejection/Coping With Revision
Parlaying Success (Acceptance!)/Meeting Goals

Whether utilizing an actual or hypothetical work, participants are expected to *identify and prioritize* 3–5 journals to which to submit, as well as describe the rationale for selection. They then compile a submission packet, as well as design a feasible system for (1) tracking their submission; (2) shepherding the work along. (This is the "keeping records" component of the plan.)

After data and actual examples of outright rejection, "split decisions," and requests for revision are shared (source: *Grad Student's Guide to Getting Published*), participants are invited to discuss strategies for coping with each example/scenario. Results are shared and further refined to individual "plans of action" participants may accept or, preferably embrace and implement (contributing source: *Professors as Writers*).

Finally, participants are requested to perform some assessment, both of themselves and of the workshop. The first exercise has to do with reflecting upon their own participation in scholarly publishing. They are asked to respond honestly to the following: Where are you now? What are you publishing/do you want to publish? Why are you publishing? Where are you going? The second exercise asks that they consider their participation in active mentorship in scholarly publishing; for example: Was this workshop of value to you, and why? Who would you suggest attend, and why? Would you like to receive more mentoring (if yes, in what area; if not, why not)? Would you like to help provide active mentorship to others, or assist in "missionary" work (source: *Professors as Writers*)?

* Participants are provided with a *Workbook in Scholarly Publishing* containing all of the worksheets, pertinent contributing source materials, and "Journal Assessment Sheet" necessary for performing the activities in the Workshop. They may also arrange to receive a personal copy of the resource text, *The Grad Student's Guide to Getting Published*.

CONCLUSION

Because individuals, institutions, and professional organizations have relied (and continue to rely) on the method of osmosis to "instruct" academics in their expected duties, there is a yawning gap in knowledge and practice at the very heart of scholarly endeavor. If colleagues are to find both their voices as authors and success as scholars, then the system itself must prepare to make active mentorship in scholarly publishing an integrated, systematic component of professional practice.

Such a transformation should not be too difficult a task, for "the system" is made up of individuals who can, and often do, effect change. The graduate students in the Department of Literatures and Languages at UC Riverside became their own advocates, and their faculty mentors responded quickly and effectively. Professional trailblazers like McKeachie and Seldin, Cross and Grasha, Boice and Boyer, have all sounded calls to action; all have evoked positive, even passionate, responses.

The *time* to start is now—now that sufficient information, tools, and strategies are at hand, right here in this volume. The *place* to start is with yourself, in your own practice and on your own campus. As I have endeavored to show in this chapter, following the path of active mentorship in scholarly publishing is neither superfluous nor difficult nor costly. It may start with a book from the bookstore, an informal conversation with peers, a seminar for graduate students, a workshop with or for colleagues. The beginning is clear. What is not known is where a trip down the freshly illuminated road of scholarly publishing may one day bring us. The question for you to answer is this: In traversing that road, what signposts do *I* want to contribute?

NOTES

1. See Chapter 2 of Ralph E. Matkin and T. F. Riggar's *Persist and Publish: Helpful Hints for Academic Writing and Publishing* (Niwot, Colo.: University Press of Colorado, 1991) for a review of studies indicating "productivity patterns expected by academic institutions" (23).

2. Boice cites J. R. Cole's article, "Women in Science," *American Scientist* 69, (1981): 385–391. In his Introduction to *Publish, Don't Perish*, Moxley cites studies by Ernest Boyer, Mary Renck Jalongo, and Charles J. Sykes, which support the conclusion that "only about 10 to 20 percent of our colleagues appear to be responsible for the bulk of what is published" (xvi).

3. For suggestions on where to look, see Chapter 7 of *The Grad Student's Guide to Getting Published*, "Using Your University Fully."

4. For guidance in both this area and the following area, collaboration, I recommend consulting Ann E. Austin's and Roger G. Baldwin's *Faculty Collaboration: Enhancing the Quality of Scholarship and Teaching*. ASHE-ERIC Higher Education Report No. 7 (Washington, D.C.: George Washington University, School of Education and Human Development, 1991).

5. Interview with Max Neiman transcribed and edited for "Start Being Professional Now," in *The Grad Student's Guide to Getting Published* 44. For more information on typical rejection rates on journal articles, see also Matkin and Riggar, *Persist and Publish*

(pp. 83–85); you may also do your own calculations based on the information found in reference works like the Modern Language Association's *Directory of Periodicals*.

6. Ornatowski describes the book as "an introduction to the lively debates that are reshaping the course of higher education in America." He further comments that "In the interstices of discussions of collegiality, research, and the mechanics of publication, the book manages to deal with other issues critical to academic life: professor/student relationships; the use (and misuse) of graduate students; the place of women in academia; the problem of finding one's place in the scholarly world and integrating one's intellectual activity with one's personal and political life; the ethics of publishing; and the present and future state of graduate education in America" (29).

REFERENCES

Allison, Alida, and Terri Frongia. *The Grad Student's Guide to Getting Published*. New York: Prentice Hall, 1992.

Boice, Robert. *Professors as Writers*. Stillwater, Okla.: New Forums Press, 1990.

—. "Foreword." *Publish Don't Perish: The Scholar's Guide to Academic Writing and Publishing*. By Joseph M. Moxley. Westport, Conn.: Greenwood Press, 1992.

Boyer, Ernest L. *Scholarship Reconsidered: Priorities of the Professoriate*. Princeton, N.J.: Carnegie Foundation for the Advancement of Teaching, 1990.

Moxley, Joseph M. *Publish, Don't Perish: The Scholar's Guide to Academic Writing and Publishing*. Westport, Conn.: Greenwood Press, 1992.

Ornatowski, Cezar M. "Harbinger of Change." Review of *The Grad Student's Guide to Getting Published*, by Alida Allison and Terri Frongia. *American Book Review* (December 1993–January 1994): 29–30.

Schuster, Jack. "Preparing Faculty for the New Conceptions of Scholarship." *New Directions for Teaching and Learning* 54 (1993): 30.

21

Mentoring and the Art of Getting Dissertations Published

Fredric G. Gale

Any discussion of how to get doctoral students' dissertations published must begin with two questions. First, why should the dissertation director want to get his or her students' dissertations published? Second, why should it be important to the student writer to get published while still a graduate student; won't there be plenty of time for that later, when the student becomes a professor? In this chapter, I will try to answer these important questions and several others that are in turn raised by the answers.

FROM THE DIRECTOR'S POINT OF VIEW

The task of directing a doctoral dissertation is an onerous one that is not usually compensated in any direct way by the university. For this reason alone, many graduate faculty members try to avoid directing dissertations—indeed, avoid the mentoring role altogether—and content themselves with sitting on dissertation committees as readers.[1] Thus, the director can be assumed to have a fairly strong sense of duty to the university, the department, and the graduate students, or he or she would not have taken on the job in the first place. The director may also be driven by a personal desire for promotion and recognition. Whatever the reasons for becoming the dissertation director, they do not obviously explain why this individual should be concerned with something that will take place *after* the student has graduated. Very likely the director's aim is to help the department maintain a vigorous doctoral program; if so, one of the ways to do so is to have as many as possible of one's doctoral students go on to success at other universities. This word-of-mouth index of success is one of the few ways by which highly rated graduate students can measure the suitability of a particular doctoral program for their needs. One of the surest ways to success, at least success as measured by promotion and tenure, is to publish a theoretical monograph, and one of the easiest ways to write one is to turn one's dissertation into a book. A dissertation director who encourages the student writer to think of the dissertation as a book and then helps the student to realize this goal helps not only the student but also the graduate program, and ultimately, the department. For successful graduate students beget future graduate students who are bright and highly motivated, and so on.

FROM THE STUDENTS' POINT OF VIEW

Many—perhaps most—doctoral students are long on information about the theoretical contents of their chosen field but painfully short on practical wisdom about how to get an academic job and keep it and about the politics of publishing. Thus, many students are unaware of the enormous benefit accruing from getting their dissertations published in the first year or so after graduation. Accordingly, dissertation directors should clearly inform their students of the facts of life. One of these facts is that, as Robert Boice and Ferdinand Jones point out: "As few as 10 percent of writers in specific areas account for over 85 percent of the literature" (1984, 568). Joseph Moxley suggests one of the reasons for this paucity of published writers: "Because our culture tends to mystify and aggrandize the creative process, many academicians are unaware of how productive authors work. They are often naive about how politics and subjective factors taint the editorial process. Many academicians are unaware of the aggressive marketing strategies they may need to publish their work" (1992, xvi–xvii).

These reasons and others account for the many doctoral students who embark on the search for academic positions without essential knowledge of how candidates prepare to get themselves hired and, having found positions, become tenured. This is why I argue that dissertation directors have a duty to inform their students and to try to persuade them to perceive the dissertation from the beginning as a book, because then it is much more likely that it will be published as a book.[2]

But what if the student does not agree and, for one reason or another, does not consider publication of the dissertation a high priority. Perhaps then the director should only make a perfunctory offer of help, and when that offer meets with disinterest he or she should simply desist. Most doctoral students recognize that, even if they are fortunate enough to achieve publication, the event is not likely to occur before they start interviewing for academic positions. Therefore, they reason, they are better off devoting their time and energy to publishing articles that will at least be accepted for publication before the job-hunting process begins. Although we may view this thinking as shortsighted, it is the natural outgrowth of the financial exigency that burdens most graduate students by the end of their final year, if not before. Many of them are very much accustomed to short-term thinking about money.

PREPARING THE STUDENT AND THE DISSERTATION

Suppose, however, that one's student sees the benefit of getting an early start on that *sine qua non* of academic advancement, the theoretical monograph, and is eager to point his or her dissertation toward publication. What determines whether the dissertation will eventually reach the public? Quite obviously, the student's writing ability and dedication are the most important factors. If the student has reached this point in his or her career and the dissertation director is not satisfied that the student has these attributes in abundance, then it is best to let the student down gently and immediately. If the student has these qualities, other contributing factors include the degree of involvement of the director and the other members of the committee in selecting the topic and developing the dissertation, beginning with the prospectus. In most cases a student can write a dissertation that will be acceptable to the committee—but is not publishable as a book—in less time than it would take to write one that could be successfully marketed as a book. Therefore, it may be necessary to push the student in the direction of a cutting edge topic instead of the one that the student has been privately cherishing and perhaps even storing up notes for. This may involve the student in writing several drafts of the prospectus and may lead the student to feel a mounting sense of frustration and impatience.

Each director may deal with this problem differently. My own approach is to sit down with the student at intervals over weeks or months *before* he or she actually starts writing the prospectus; I review successive drafts of his or her extended thesis statement, until I get what I consider to be a current topic of sufficient complexity and intellectual content. I do not tell the student what to write, but if I am dissatisfied, I will ask the student to read more, suggesting additions to his or her reading list. When both the student and I are satisfied, then the student will write the prospectus that all the committee members will review and comment on. Some committee members object to this method because they want to be fully involved from the beginning. The enlightened dissertation director deals with this political problem out of the student's sight and hearing and resolves it before the process is very far along.

It is difficult to generalize about what is a publishable topic; obviously, that depends on the particular discipline. Some dissertations have little or no hope because they are either too arcane, thus limiting their market, or too out of date, that is, not in the current conversation among experts on the topic. In the field of English, for example, a dissertation today that deconstructs the work of a prominent writer would find little audience and no publisher. While Jacques Derrida is still an important figure in the humanities and the social sciences, the application of the deconstructive strategy has been done and redone and is no longer interesting. We must remember that publishing, even academic publishing, is a business. Even though university presses do not expect to make money on every book they publish, they do not want to commit financial suicide either.

Some of them will take a risk on some books, but not much of a risk and not on many books, or they will not survive for long. In short, the student must find *for himself or herself* a topic of current interest, one that is being talked about in the prominent journals. The dissertation director should not actually suggest topics to the writer; rather, he or she should guide the student away from the wrong topic. I will discuss why later in this chapter when I discuss the topic of mentoring and its implications. Thus, it may be weeks or even months before the student defines a satisfactory topic and writes an acceptable prospectus. Some students and some professors may be unwilling to devote this kind of time to the project even before the student begins to write in earnest.

THE WRITING PROCESS

Nevertheless, let us suppose that you have influenced your student to select a topic that at least has publication potential. The student has submitted a first draft of the first chapter. What you, as the director, choose to do at this point will determine how the writing process will proceed, and therefore the student has a choice to make. The student may write the dissertation *as a book* from the beginning, or may write it as a dissertation and hope to revise it sufficiently later to get it published. Both choices pose difficulties, and the better choice depends on the student's priorities. Many universities—because of bad experiences and also because it is an employer's market today—are now willing to hire only those people who already have their Ph.D. in hand when they start work as a brand–new faculty hire in the August following their campus interview. Thus, some doctoral candidates must defend their dissertations in the June or July preceding. Depending on when they have started their dissertations, this may mean defending a somewhat imperfect dissertation: one that is finished but not very polished. In such cases, some committees may show a little leniency, but such a dissertation is far from being a publishable book. It may need several more revisions that the writer simply has no time to prepare. Students who can put off the job search for another year might well be able to turn out a dissertation that is a finished book. Even so, it will likely require revisions for the referees for the publisher may require further changes. All of this takes time, time that the student does not have, perhaps because he or she has exhausted his or her financial resources.

On the other hand, the student may decide (or may be forced to decide) to proceed with the minimum dissertation and to revise it following safe employment somewhere. This is not any easy route to take either, for every dissertation requires extensive revision, which cannot be rushed. Typically, a dissertation contains some material that we describe as a review of the literature"; this is the part that students usually find easiest to write. It demonstrates that the student has read all of the relevant literature on the general topic in which his or her dissertation is situated. However, this part is too long for most readers of the book, and they, unlike the members of the committee, are not a captive audience. Some ruthless cutting is necessary in this part and in any other parts inserted as padding. It must be replaced by some new material that is more argumentative and groundbreaking than the student writer is usually prepared to risk in the dissertation. But when it comes to marketing the dissertation as a book, the director should advise budding authors that they have nothing to lose and everything to gain from intellectual pioneering, however risky that may seem.

FINDING A PUBLISHER

This is what it takes to get an academic book published today: one cannot, like Alexander Pope, say what has oft been said before, howsoever cleverly one says it; one must have something new to say, and it must be most definitely an addition to the ongoing conversation in the discipline. Therefore, both student and director must be right up to the minute on what is being said on the dissertation topic in the academic journals and newest academic books. A dozen publishers stand ready to publish the latest book by Stephen Hawking or Stephen King, but if I want my work published, I must find a topic that will interest at least a thousand readers enough to make them buy the book. Since my name will not do it, my text must.

This is what publishers are looking for, but they will not come looking for your student; publishers must first be sold the idea of the book. And before this, one must help select likely publishers for the student's book. Assuming the director is active in publishing in the field (presumably he or she would not otherwise be directing a doctoral dissertation), he or she knows that you select a publisher as you would select an academic journal for your article. Just as you read journals and know that each is likely to publish, so you follow what various book publishers have published in your field. This suggests that publishers never change, and of course this is not true. Publishers occasionally do branch out into new fields, but this sort of breakout is unpredictable; in any case, it is usually introduced by a book written by, or a series of books edited by, someone prominent in the field. It rarely begins with the publication of someone's dissertation in a new field.

One can begin, therefore, by eliminating publishers outside one's field and publishers who do trade books and textbooks. For example, a book on composition theory may have a good chance at Southern Illinois University Press but little chance at Oxford University Press. Many textbook publishers like St. Martin's Press are not very interested in critical monographs because they are looking for a large readership. This narrows the list considerably, and it can be narrowed further by looking at what the remaining publishers have done recently and talking to colleagues who are active, until one has a list of perhaps three or four likely publishers. The student may be able to do this but usually has much less information than the director and lacks the director's contacts among active writers in the field.

Almost as important as knowledge of what publishers to target is personal contact with editors. The best place to make this contact is at professional conferences where publishers may often be represented, and this is something that students can only do for themselves. The student, who by now is a faculty member somewhere with students of his or her own, must be advised to approach editors at conferences and open the conversation by discussing a book the editor has recently brought out and then leading the conversation around to his or her own book. Even if the editor does not show more than perfunctory interest, the prospective author is still better off. He or she can now write a cover letter to the editor (enclosing a prospectus for the book) using the editor's name, perhaps even first name, and referring to their earlier conversation. This definitely improves the chances that the editor will at least read the prospectus and perhaps send the book out to reviewers, as opposed to simply sending the manuscript back with a short, polite note.

The prospectus itself is nearly as important as the book, at least in getting the book through the first gate and into the hands of reviewers. Before anything else, the publishers must be convinced that the subject of the book and the author's treatment of it are interesting enough to a broad enough readership that it is worth a financial gamble of thousands of dollars. Accordingly, the key to the prospectus is the section that addresses the market for the proposed book. Here is where one describes what else has been published in the same area as the proposed book and explains how the new book is different and yet interesting to many of the same readers. One must explain why readers will want to read the book and must suggest who the readers might be, that is, in what academic disciplines and other occupations. The book must have merit, of course, and that will be established by sending the book out to referees. First, however, the editor must be convinced that it is marketable. The former student, perhaps now a colleague and friend at another university, must be persuaded to spend a great deal of time on this part of the prospectus, doing careful research and careful writing. It is time well spent.

MENTORING AND OTHER RELATIONSHIPS WITH STUDENTS

Let us now present some useful advice about conducting oneself in the role of dissertation director and how that role may be transmuted into other roles. First, it should be clear that being an advisor is not the same thing as being a mentor. Shapior, Haseltine and Rowe describe a number of hierarchical relationships that may be suggested, created, or implied by the relationship between professor and student, such as that of dissertation director and writer. These include relationships from the most evenly balanced or symmetrical to the most unbalanced: "peer pal," "guide," "sponsor," "patron," and, finally, "mentor." The peer pal is someone at the same level with whom one shares information; at the other end of the scale is the mentor: "An individual who assumes the role of both teacher and advocate in an intense *paternalistic* relationship" (quoted in Merriam, 1983, 164; emphasis added).

Clearly, one can discharge the obligations of dissertation director without assuming the role of mentor; therefore, one might examine why he or she should take on this role that entails so much more. Perhaps the mentor does it for a student thought to be exceptional, as a contribution to the profession and perhaps as a repayment, in a sense, of one's own mentor. Whatever the reason, as extensive research into mentoring argues persuasively and as Lyons, Scroggins, and Rule point out, the mentor "plays an almost spiritual role in the life of the graduate student" (1990, 277). They add that, "While mentoring *can* lead to success in business and the professions, having a mentor is absolutely *essential* for success in graduate school. Graduate school mentors and their protégés share a comradeship of such extraordinary intensity that it transcends the normal teacher/student relationship" (279).

Similarly, John Kronik, writing about the special mentoring relationships between men and women, notes that, "By tradition the mentor is protective, knowing, trustworthy, caring. The mentor-mentee relationship includes but goes well beyond teaching and advising. It stems from a mutual attraction that involves friendship and that provides guidance and nurturing of a broadly professional sort while bearing on the private dimension as well" (1990, 53). The relationship is a complex one and subject to both creative interpretation and misinterpretation. Moreover, as Gary A. Olson and Evelyn Ashton-Jones argue, "The subject of mentoring becomes even more complex when you introduce the factor of gender" (1992, 118).

The obvious dangers associated with cross-gender mentoring are not the only problems that may be just below the surface of the mentoring or even advising relationship. As C. E. Weber notes, "Mentors may be unfulfilled individuals who try to live through an alter-ego in an attempt to gain some sort of immortality" (1980, 21). Although Weber's allusion to the *Pygmalion* mentality does not apply to most of us, I think we might all admit to a strong sense of fulfillment when our favorite students do well and go on to success (sometimes greater than our own). We must be on guard and sufficiently self-reflective to avoid falling into the trap of becoming too involved in our students' dissertations and—worse still—in our students' lives. It is very easy to cross the line unwittingly from advisor to collaborator, because newly graduated students are quite accustomed to looking to their major professors for guidance and encouragement. These new graduates are vulnerable and in some cases may draw the mentor into a new relationship that carries over the support of the old one.

The best thing that can happen if you stray across the line from former mentor or advisor or guide to present collaborator is that the book gets published and you are thanked publicly or privately for your contribution. The worst thing that can happen is that the dissertation never gets published, and you are blamed for it. The risk that the worst will happen is not adequately compensated for by the chance that the best will happen. Therefore, dissertation directors are urged to develop a mentoring relationship with their doctoral students, and be very careful not to become anything more.

NOTES

1. The role of the second, third, fourth, or fifth reader may range from the merely ceremonial to active involvement, depending, of course, on the style of the dissertation director and the customary practice of the department. In any case, I am not denigrating the role of readers, but am merely pointing out that their job is easier than that of the chairperson of the committee, though not to be undertaken lightly.

2. We should remember that I am using the word "likelier" in a relative sense, for, as Stanley Aronowitz has pointed out, only 2 to 3 percent of all manuscripts make it into book form (1988, 44).

REFERENCES

Aronowitz, Stanley. "A Writer's Union for Academics?" *Thought & Action* 4, 2 (Fall 1988): 41–46.

Boice, Robert, and Ferdinand Jones. "Why Academicians Don't Write." *Journal of Higher Education* 55 (September/October 1984): 567–582.

Kronik, John W. "On Men Mentoring Women: Then and Now." *Profession 90* (1990): 52–57.

Lyons, William, Don Scroggins, and Patra Bonham Rule. "The Mentor in Graduate Education." *Studies in Higher Education* 15 (1990): 277–285.

Merriam, Sharan. "Mentors and Protégées: A Critical Review of the Literature." *Adult Education Quarterly* 33 (1983): 161–173.

Moxley, Joseph M. *Publish, Don't Perish.* Westport, Conn.: Greenwood Press, 1992.

Olson, Gary A., and Evelyn Ashton-Jones. "Doing Gender: (En)gendering Academic Mentoring." *Journal of Education* 174 (1992): 114–127.

Weber, C. E. "Mentoring." *Directors and Boards* (1980): 17–24.

Annotated Bibliography of Academic Publishing Sources

Bruce W. Speck

INTRODUCTION

Most academicians have had no formal training in the art and business of publishing scholarly books and journal articles. This gap in their formal education may explain why so much has been written about how to publish scholarly works. In fact, academicians—particularly new tenure-track professors—may not be aware of the print resources available to them. To provide budding scholars with a resource for studying the publishing process for scholarly books and journal articles, I have selected, arranged, and annotated sources that provide an overview of the entire process. Although this section does not include my bibliography *Editing: An Annotated Bibliography*, I recommend it for authors who are interested in locating sources that explain how editors fit into the manuscript publishing process.

WHAT COMPREHENSIVE SOURCES ARE AVAILABLE?

Benjaminson, Peter. *Publish Without Perishing: A Practical Handbook for Academic Authors*. Washington, D.C.: NEA, 1992. Benjaminson says little about writing a book, focusing instead on decisions related to publishing a book. For instance, he discusses contracts, agents, book proposals, advances, royalties, subventions, copyright, indexes, subsidiary rights, reprints, and author–publisher negotiations.

Boice, Robert. *Professors as Writers: A Self-Help Guide to Productive Writing*. Stillwater, Okla.: New Forums Press, 1990. Boice explains blocks to writing productivity and provides short- and long-term solutions to overcoming those blocks. The long-term strategy for productive writing is the Four-Step Plan, the heart of Boice's advice to blocked writers.

Cummings, L. L., and Peter J. Frost, eds. *Publishing in the Organizational Sciences*. Homewood, Ill.: Richard D. Irwin, 1985. Written from the perspectives of authors, editors, and reviewers, the essays in this volume provide insight into ways participants in the journal publication process view that process. One theme that runs throughout the essays is manuscript rejection.

Day, Robert A. *How to Write and Publish a Scientific Paper*. 3rd ed. Phoenix: Oryx Press, 1988. Day explains how to write the components of a scientific paper and what happens to the paper during the publication process. When preparing a scientific paper, authors should know how to prepare a title, abstract, introduction; how to follow the Introduction, Methods, Results, and Discussion (IMRaD) formula; how to cite references; and how to prepare figures and tables. Once the paper is prepared, authors should know how to submit the manuscript, work with editors, read proofs, and order reprints. In addition, Day explains how authors can prepare a review paper, conference report, book review, and Ph.D. thesis; how to deliver an oral presentation of a paper; and how to prepare a poster. He also discusses English usage.

Dorn, Fred J. *Publishing for Professional Development*. Muncie, Ind.: Accelerated Development, 1985. Dorn's book can be divided into three parts: the writing process, the publishing process, and written products. Under the writing process, Dorn explains why an academician should write and how to generate and evaluate ideas. Under the publishing process, he discusses how to evaluate journals, write query letters, prepare manuscripts, and understand the editorial process, including rejection. Under written products, Dorn discusses book reviews, journal articles (experimental, review, and theoretical articles), book proposals, books, and freelance opportunities for magazine articles.

Fox, Mary Frank, ed. *Scholarly Writing & Publishing: Issues, Problems, and Solutions*. Boulder, Colo.: Westview Press, 1985. The ten essays in this book cover the following topics: making the transition from writing a dissertation to publishing scholarly works, preparing articles for journals, working with book publishers (and publishing textbooks), learning how to be a productive scholar, using writing support groups, collaborating to produce scholarly research, analyzing publishing genres, and improving productivity for women scholars.

Harman, Eleanor, and Ian Montagnes, eds. *The Thesis and the Book*. Toronto: University of Toronto Press, 1976. These essays about the thesis or dissertation as a published book describe how university presses evaluate a dissertation, differences between a book and a thesis/dissertation, and ways to revise a dissertation so that it will be a publishable book.

Luey, Beth. *Handbook for Academic Authors*. Rev. ed. New York: Cambridge University Press, 1990. Luey explains the publishing process for journal articles, revised dissertations, books, anthologies, and textbooks, while giving authors advice about how to work with publishers, prepare manuscripts (especially with the use of electronic equipment), and understand the economics of publishing.

Matkir., Ralph E., and T. F. Riggar. *Persist and Publish: Helpful Hints for Academic Writing and Publishing*. Niwot, Colo.: University Press of Colorado, 1991. The authors first itemize different types of academic writing, explaining the role of writing in academic life, and note that writing is demanding and requires a plan of action. The authors then discuss the journal-article production process, elements of journal articles (including a checklist for authors), and rejection; characteristics of monographs and technical reports; book publishing, including an overview of the book industry, proposals, contracts, and author-editor relations; and professional meetings, book reviews, editorial appointments, and calls for papers.

Moxley, Joseph M. *Publish, Don't Perish: The Scholar's Guide to Academic Writing and Publishing*. Westport, Conn.: Praeger, 1992. Divided into four parts, Moxley's book provides an overview of creating and publishing scholarly works. Part one discusses how to get started writing, including refutations of common misconceptions about writing, ways to develop scholarly projects, and advice on submitting work to a publisher. Part two focuses on components of a scholarly work (abstracts, introductions, conclusions, paragraphs), particular genres (book reviews, quantitative and qualitative research reports, literary nonfiction, anthologies, book proposals, grants), and issues related to documentation of sources, copyright, and acknowledgments. Part three discusses revising and editing a manuscript, with a particular view toward the way editors evaluate manuscripts. Part four discusses the redefinition and financial support of scholarship.

—, ed. *Writing and Publishing for Academic Authors*. Lanham: University Press of America, 1992. The essays in this anthology are divided into four parts. Part one includes a nineteen-point list of work habits, ways to increase productivity, and uses of freewriting. Part two examines academic genres, beginning with theoretical views on humanistic scholarship, technical papers, and literary criticism. Then the essays discuss book reviews, books composed of conference papers, publication of dissertations, publication policies at university presses, textbook proposals, grant proposals, and commercial (crossover) writing for academicians. Part three includes chapters on revising, editing, and proofreading. Part four discusses current issues: coauthorship, author-editor relationships, computer databases as a research tool, and other references for scholarly publishing.

Smedley, Christine S., and Mitchell Allen. *Getting Your Book Published*. Newbury Park, Calif.: Sage, 1993. The authors have prepared a primer on book publishing, starting with a view of publishing as a business. Then the authors move through the publishing process: finding and writing about topics, selecting an appropriate publisher, writing a book prospectus, understanding the review process, interpreting a publishing contract, working with an editor, and understanding the book production and marketing process. A concluding chapter discusses twenty common publishing problems related to issues raised in previous chapters.

Thyer, Bruce A. *Successful Publishing in Scholarly Journals*. Newbury Park, Calif.: Sage, 1994. Thyer begins by explaining the importance of journal articles and reasons that a scholar should publish a journal article. Then he leads the reader through a series of questions as an aid in selecting an appropriate journal. Thyer tells how to prepare and submit the manuscript and how to revise an accepted manuscript or deal with a rejected manuscript. Then he explains the publishing process—author's agreements, proofs, reprints—and ways an author can market the published manuscript. To increase productivity, Thyer counsels authors to collaborate; write book reviews, letters to editors responding to articles, and editorials; serve on editorial boards; and guest edit a special issue of a journal.

Van Til, William. *Writing for Professional Publication*. 2nd ed. Boston: Allyn and Bacon, 1986. Van Til's book is divided into four parts. Part one discusses genres—books, professional magazines, scholarly journals, yearbooks, anthologies, textbooks, trade books, and specialized books—and book reviews and columns. Part two explains how to go about the writing process, from finding time to write and generating ideas to finding a publisher and preparing a book index. Part three explains how editorial offices operate, including the review process, copyediting, journal production, economics, and marketing. Part four is a sample of questions about publishing and their answers.

HOW DO PUBLISHERS ACQUIRE SCHOLARLY WORKS?

Davis, Richard M. "Publication in Professional Journals: A Survey of Editors." *IEEE Transactions on Professional Communication*, PC–28, 2 (1985): 34–42. Davis, in reporting on questionnaires he sent to editors of journals in technical fields, provides insight into refereeing, instructions to authors, and processing of manuscripts (including how editors evaluate manuscripts and types of common mistakes authors make). Davis concludes his article by listing a ten-step sequence authors should use to publish an article.

Fitchen, Allen N. "The Selection Process in Scholarly Publishing." *Humanities* 8, 3 (1987): 30–32. According to Fitchen, the first decision in a series of publishing decisions made by university presses is to send a manuscript out for peer review. If a manuscript receives a favorable review, it must be approved by a committee representing the university. During the selection process, editors continually ask questions about cost and audience.

Parsons, Paul. *Getting Published: The Acquisition Process at University Presses*. Knoxville: University of Tennessee Press, 1989. Based on research involving fifty–two university presses, Parsons found that presses acquire manuscripts using the following methods: author–initiated, editor-initiated, and prior association. In addition, Parsons discusses peer review, editorial committees, and the transformation of dissertations into books. Parsons makes eight predictions about future acquisition processes at university presses.

Schmitt, Albert R. "What Makes a Paper Publishable?" *Editors' Notes* 1, 1 (1982): 3–6. Schmitt claims that peer reviewers opinions make a paper publishable or not publishable. However, Schmitt recognizes that peer reviewers may not agree on the merits of a paper and, therefore, gives examples of how conflicts among reviewers were resolved. He counsels authors to prepare a manuscript for peer reviewers with great care, using good style and correct spelling, but he notes that luck also has a role in making a paper publishable.

Smith, Frank R. "The Etiquette of Submitting an Article for Publication." *Journal of Technical Writing and Communication* 17, 3 (1987): 207–214. In explaining a protocol for authors who submit manuscripts to journals, Smith discusses the overall journal publication process and then explains an author's obligations during that process. For example, an author should submit a manuscript free of mechanical errors, select a topic that fits the journal's needs, produce a manuscript based on a thorough literature review, send the manuscript to only one journal at a time, consider carefully reviewers' comments, work with the editor to make useful changes in the manuscript, and return corrected galleys and proofs promptly.

Talbot, John. "The Book Acquisition Process: Why a Few Get Published While Most Don't." *The Insider's Guide to Book Editors and Publishers*, 1990–1991. Ed. Jeff Herman. Rocklin, Calif.: Prima Publishing and Communications, 1991. 1–6. Talbot claims that much of publishing is a matter of timing, so authors can get into a book-publishing house by submitting a manuscript with a professional appearance and a convincing cover letter, thus avoiding the slush pile. The manuscript must also meet the publisher's needs.

Thatcher, Sanford G. "Competitive Practices in Acquiring Manuscripts." *Scholarly Publishing* 11, 2 (1980): 112–132. Thatcher explains data about acquisition processes as collected by questionnaires from twelve university presses. Included are questions about simultaneous submissions, editorial decision making, advance contracts, the first-option-on-next book clause, author inducements (special royalty rates, monetary advances, fast production schedules, and so on), and book bidding.

Wasserman, Marlie Parker. "Proximity Breeds Discontent." *Scholarly Publishing* 22, 1 (1990): 23–27. Because university presses often have difficulty publishing manuscripts from faculty members from the campus on which the press is located, Wasserman gives three suggestions to presses for acquiring manuscripts. One suggestion is to use faculty members as reviewers and manuscript scouts.

Wendroff, Michael. "Should We Do the Book?: A Study of How Publishers Handle Acquisition Decisions." *Publisher's Weekly* 218, 7 (1980): 24–30. Marketing is one of the critical issues in the acquisition process of publishing houses; however, most houses equate marketing with sales. Ironically, acquisition decisions fit on a continuum of sales being essential to sales being unimportant. When making their acquisition decisions, publishers also consider author's reputation, paperback sales, timeliness, pricing, and backlist sales when making acquisition decisions.

WHAT SHOULD AN AUTHOR KNOW ABOUT HOW TO CREATE SCHOLARLY WORKS?

Bailey, Herbert S., Jr. "How to Publish Your Book at a University Press." *Humanities* 6, 6 (1985): 31–32. According to Bailey, authors who want to publish a book should (1) write the book, (2) choose a publisher, (3) write to several presses, and (4) wait. Although this formula seems simple, Bailey provides details for each step. For instance, when writing to several presses, authors should not send the manuscript but should instead prepare a letter with a one-page description of the manuscript.

Barlow, Richard G. "Literary Research and the Preparation of Scholarly Manuscripts for Journal Publishing." *Editors' Notes* 13, 1 (1994): 21–29. Recognizing that new faculty members have not had formal training in publishing scholarly journal articles, Barlow lists ten reasons why manuscripts are rejected. In an eighteen-point list, he explains what authors should do in preparing manuscripts for publication.

Boice, Robert. "The Neglected Third Factor in Writing: Productivity." *College Composition and Communication* 36 (1985): 472–479. In an experiment using academicians, Boice found that experimental subjects who were forced to write regularly produced eight times more writing than either subjects who were instructed to write very little or subjects who wrote spontaneously. In addition, experimental subjects had twice as many creative ideas as the subjects who wrote spontaneously and twelve times the creative ideas of subjects who wrote very little. Boice concludes that creativity is not spontaneous and internally motivated; contingency or forced writing is the source of creative ideas. Indeed, "productivity precedes creativity" (477).

Boice, Robert, and Ferdinand Jones. "Why Academicians Don't Write." *Journal of Higher Education* 55, 5 (1984): 567–582. Among the reasons why academicians don't write are distractions and lack of time (for instance, teaching responsibilities), writing blocks (several types), personality and gender, exclusionary factors (reviewing practices and increased number of publications necessary for academic success), the possibility that writing is an unhealthy act, the hard work required in writing, and poor instruction in writing. However, the authors argue that hindrances to writing can be dealt with when the publishing process is more democratic than it is now; when writing is seen (and taught) as a cognitive process that requires effort, not as a romantic ideal that requires a muse; and when electronic journals reduce the need for publication in paper journals and encourage an informal writing style.

Boor, Myron. "Suggestions to Improve Manuscripts Submitted to Professional Journals." *American Psychologist* 41 (1986): 721–722. Speaking as a reviewer, Boor explains how to improve specific parts of the manuscript—introduction, methods, results, discussion, and abstract—noting that the length of most manuscripts can be reduced by 15 percent.

Bostian, Lloyd, and Barbara Hollander. "Technical Journal Editors and Writing Style." *Journal of Technical Writing and Communication* 20, 2 (1990): 153–163. Scientists who are editors of scientific journals generally do not have training in writing or editing, are more concerned with precision of concepts rather than writing style, do not believe that a journal editor's role is to help writers improve their style, claim they have style preferences but do not apply those preferences in editing their journals, and do not give authors adequate instructions about appropriate style.

Buehler, Mary Fran. "Creative Revision: From Rough Draft to Published Paper." *IEEE Transactions on Professional Communication*, PC-19, 2 (1976): 26–32. Buehler identifies seven types of revision—substantive, policy, language, mechanical style, format, integrity, and copy clarification—and explains how an author can use each type to revise a manuscript.

Byford, G. H. "Your Scientific Paper: An Editor's Point of View." *Proceedings 1990 International Professional Communication Conference. Communication Across the Sea: North American & European Practices*, 183–185. IEEE Professional Communication Society. Speaking as an editor, Byford gives authors four points of advice about preparing a manuscript. Then he discusses graphics, manuscript page layout, references (advising authors not to use references, such as conference proceedings or personal correspondence, that are not commonly available to readers), mathematics, and statistics (noting that statistics do not prove a point but provide evidence).

Deitrich, Margaret A. "Beating the Odds: Getting a Manuscript Published." *Teacher as Writer: Entering the Professional Conversation*. Ed. Karin L. Dahl. Urbana, Ill.: NCTE, 1992. 188–192. Teachers can increase their chances of getting published by writing regularly, sending their manuscripts to appropriate journals, including classroom examples in manuscripts, scheduling time to revise and refine a manuscript, and either sending rejected manuscripts out immediately after they are rejected or revising a rejected manuscript and sending it to another journal.

Dieterich, Dan. "Writing by Academic Professionals." *Writing in the Business Professions*. Ed. Myra Kogen. Urbana, Ill.: NCTE, 1989. 174–184. Dieterich criticizes academic writing for focusing on the message, not the audience. He suggests that academic writing can be improved when academicians consider themselves professional writers and use the writing process to plan and prepare administrative documents, particularly letters and memos. Dieterich's advice could be applied to query letters.

Donelson, Ken. "Writing, Editing, and Miracles." *Teacher as Writer: Entering the Professional Conversation*. Ed. Karin L. Dahl. Urbana, Ill.: NCTE, 1992. 95–106. As a former editor, Donelson explains what he and his co–editor looked for in manuscripts, how they made editorial policy, and why they accepted some manuscripts and rejected others. Donelson outlines ten topics English teachers could write about for the journal he edited.

Dressel, Susan. "Generating a Quick First Draft." *IEEE Transactions on Professional Communication*, PC–26, 4 (1983): 172–174. Authors can generate a first draft by using a tape recorder or having a preliminary oral presentation of their paper video recorded.

Dunn, George R. "Guidelines for Writing for Publication." *IEEE Transactions on Professional Communication*, PC–24, 4 (1981): 172–175. Dunn explains how to develop a topic and an outline, how to write a manuscript, how to review a manuscript, how to submit a manuscript to an editor, and how to respond to an editor's evaluation of the manuscript.

Estrin, Herman A. "How to Write for Scientific and Technical Journals." *IEEE Transactions on Professional Communication*, PC–25, 1 (1982): 32–33. Estrin tells authors how to choose a topic using five guidelines, how to select a journal, how to format the manuscript, and how to develop an outline.

Farkas, L. L. "Writing Better Technical Papers." *A Guide for Writing Better Technical Papers*. Eds. Craig Harkins and Daniel L. Plung. New York: IEEE Press, 1982. 119–122. To prepare a paper for publication or a presentation, authors should show that the proposed idea is needed, consider the paper's audience, prepare a summary and outline, and plan for illustrations, prepare an initial draft (including reading the draft aloud or tape recording it and listening to the recording), edit the manuscript, and prepare a final draft for an editor.

Garvey, William D. "The Scientific Journal Article." *Communication: The Essence of Science*. Oxford: Pergamon Press, 1979. 69–90. Although Garvey provides an overview of how to write an article for a journal, he emphasizes that journal editors and reviewers have theoretical positions that play a large part in the peer-review process. Thus, authors need to recognize that a manuscript may not be rejected because it is not valid, but because it does not fit editors and reviewers theoretical positions. In addition, Garvey tells authors to expect to revise their manuscripts because virtually all manuscripts that survive the review process must be revised.

Giltrow, Janet. *Academic Writing: How to Read and Write Scholarly Prose*. Peterborough, Ontario: Broadview Press, 1990. Giltrow explains basic scholarly activities: summarizing, analyzing audience, organizing academic arguments, using sources to document an argument, understanding scholarly styles, and making presentations.

Haness, Joel. "How to Critique a Document." *IEEE Transactions on Professional Communication*, PC–26, 1 (1983): 15–17. Haness provides manuscript reviewers with a three-stage checklist to critique documents, listing questions for each stage. Stage one deals with the writer's purpose, stage two with grammar and style, and stage three with readability, loose ends, and inconsistencies.

Helms, Sandy. "Courtesy in Print: The Acknowledgment." *Medical Communications* 13, 4 (1985): 80–82. Helms explains when and how an author should make an acknowledgment. For instance, authors should acknowledge assistance from other professionals and the use of certain information, such as illustrations. (The use of some information may require written permissions.)

Laermer, Richard. "How to Use Your Time as a Writer Effectively." *The Insider's Guide to Book Editors and Publishers*, 1990–1991. Ed. Jeff Herman. Rocklin, Calif.: Prima Publishing and Communications, 1991. 39–43. Writers should take their time to write, that is, prepare professional manuscripts; find a place to write; keep a telephone and answering machine at that place; keep a list of ideas for articles; and send out query letters to editors.

Lindeborg, Richard A. "Faster Manuscript Publishing: A Case Study." *IEEE Transactions on Professional Communication*, 33, 1 (1990): 7–11. In reporting generally positive results of one organization's efforts to decrease in-house publishing time, Lindeborg also notes that the time increased for articles that were published by out-of-house journal publishers. The reasons for that increase include budget cuts, failure of authors to followup on the processing of their manuscripts, and poor management of the publication process.

MacNealy, Mary Sue. "Practical Tips for Aspiring Authors." *Proceedings 40th Annual Conference Society for Technical Communication: Communication Roundup*. Arlington, Va.: STC, 1993. 87–90. Based on three empirical studies she conducted, MacNealy provides ten tips for authors, including advice about generating ideas (dissonances are the key), getting feedback on a manuscript, analyzing journals, following up when an editor is slow to respond to the manuscript, and revising an article that has been conditionally accepted for publication.

MacNealy, Mary Sue, Bruce W. Speck, and Noel Clements. "Publishing in Technical Communication Journals from the Successful Author's Point of View." *Technical Communication* 41 (1994): 240–259. The article reports the results of a questionnaire sent to authors who had published in technical communication journals, and it provides insights into the ways prospective authors can maximize their chances of being published in technical communication journals. In addition, the results provide authors with information about what to do when editors are slow in communicating with authors and how authors can negotiate manuscript revisions with editors. The ways editors can improve the author-editor relationship are also included.

Mahoney, Michael J. "Publication: The Endless Quest." *Scientist as Subject: The Psychological Imperative*. Cambridge, Mass.: Ballinger, 1976. 79–107. Mahoney heavily criticizes the journal publication system, noting that bias among editors and reviewers produces unreliable and prejudicial publication decisions. To reform the system, Mahoney recommends the elimination of referees (or replacing them with graduate students), the evaluation of manuscripts based on their relevance and methodology, the use of contract publishing (meaning that editors promise to publish papers based on a proposal to conduct the research), the use of blind review, and the allowance of multiple submissions.

Manley, Richard, Judith Graham, and Ralph Baxter. "Some Guidance on Preparing Technical Articles for Publication." *IEEE Transactions on Professional Communication* 32, 1 (1989): 5–11. The authors suggest that, although a technical report can be turned into a journal article, potential authors of journal articles need to be made aware of writing opportunities, ways to reshape a technical report for a journal article, the nature of the publication process for journals and conference proceedings, and the use of time to complete a manuscript.

Michaelson, Herbert B. "How to Write and Publish a Dissertation." *Journal of Technical Writing and Communication* 17, 3 (1987): 265–274. Michaelson gives eight criteria for choosing a thesis or dissertation topic that will be publishable; he discusses a process for preparing the thesis or dissertation.

Morgan, Peter P. "Author, Editor and Reviewer: How Manuscripts Become Journal Articles." *Canadian Medical Association Journal* 124,6 (1981): 664–666. The process that results in a published journal article begins with the author's preparation of a manuscript. That manuscript is peer reviewed, and most likely, reviewers will require revisions in the manuscript. Morgan stresses the responsibility of peer reviewers to document their critiques and support their judgments.

Nicosia, Gerald. "What Every Writer Should Know about Research." *The Insider's Guide to Book Editors and Publishers,* 1990–1991. Ed. Jeff Herman. Rocklin, Calif.: Prima Publishing and Communications, 1991. 35–38. Every writer should know how to use the library, including computerized databases, and how to interview people to gather information. Nicosia focuses on the personal interview, explaining how to conduct one.

Pasco, Allan H. "Basic Advice for Novice Authors." *Scholarly Publishing* 23, 2 (1992): 95–104. Given the current state of publishing, academic authors must learn about the business of publishing to act as full partners with editors, printers, and publishers in the publication process. Thus, authors should learn which publishers are best suited to publish a particular book the author writes and which publishers are dependable. Authors should learn to take revision suggestions humbly. Authors should also help sell their books, once they are published.

Philipson, Morris. "The Scholar as Publishing Author." *Scholars and Their Publishers.* Ed. Weldon A. Kefauver. New York: Modern Language Association, 1977. 27–33. Philipson answers eleven questions that authors often ask about publishing. The topics he addresses are preliminary inquiries to publishers, multiple submissions, scholars' disenchantment with learned journals, editors' power over authors, the role of microforms in book publishing, page charges, submission fees, royalties, permission fees, copyright, and advertising.

Prater, Doris L. "Decisions Authors Make While Writing." *Teacher as Writer: Entering the Professional Conversation.* Ed. Karin L. Dahl. Urbana. Ill.: NCTE, 1992. 218–224. To prepare an article for a journal, a writer needs to make four major decisions: What will be the topic for the article? How will the article be organized? Who is the audience for the article? From what viewpoint will the author write? Prater discusses each decision, providing information, for instance, on how to generate a topic and organize an article.

Presser, Stanley. "Collaboration and the Quality of Research." *Social Studies of Science* 10 (1980): 95–101. Presser compared the papers submitted to a journal over a year's time with editorial decisions about those papers and found that collaboration has some relation to quality based on editorial decisions about papers. Collaboration, however, kept authors from writing bad papers, not necessarily producing good papers. Presser also found that regardless of the authors' discipline, collaboration increased the quality of their papers.

Reitt, Barbara B. "An Academic Author's Checklist." *Scholarly Publishing* 16, 1 (1984): 65–72. Under five headings (completeness, authority, expertness, singularity, and finesse), Reitt lists questions that authors, editors, and reviewers can ask to evaluate a manuscript. In addition, Reitt lists questions for evaluating a cover letter.

Riggar, T. F., and R. E. Matkin. "Breaking into Academic Print." *Scholarly Publishing* 22, 1 (1990): 17–22. Beginning scholars can begin a publishing career by attending conferences, communicating with editors, preparing book reviews, seeking work as a journal referee, preparing commentaries of published articles, and writing a manuscript for a journal's theme issue. In short, beginning scholars should seek a wide range of publishing opportunities.

Tompkins, Gail E. "Nuts and Bolts of Writing a Manuscript." *Teacher as Writer: Entering the Professional Conversation.* Ed. Karin L. Dahl. Urbana, Ill.: NCTE, 1992. 137–149. Tompkins explains how to use a process, instead of a product, approach to preparing a manuscript for publication. She discusses prewriting, drafting, revising, editing, and submitting a manuscript. She also provides checklists authors can use to determine whether they have satisfied the requirements for each stage in the process approach to writing.

HOW DO EDITORS MAKE DECISIONS ABOUT PUBLISHING SCHOLARLY WORKS?

Conarroe, Joel. "I Wish I Had Said That!" *Editors' Notes* 3, 2 (1984): 27–28. The editorial board of the PMLA selects manuscripts by comparing them to each other, evaluating readers' reports, and considering the audience for PMLA. Conarroe also lists five specific criteria the board uses.

Cuningham, Charles E. "Authors Need to Be Told." *Scholarly Publishing* 6, 3 (1975): 249–256. Economics is a significant factor in a university press's publishing decision, so authors should write books that do not appeal to limited audiences.

Giamatti, A. Bartlett. "Safeguard of Process: The Editorial Committee." *Scholarly Publishing* 7,2 (1976): 129–133. At university presses, an editorial committee is responsible for safeguarding the publishing process. At the same time, the editor is responsible for producing books. Thus, Giamatti believes that the decision-making process is inherently antagonistic, and should be so, though characterized by "affectionate antagonism." Such antagonism is necessary to ensure that quality manuscripts are published.

Horowitz, Irving Louis. "Gatekeeping Functions and Publishing Truths." *Communicating Ideas: The Crisis of Publishing in a Post-Industrial Society.* New York: Oxford University Press, 1986. 162–168. Scholarly and commercial presses are quite effective in sifting manuscripts to publish quality books. The success of such sifting is due largely to the presses' use of outside reviewers. Nevertheless, publishers' cautiousness in making publishing decisions can be a form of censorship that stops the publication of useful books, although such books at first blush appear to be risky publishing endeavors.

—. "New Technology and the Changing System of Author-Publisher Relations." *New Literary History* 20, 2 (1989): 505–509. In large publishing houses, the decision to publish a book is based in large part on the recommendations of outside reviewers. However, large firms do not want to publish scholarly books that will not be highly profitable. Large firms' divestment of low-profit scholarly books has opened opportunities for small presses to publish such books. In small presses, the decision-making process is generally focused on one person, and thus, the division of labor via outside reviewers that large houses use in the editorial process is circumvented.

Parsons, Paul F. "The Editorial Committee: Controller of the Imprint." *Scholarly Publishing* 20,4 (1989): 238–244. The editorial committee of a university press approves works that the press publishes; however, most of the time, the committee accepts the editor's recommendation to publish a book. Members of the committee serve two- to five-year terms, are generally tenured faculty, and are not paid for their service.

Pfeffer, Jeffrey, Anthony Leong, and Katherine Strehl. "Paradigm Development and Particularism: Journal Publication in Three Scientific Disciplines." *Social Forces* 55, 4 (1977): 938–951. The authors analyzed journal articles in chemistry, sociology, and political science and found that the social science journals used particularistic standards in evaluating manuscripts, but the journals in chemistry used universalistic standards. The authors suggest that journals representing fields without well-established paradigms tend to use particularistic standards to evaluate manuscripts. Conversely, journals representing fields with well-established paradigms tend to use universalistic standards to evaluate manuscripts.

Powell, Walter W. *Getting into Print: The Decision-Making Process in Scholarly Publishing.* Chicago: University of Chicago Press, 1985. Powell conducted case studies of two publishing houses and found that the decision-making process for publishing a book is complex and guided by unstable preferences. For instance, editors tend not to choose complex books (books they don't understand) because complex books don't sell well, but an editor might choose such a book because it could be a good public relations strategy. In addition, reviewers' comments are valued in relation to an editor's commitment to a manuscript. Thus, an editor tends to select reviewers who will mirror the editor's choice. Also, time spent on a publishing decision is related to an author's status. In sum, the decision-making process in a publishing house is made by a tight–knit group of people whose function is to limit publication so that the house's prestige is maintained.

——. "Publishers' Decision Making: What Criteria Do They Use in Deciding Which Books to Publish?" *Social Research* 45, 2 (1978): 227–252. Powell conducted research at two scholarly book publishing houses and determined that when selecting books, editors tend to use particularistic standards—time expended to review a work, the editor's particular publishing interests, and the need for a steady flow of manuscripts. Powell also identified three queues, noting that the high-priority queue is reserved for authors or friends of authors the editor knows.

Smigel, Erwin O., and H. Laurence Ross. "Factors in the Editorial Decision." *The American Sociologist* 5, 1 (1970): 19–21. After studying manuscript decisions at a journal, the authors found that a referee's status as an expert or nonexpert had nothing to do with how the referee evaluated a manuscript. In addition, editors accept or reject manuscripts for the same reasons.

Tripp, Edward. "Editors and the Editorial Committee." *Scholarly Publishing* 8, 2 (1977): 99–109. Editorial committees at a university press are not involved early enough in the acquisition process to ensure quality control. However, editorial committees could become involved in the process earlier by working with editors to build lists, identifying emerging areas of scholarship and the scholars working in those areas, accepting manuscripts that do not fit the pattern of tradition scholarship, and promoting the publication of books about teaching.

HOW CAN AN AUTHOR REVISE A SCHOLARLY WORK AFTER IT'S BEEN REVIEWED?

Bakanic, Von, Clark McPhail, and Rita J. Simon. "If at First You Don't Succeed: Review Procedures for Revised and Resubmitted Manuscripts." *The American Sociologist* 21, 4 (1990): 373–391. In evaluating the manuscript decision-making process at one journal, the authors found that 9 percent of all submitted articles were accepted for publication without revisions. However, 62 percent of revised and resubmitted articles were accepted for publication. A manuscript's fate is closely identified with referees' comments; manuscripts reviewed by more than one referee were rejected if only one referee gave a negative report, while manuscripts reviewed by only one referee who gave a positive report were accepted.

Daft, Richard L. "Why I Recommended That Your Manuscript Be Rejected and What You Can Do about It." *Publishing in the Organizational Sciences*. Ed. L. L. Cummings and Peter J. Frost. Homewood. Ill.: Richard D. Irwin, 1985. 193–209. Because refereeing is a subjective process, style and tone can have an impact on a referee's evaluation of a manuscript. However, Daft cites eleven problems in 111 manuscripts he has reviewed. In particular, he recommends that authors take care in theory development and research design.

DeBakey, Lois, and F. Peter Woodford. "Extensive Revision of Scientific Articles—Whose Job?" *Scholarly Publishing* 4, 4 (1973): 147–151. Editors should not revise authors' manuscripts extensively but should help the author revise his or her manuscript by providing examples of edited paragraphs.

Howe, M. Rita. "Editor and Author: A Professional Relationship." *CBE Views* 9, 3 (1986): 69–74. When editors and authors work together to revise a manuscript, they can learn to respect each other. Howe provides a scale to measure an author's level of cooperation, but notes that an author does not lose control of his or her manuscript by cooperating with an editor.

Markland, Murray F. "Taking Criticism—and Using It." *Scholarly Publishing* 14, 2 (1983): 139–147. Authors should not try to prove that the criticism a reviewer offers is wrong; rather, authors should learn how to interpret reviewers' remarks. Markland cites eight standard reviewers' remarks and explains how to interpret those remarks to revise a manuscript.

Silverman, Robert J., and Erik L. Collins. "Publishing Relationships in Higher Education." *Research in Higher Education* 3, 4 (1975): 365–382. In their study of higher education journals, the authors found that editors do not want to share their power with authors. Thus, although authors want editors to publish policies about peer-review procedures, editors tend not to see a need for publishing such policies.

Simon, Rita, Von Bakanic, and Clark McPhail. "Who Complains to Editors and What Happens." *Sociological Inquiry* 56, 2 (1986): 259–271. In studying the manuscripts submitted to a particular journal, the authors found that editors reconsidered and published 13 percent of complainants' manuscripts. Associate and full professors

constituted 60.7 percent of complainants, and those who received their doctorates from
highest ranking universities were overrepresented among complainants.

Stainton, Elsie M. *Author and Editor at Work: Making a Better Book.* Toronto:
University of Toronto Press, 1982. Divided into three parts, Stainton's book addresses
authors and editors. Part one, intended for authors, advises authors to be open to
editors' comments. Part two, addressed to editors, counsels editors to compromise. In
part three, focusing on the author-editor relationship, Stainton notes that good writers
are more open to editorial suggestions for revision than are bad writers.

Streufert, Siegfried. "Not to Perish: Recommendations from an Outgoing Editor." *Journal
of Applied Social Psychology* 12, 5 (1982): 420–428. Authors can be involved actively
in the journal publication process by (1) referencing the work of prominent research
early in a manuscript, (2) participating in a dialogue with the editor if a manuscript is
rejected, and (3) explaining where reviewers misread a manuscript.

Swinger, Alice K. "Rejection: Who Needs It?" *Teacher as Writer: Entering the Professional Conversation.* Ed. Karin L. Dahl. Urbana, Ill.: NCTE, 1992. 243–249.
Swinger wrote to writers, asking them about rejection. In general, those writers initially
responded negatively to the editor's rejection. However, writers also learned how to
deal with rejection: not writing, keeping several projects in circulation, learning to
accept the risk of rejection when writing in new areas or using new genres, and
preparing manuscripts carefully.

Williams, Miller. "The Writer and the Editor." *Scholarly Publishing* 14,3 (1983):
149–154. Author-editor conflicts are based primarily on the editor's style in personal
relations. Williams suggests ways editors can have a pleasing style, and notes that
authors will accept editorial changes if the editor can demonstrate with sensitivity and
common sense that the changes should be made.

Willis, Cecil L., and Richard S. Bobys. "Perishing in Publishing: An Analysis of
Manuscript Rejection Letters." *The Wisconsin Sociologist* 20, 4 (1983): 84–91. Based
on the rejection letters they studied, the authors found that the letter resulting from a
short review process provides some justification for the rejection. However, the letter
resulting from a long review process provides no justification. The authors also found
that small journals have the lowest rejection rates of small, medium, and large journals
and send the most supportive and helpful rejection letters of all three type of journals.

WHAT SHOULD AN AUTHOR KNOW ABOUT CONTRACTS FOR SCHOLARLY WORKS?

Fox, James, and Linda K. Rawson. "The Publishing Contract: An Introductory Overview
to Publishing and the Law." *The Business of Book Publishing: Papers by Practitioners.*
Eds. Elizabeth A. Geiser, Arnold Dolin, and Gladys S. Topkis. Boulder., Colo.:
Westview Press, 1985. 86–104. Book contracts should be written clearly to avoid legal
entanglements. Thus, a publisher's criteria for an acceptable manuscript should be
stated unambiguously. In addition, the authors discuss libel, product liability, copyright,
subrights, and reversion of rights.

Harvey, William B. "The Publishing Contract." *Scholarly Publishing* 8, 4 (1977):
299–314. Ambiguities in publishing contracts are resolved legally against the party that
prepared the contract—the publisher. Harvey explains four features that are essential

to all publishing contracts, discusses the satisfaction clause, provides a list of subsidiary rights, and reviews royalty payments to deceased authors. The Princeton University Press contract is appended.

Oskam, Bob. "Negotiating a Publishing Contract." *Editors on Editing: An Inside View of What Editors Really Do.* Rev. ed. Ed. Gerald Gross. New York: Harper and Row, 1985. 90–100. Although an author, an editor, or an author's agent can negotiate a publishing contract, Oskam explains how first-time authors can negotiate directly with editors. Oskam focuses on negotiating an advance and advises authors to work with a conscientious editor.

Sisler, William P. "Workshop: The Publishing Contract." *Scholars and Their Publishers.* Ed. Weldon A. Kefauver. New York: Modern Language Association, 1977. 40–47. Sisler explains standard provisions in the publishing contract and answers questions about copyright, royalties, permission fees, and subsidiary rights.

WHAT ARE SOME OF THE ETHICAL/LEGAL ISSUES IN SCHOLARLY WRITING?

Brock, Thomas D. "Assignment of Copyright by Authors to Journals: Is It Necessary?" *CBE Views* 6, 4 (1983): 5–6. Journal editors should only require an author to assign copyright for the use of his or her article in a specific issue of a journal. Brock lists four consequences for publishers if authors do not assign all rights to a journal and three disadvantages to authors when they assign all rights to a journal.

Coughlin, Ellen K. "Concerns about Fraud, Editorial Bias Prompt Scrutiny of Journal Practices." *The Chronicle of Higher Education*, February 15, 1989: A4–A7. One reason why peer review has been called into question is publication fraud. Coughlin gives the pros and cons of issues surrounding publication fraud, including detecting fraud through the use of random audits of raw data, determining authorship when a manuscript has more than one author, and using blind review.

De George, Richard T., and Fred Woodward. "Ethics and Manuscript Reviewing." *Scholarly Publishing* 25,3 (1994): 133–145. The authors base their discussion of ethics on rights, duties, and obligations. Editors carry the responsibility for fulfilling the bulk of the duties and obligations because editors have the most power in the author-editor-referee-editorial board relationship. Thus, editors must inform authors of what the manuscript review process entails and must inform authors of deviations in the process. However, editors are not required morally to review authors' works, and editors can select reviewers that editors believe will report that an author's work should not be published. Authors have the responsibility to be truthful and disclose information, particularly about multiple submissions. Reviewers have the obligation to be objective and the right to remain anonymous.

Johnson, William Bruce. "Ethical Procedures for Authors and Publishers." *Scholarly Publishing* 7, 3 (1976): 253–260. Clear communication in the author-publisher relationship is critical for a smooth relationship. For instance, publishers should explain to authors how the review process works and ensure that the review process is ethical, including selecting disinterested, competent reviewers. Publishers should also give authors an opportunity to evaluate reviewers' comments.

LaFollette, Marcel C. *Stealing into Print: Fraud, Plagiarism, and Misconduct in Scientific Publishing.* Berkeley: University of California Press, 1992. LaFollette provides ways to classify violations of publishing conduct, discusses the role of journals in scientific publishing (and the assumption that journal norms are well known and clearly articulated), explores what constitutes authorship of a manuscript, explains the ethical issues related to peer review, investigates the ramifications of exposing misconduct (and the role of the press as a watchdog), outlines the types of action that are useful in investigating allegations and what counts as evidence in an investigation, discusses corrective action called for by an investigation (e.g., retractions and punishments), and explores five issues that impinge on future discussions about fraud in scientific publishing.

Michaelson, Herbert. "How an Author Can Avoid the Pitfalls of Practical Ethics." *IEEE Transactions on Professional Communication* 33, 2 (1990): 58–61. Authors can make two major types of ethical errors: intentional and unintentional. Michaelson warns against both and gives examples of each. Under unintentional errors, he lists ten traps to avoid, including not giving credit to others' accomplishments, withholding contradictory data, and not reporting limitations of test results. Under intentional errors, Michaelson discusses unfair bias, ambiguity and speculation (including the use of nonexistent references), plagiarism, and indiscriminate publication (self-plagiarism, premature publication, and multiple submissions).

"Multiple Submissions." *Editors' Notes* 1, 1 (1982): 9–26. "Multiple Submissions" is the heading for three articles on that topic. The first article by David Hirsch discusses the pros and cons of multiple submissions. The second article by Anne Paolucci discusses the need for guidelines about multiple submissions. The third article by William Pryor discusses the need to process manuscripts quickly.

Scott, David P., and Lorraine C. Smith. "Duplicate Publication: An Increasing Problem." *CBE Views* 9, 1 (1986): 4–8. The authors cite the pressures on authors leading to duplicate publication, including pressure from funding agencies; assessment of the quantity, not the quality, of publications; and page limitations for manuscripts. The authors also suggest that editors should have a clear idea of what constitutes duplicate publication.

Index

About the Editors and Contributors

Joseph M. Moxley is professor of English at the University of South Florida. He has edited, authored, or coauthored six books, including *Publish, Don't Perish* (Praeger, 1992). He has published over thirty articles and stories and served as an editor for several academic journals. In 1994 and 1990, he received Florida Board of Regents Awards for Excellence in Undergraduate Teaching. He offers academic writing workshops for faculty at numerous universities.

Lagretta T. Lenker is co-director of the Center for Applied Humanities and director of the Division of Lifelong Learning at the University of South Florida. Dr. Lenker is also the co-editor of *Youth Suicide Prevention: Lessons from Literature*, *The Aching Hearth: Family Violence in Life and Literature*, and *Gender and Academe: Feminist Pedagogy and Politics*. She currently serves on the editorial board of the *Continuing Higher Education Review*.

Elizabeth S. Blake is vice chancellor for Academic Affairs, dean, and professor of French at the University of Minnesota, Morris. Before going to Minnesota-Morris as dean in 1979, she held faculty and administrative positions at Barnard College and at Wellesley College. She has presented papers on different aspects of the values conflict in higher education at the annual meeting of the Association of American Colleges in Seattle, Washington (1993), at the University of Southern Maine, and at Keene State College, New Hampshire. She is preparing an article on that topic as it relates to the development of small public liberal arts colleges.

Robert Boice is professor of psychology at the State University of New York at Stony Brook. He teaches courses on the psychology of writing, on teaching for graduate teaching assistants, and on the history of psychology. His books include *The New Faculty Member*, *Building a Diverse Faculty*, and *How Writers*

Journey to Comfort and Fluency. Dr. Boice is a licensed psychotherapist with a practice limited to writers and springer spaniels.

Robert M. Diamond is assistant vice chancellor for Instructional Development at Syracuse University, where he directs the Center for Instructional Development and serves as professor of design, development, evaluation, and higher education. Dr. Diamond directs a national project, Institutional Priorities and Faculty Rewards.

David Erben teaches in and is co-director of the computer and writing program in the Department of English at the University of South Florida. He is the founder/editor of *Seulemonde*, an electronic journal and internet consortium.

Sandra Featherman is president of the University of New England. She formerly served as vice chancellor for Academic Administration at the University of Minnesota, Duluth, and at Temple University as assistant to the president and as director of the Center for Public Policy, a center with six institutes and centers reporting to it. Dr. Featherman is a director of several private foundations and has served on public funding agencies as well.

Terri Frongia is currently director of Distance Learning and Instructional Development at the University of California at Riverside. Author of a monograph on seventeenth-century literature and art, *The Aesthetics of the Marvelous*, she has published articles on Shakespeare's *Othello*, the works of modern Italian poets and fantasists, hypertext and cyberpunk, children's literature, and the image of the female hero. She also coauthored a book, *The Grad Student's Guide to Getting Published* (1992).

Fredric G. Gale is assistant professor at the University of Arkansas, where he teaches undergraduate and graduate rhetoric and writing courses. He practiced law before returning to the academy in 1990. Professor Gale has published three books in the last three years and is at work on a fourth book. He has also published more than a dozen articles and book reviews in a variety of scholarly journals. In addition, he is editor of the *Forum*, a scholarly journal published by the Association of Teachers of Advanced Composition.

Richard C. Gebhardt has been chair of the English Department of Bowling Green State University since 1989. He was Humanities Division chair and assistant academic dean at Findlay College. He served as editor of *College Composition and Communication* from 1987 to 1994.

Douglas Harper is professor and chair of the Department of Sociology at the University of South Florida. He has also taught at the University of Amsterdam, the University of Bologna, Italy, and SUNY Potsdam. His books include *Good Company* and *Working Knowledge: Skill and Community in a Small Shop*. He is founding editor of the journal *Visual Sociology*, now in its tenth year. His current research is on agricultural communities and on the epistemology of visual sociology.

Maggie Johnson is the head of the chemistry/physics library at the University of Kentucky. Previously, she was assistant director of the Greater Kansas City Center for Economic Education and coordinator of the Government Documents Division of the Missouri State Library.

Paul LeBlanc is associate professor of English at Springfield College, Massachusetts. He is on leave of absence, working for Houghton Mifflin Company as vice president in charge of College New Media. He has published widely on the topic of technology, education, and scholarship, including a text on software development and the history of computers and composition studies.

James Lichtenberg is vice president of the Higher Education Division of the Association of American Publishers. He has worked for Columbia Pictures in Rome and New York. As a freelance journalist, he has published in the *New York Times*, *The Journal of Contemporary Business*, *Change* magazine, and *Department Chair*.

Robert A. Lucas is director of the Institute for Scholarly Productivity, a private consulting firm in San Luis Obispo, California. He was director of Research Development and associate vice president for Graduate Studies, Research, and Faculty Development at Cal Poly State University, San Luis Obispo, before leaving the university in 1992. Dr. Lucas is the author of over fifty articles, chapters, and books, and has served on the editorial boards of *Grants Magazine* and *Research Management Review*. He is nationally known for his column "Ask Ann Granters," published in the NCURA *Newsletter*. His book *The Grants World Inside Out* was published in 1992.

Ralph Norman is editor of *Soundings: An Interdisciplinary Journal*, the official publication of the Society for Values in Higher Education. A professor of Religious Studies at the University of Tennessee, he founded the Department of Religious Studies there in 1966. He has served as head of the department, associate dean of the College of Liberal Arts, vice provost, and associate vice chancellor (1990–present). Dr. Norman is author, with Charles Reynolds, of *Community in America*, and of numerous essays, articles, and reviews.

R. Eugene Rice is scholar in residence and director of the Forum on Faculty Roles and Rewards at the American Association for Higher Education,

Washington, D.C. Until recently, he was vice president and dean of the faculty at Antioch College, where he continues to have an appointment as professor of sociology and religion. He moved to Antioch from the Carnegie Foundation (Princeton) where he was a senior fellow engaged in the national study of the scholarly work of faculty, a topic on which he has published extensively. His teaching and research focus on the sociology and ethics of the professions and the workplace.

Patsy P. Schweickart is professor of English and women's studies at the University of New Hampshire. She is the editor of the *NWSA Journal*, the scholarly publication of the National Women's Studies Association. She is also author of "Reading Ourselves: Toward a Feminist Theory of Reading," and co-editor with Elizabeth Flynn of *Gender and Reading: Essays on Readers, Texts and Contexts*. Her most recent article will appear in *Provoking Subjects*, which is forthcoming.

R. A. Shoaf is alumni professor of English at the University of Florida. He is the founding editor of *Exemplaria: A Journal of Theory in Medieval and Renaissance Studies*, president of the Council of Editors of Learned Journals, and a member of the Advisory Boards of *Chaucer Review* and SEENET, the Society for Early English and Norse Electronic Texts.

W. A. Sibley is vice president for Academic Affairs at the University of Alabama at Birmingham. He is currently responsible for the undergraduate and graduate education programs in the schools of Arts and Humanities, Business, Education, Engineering, Natural Sciences and Mathematics, Social and Behavioral Sciences, Special Studies, and the Graduate School. He has published over 200 papers on research and research administration.

George Simson is professor of English and founder of the Center for Biographical Research at the University of Hawaii, and founder and for seventeen years editor of *Biography: An Interdisciplinary Quarterly*. He was board member, vice president, and president of the Conference (now Council) of Editors of Learned Journals, and a founder of the Mediation Committee of CELJ. He is also a founding member of the Matsunaga Institute for Peace at the University of Hawaii and of the Center for Global Non-Violence, an independent nonprofit institute.

Richard Smyth is assistant professor of English at Hamline University in St. Paul, Minnesota. He has published an essay in *Inner Space Outer Space: Humanities, Technology, and the Postmodern World*, edited by Daniel Schenker, Craig Hanks, and Susan Kray. He also coedits and publishes the poetry journal *Albatross* and has published poems in various journals.

Bruce W. Speck is director of the Professional Writing Program and coordinator of Writing-across-the-Curriculum at the University of Memphis in Tennessee. He has published *Editing: An Annotated Bibliography* and *Publication Peer Review: An Annotated Bibliography*. A third volume, *Managing the Publishing Process: An Annotated Bibliography*, is in press. With colleagues, he has conducted empirical research on the publication process at technical writing journals and has published the results in *Technical Communication*.

Todd Taylor teaches in and is co-director of the computer and writing program in the Department of English at the University of South Florida. He is the founder/editor of JAC Online, an internet version of an already established print journal in composition theory.

Brian J. Thompson is provost emeritus, distinguished university professor and professor of optics at the University of Rochester. He is the author of more than 180 scientific and technical papers. His book on physical optics has been translated into Russian, Polish, and Chinese. He is currently the editor of the monthly international journal *Optical Engineering*; editor of the *Milestone Volumes of Selected Papers in Optics,* which now include over 100 titles; editor of the Marcel Dekker series of books on optical engineering, with 48 titles printed. He is the chair of the editorial board of the University of Rochester Press, which he founded five years ago.

David Watt is the vice chancellor for Research and Graduate Studies and the director for the Advanced Science and Technology Commercialization Center at the University of Kentucky. His current responsibilities involve all aspects of the research and creative works of the faculty.

Morton Winston is professor of philosophy at Trenton State College and coordinates the development of an interdisciplinary, core general education course on ethics and technology. He served previously as director of the Center for Instructional Enhancement. He has published in the fields of the philosophy of science, cognitive science, ethical theory, biomedical ethics, pedagogy, and human rights.

ISBN 0-313-29572-7